THE MARTYRED PRINCES
BORIS AND GLEB

UCLA Slavic Studies
Volume 19

THE MARTYRED PRINCES BORIS AND GLEB:
A SOCIO-CULTURAL STUDY OF THE CULT AND THE TEXTS

by

Gail Lenhoff

Slavica Publishers, Inc.

Slavica publishes a wide variety of books and journals dealing with the peoples, languages, literatures, history, folklore, and culture of the peoples of Eastern Europe and the USSR. For a complete catalog with prices and ordering information, please write to:

> Slavica Publishers, Inc.
> P.O. Box 14388
> Columbus, Ohio 43214
> USA

ISBN: 0-89357-204-7.

Copyright © 1989 by the author. All rights reserved.

Text set by Randy Bowlus and Mary Lou Blum at the East European Composition Center, supported by the Department of Slavic Languages and Literatures and the Center for Russian and East European Studies at UCLA.

Printed in the United States of America.

CONTENTS

PREFACE 7

ABBREVIATIONS 10

1. APPROACHING THE LITERATURE OF MEDIEVAL RUS' ... 11
   The Critical Tradition 11
   Early Russian Writing: Theory and Praxis 16
     Anomaly as Rule 20
     Protogenres 24
     The Loci of the Saint's Life 26
     Plotting the Matrices of the Cult Texts 30

2. THE KIEVAN CULT 32
   The Syncretic Response 32
     Blood Revenge and Ancestor Worship 34
     The Fire Miracles 37
   The Christian Response 41
     Boris' and Gleb's Burial 41
     The Miraculous Evidence 43
     The Protocol of Canonization 45
     The Veneration of the Princes' Relics 48

3. RITUAL COMMEMORATION 55
   The Saints' Office 56
     Metropolitan John's Office 56
     The Novgorod Sticherarion Office 65
     The Ivaniči Menaion Office 67
     The Fifteenth-Century Office 70
   The Homiletic Tradition 71
     The Eulogies 72
     The Paremia Readings 75

4. TESTIMONIALS 78
   The "Narration" 79
   The "Lection" 88

5. CHRONICLES 101
   Redactions 102
   Point-of-View 107
     The Socio-Political Model 109
     The Ethical Models 113

CONCLUSION	122
NOTES	126
BIBLIOGRAPHY	143
INDEX	160

PREFACE

This monograph is part of a long-term project to reassess the nature of Old Russian writing in terms of the socio-cultural systems of Medieval Rus'. For many decades it was taken for granted that Old Russian writers imitated the literary models they inherited from Byzantium, and that the corpus of medieval written texts could be systematically described, and defective texts reconstructed, with reference to these models. Today most medievalists recognize the inadequacy of a literary-generic approach to account for the sort of texts that were produced in pre-Petrine Rus'. Among the most promising alternatives is to approach such texts as the products of broader cultural systems that ordered the life of the community.

This methodology finds its inspiration and closest analogy in the work of the *Formgeschichte* critics, who sought to clarify the norms and customs that produced elementary literary forms in the early Christian period. Such an approach acknowledges that the writings of medieval Rus' differ from belletristic literature in their etiology as well as their function and form. This premise serves as the point of departure for the theory, elaborated in the opening chapter, that the kinds of texts composed in Kievan and Muscovite Rus' are most productively conceptualized as "protogenres." The process of literary analysis, from this standpoint, begins with the identification of a work's socio-cultural context, its provenance, and its probable functions for the community. Then and only then can we pinpoint the factors which account for the production and shape of the text as well as for later modifications made by medieval editors.

How does a socio-cultural institution generate a written text? Is it possible to compose a text without being conscious of literary-generic conventions? What is the place of rhetoric in the writing of Old Rus'? To what extent are we dependent upon literary texts when we attempt to reconstruct what the *Formgeschichte* critics called a work's *Sitz im Leben*? Does this dependency invalidate our findings? These are only a few of the questions which a protogeneric approach provokes. I have responded to such questions on a general theoretical level, but the test of a theory ultimately lies in its accountability to real texts. The following study of SS Boris and Gleb was initially conceived as just such a test case, illustrating the potential of a protogeneric approach and providing a concrete picture of the writing process in the Kievan period.

An unusual variety of texts and material artifacts devoted to Boris and Gleb have survived from this time, many of relatively early provenance. They have inspired extensive, occasionally brilliant, commentary from medievalists and cultural historians. To review the history of their study is, in a sense, to review the history of medieval Slavic studies as a discipline. It is not without its biases, however, and the scholarship has yet to circumscribe the object of investigation. The cult has too often been treated synchronically as all of a piece. Christian aspects of the cult have, at times, overshadowed its more archaic features and vice versa. All too frequently philologists have chosen to overlook the contributions of scholars in other disciplines, an isolationism that has proven to be mutual. The texts that make up the rich liturgical tradition, though of primary importance for the saints' veneration, have been virtually ignored, probably because they do not fit into mainstream "genres" of investigation.

The socio-cultural approach advanced here is intended to correct these deficiencies and fill in major lacunae in our understanding of Boris' and Gleb's legacy. My primary purpose, to illustrate the specific relation of the cult's *Sitz im Leben* to the kind of texts that were produced at any given stage in its development, has dictated the structure of the presentation. Chapter One reviews the critical tradition and sets forth the theoretical premises behind the investigation. Chapter Two focuses on the early stages of the Kievan cult, which are particularly crucial to an understanding of the texts. The following chapters treat the minimal set of texts necessary for formal veneration and the texts which are optional or desirable as a means of promoting the veneration of the saints. In each section I discuss the way in which the texts depart from the generic models that have been ascribed to them, and then illustrate how their apparently anomalous features can be accounted for in terms of extra-literary systems, subsystems and functions. The capacity of a protogeneric approach to explain apparent anomalies in a systematic fashion, and the insights it provides into the community's perception will, I hope, inspire further case studies of Old Russian writings and lead to a much-needed reassessment of the pre-Petrine literary corpus.

In the interim between the conception of this monograph and its publication, I published several articles setting forth the basic theoretical tenets of a protogeneric approach. A few brief excerpts from these, integrated into individual chapters, are reproduced here with the publishers' permission. Biblical citations, except when noted, are taken from the King James translation. References to psalms follow the Septuagint in accordance with Orthodox practice. All citations from cult texts are rendered in the original with ligatures opened and punctuation added, when required for clarity's sake. Orthographical modifications, while regrettably necessary for pragmatic considerations, have been kept to a minimum. English translations of all Slavonic texts have been provided in the footnotes. Where possible, I have used published translations, amending them as needed. All other translations are my own. I have attempted to deal with the various sets of specialized terms and international nomenclature as consistently as possible. The names of East Slavic saints, clerics, and historical characters are rendered in exact transliteration. Patronymics, geographical names and pre-

Revolutionary orthography (in the case of bibliographical data) have been standardized. Greek, Latin and Scandinavian names are rendered according to the customary scholarly conventions. Liturgical terminology follows the system used in the English translation of Gardner [1976, 1980]; occasionally, for the sake of clarification, Greek or Cyrillic terms have been provided in brackets.

The project has benefited from the generous advice and criticisms of fellow medievalists. Henrik Birnbaum, Jesse Byock, Christian Hannick, Norman W. Ingham, Ann M. Kleimola, Andrzej Poppe, William Veder and Dean S. Worth have commented on various drafts. They are not responsible for the errors of the book, but they have surely contributed to its successes. A debt of thanks is due to the colleagues who made available to me forthcoming articles, monographs and studies-in-progress. I was unable to obtain Giorgetta Revelli's monograph [1987] before my own book went to press. Paul Hollingsworth's dissertation [Berkeley, 1988] reached me too late to be discussed in the body of this study, but served as a useful source for cross-checking bibliographical references. I would also like to express my gratitude for assistance from the International Research and Exchanges Board (IREX); Edward Kasinec of the New York Public Library; the Slavic Reference service of the University Library at Urbana-Champaign; Klaus-Dieter Seemann and Wolf-Heinrich Schmidt of Berlin's Freie Universität, together with other members of the Forschungsgruppe "Ältere Slavische Literaturen"; the State Lenin Library and Manuscript Repository (GBL); the Central State Archive for Ancient Documents and Acts (CGADA); the Institute of Russian Literature (IRLI, Puškinskij dom); the Library of the USSR Academy of Sciences (BAN); and the Saltykov-Ščedrin Library and Manuscript Repository (GPB). Finally, I must acknowledge the unceasing editorial labors of my husband and colleague, Ronald Vroon, whose contribution to the final product is truly beyond my capacity to measure.

ABBREVIATIONS

BAN	Biblioteka Akademii nauk, Leningrad
ČOIDR	Čtenija v Imperatorskom Obščestve istorii i drevnostej rossijskix pri Moskovskom universitete
CGADA	Central'nyj gosudarstvennyj arxiv drevnix aktov, Moscow
GBL	Gosudarstvennaja biblioteka im. Lenina, Moscow
GIM	Gosudarstvennyj Istoričeskij Muzej, Moscow
GPB	Gosudarstvennaja publičnaja biblioteka im. Saltykova-Ščedrina, Leningrad
IORJAS	Izvestija Otdelenija russkogo jazyka i slovesnosti Akademii nauk, St. Petersburg
IRLI	Institut russkoj literatury (Puškinskij dom) Akademii nauk, Leningrad
JEV	Jaroslavskie eparxial'nie vedomosti
Lection	Čtenie o žitii i o pogublenii blažennuju strastoterpca Borisa i Glěba
Narration	S"kazanie i strast' i poxvala svjatuju mučeniku Borisa i Glěba
NPL	Novgorodskaja pervaja letopis'
PSRL	Polnoe sobranie russkix letopisej
PVL	Povest' vremennyx let
SORJAS	Sbornik Otdelenija russkogo jazyka i slovesnosti Akademii nauk, St. Petersburg
TODRL	Trudy Otdela drevnerusskoj literatury
ZSPh	Zeitschrift für slavische Philologie

1

APPROACHING THE LITERATURE OF MEDIEVAL RUS'

> *Our task is not to analyze the originality or the art of individual authors, but to describe the laws which operate as formative factors in the popular tradition. The ultimate source of such forms is . . . life itself. To understand how such writings came to be produced by people who were not literati, we must examine their life and, since we are dealing with religious texts, the customs of their cult. We must ask what categories are possible or probable in this sociological context. . . .*[1]
> Martin Dibelius

> Се же житие преподобьнааго и блаженааго отьця нашего Феодосия, еже от оуны вьрьсты до сьде от многаго мало въписахъ. Кьто бо довъльнь вься по ряду съписати добрая оуправления сего блаженааго моужа, кьто же възможеть по достоянию его похвалити. . . .[2]

The murdered princes Boris and Gleb have come to occupy a special place in the pantheon of Russian saints. Their commemoration, in the broadest sense of the word, reaches across ecclesiastical boundaries: they are regularly "called to remembrance," not only in the cycle of Orthodox worship and its texts, but also in modern histories and professional forums. Their privileged status in the cultural sphere may, in part, be attributed to the fact that Boris and Gleb were the first Kievans to be formally canonized, and are even today regarded as patron saints of imperial power. But the attention paid to Boris and Gleb beyond the confines of the Church is in great measure due to the mystery that still surrounds their life and death, the propagation of their story, and the nature and history of their veneration.

The Critical Tradition

So much has been written on the subject of Boris and Gleb in recent years that one would expect to find broad areas of scholarly consensus.

Nothing could be farther from the actual state of affairs. Though many leading medievalists in the fields of East Slavic philology, literary criticism, art history, archaeology, and history proper have taken a stand on the issues in question, the most elementary claims about the princes still require stringent and continual qualification. Even the basic sequence of events underlying the extant narratives is not a matter of universal agreement.

The most commonly accepted story is found in the Laurentian Chronicle entry for the year 1015. According to this version the Kievan grand prince Vladimir succumbed to a sudden illness before he could name an heir. One son, Prince Svjatopolk, immediately occupied the throne, then moved to secure it by eliminating all contenders among the other sons. He hired assassins to kill his rivals, among them Boris and Gleb. His power, however, was challenged by a third brother, Jaroslav, who did battle for the Kievan throne. Jaroslav eventually drove Svjatopolk from the land, winning the title of grand prince. Miraculous signs were manifested by the bodies of the murdered princes, which were recovered by Jaroslav and given honorable burial. The brothers were canonized in the prelacy of Metropolitan John I (1019-1035).

Another version, inspired by parallels with the tale of Eymundr, a Varangian mercenary who was for a short time in Jaroslav's guards, reconstructs events very differently. Svjatopolk, it is argued, occupied Vladimir's throne for a few weeks before he was attacked by Jaroslav and forced to flee to Poland. He returned later, with his father-in-law, the Polish king Bolesław, to do battle for Kiev. In the interim, Boris, a rival contender for the Kievan throne, was murdered by Jaroslav's Varangian guards. The murder was initially concealed by Jaroslav. When it was discovered, it was blamed on Svjatopolk's desire to usurp the throne and dated 1015 to coincide with the year of Vladimir's death. The version told in the Laurentian Chronicle and narrative lives, according to this theory, was composed in conjunction with the official canonization which took place in 1072, during the reign of Izjaslav and in the prelacy of Metropolitan John II [Il'in, 1957].

These are two of many possible scenarios that could be pieced together from the available materials. The efforts to make these pieces cohere, however, have been impeded by the lack of a theoretical apparatus sufficiently broad to deal with the interdisciplinary nature of the problem. The need for such an apparatus is readily apparent when we survey the sorts of questions that remain unresolved. They may be divided into the broad categories of history and philology, each with its own scholarly biases. Historians have sought, above all, to clarify the ambiguities implicit in the surviving sources in order to reconstruct the actual course and logic of events. Literary scholars have been preoccupied by the need to account for anomalous texts produced in connection with the documentation and dissemination of the cult.

Looking first to the historical commentary, we find that a good deal of attention has been devoted to the issue of responsibility for the cult. Why were Boris and Gleb the first Kievans to be officially sainted, rather than other royal figures such as Princess Ol'ga, the first ruler to convert to Christianity, or Prince Vladimir, the Baptizer of Rus'? The high political stakes and the fact that the act of fratricide was committed during a power struggle has led many scholars to hypothesize that the cult was initiated from above. There is a widespread assumption that Jaroslav arranged to have the murdered princes canonized in order to whitewash his tarnished image and to bolster his claims to authority. This assumption finds its counter and parallel in the deduction that Izjaslav Jaroslavovič arranged to have the princes canonized in 1072 because his claims to the Kievan throne had been challenged and he hoped to unite the population behind him under the banner of a divinely-blessed dynasty.

From here, the variations are almost exponential. Some categorically deny that Boris and Gleb were sincerely venerated in the years immediately following their death, while others accept that veneration with qualifications. Cherniavsky, for example, characterizes the cult as highly syncretic with the emphasis on the element of prince rather than on the element of saint [1961: 9; see also Maczko, 1975: 72-76]. Several historians go so far as to claim that the saints' cult was essentially pagan in motivation and observance. Reisman identifies the cult as a remnant of Varangian worship of a "priest-king" [1978], while Rybakov [1965] and Sciacca [1985] explain the motivations and rituals in terms of native Kievan pagan traditions.

The discrepancy between Boris and Gleb and the majority of early Christian martyrs has prompted a variety of other theories which allow for the possibility of a genuine Christian veneration. In his monograph on Russian saints and a subsequent study, *The Medieval Russian Mind*, Fedotov expresses the view that Boris and Gleb are the first representatives of a special, uniquely Russian class of saint, the passion-sufferer [*strastoterpec*], who is venerated for submitting to a violent and undeserved end on the model of Christ [1931: 30; 1946: 97-105]. Ingham has countered Fedotov's claim by pointing out precedents where the Christian Church has venerated political victims in the form of sovereign martyrs, foremost among them the Czech saint Wenceslas [1963; 1973; 1984]. What serves as an argument for a Christian basis of veneration has also been taken as evidence of the cult's imposition from above [Il'in, 1957: 53-65].

Archaeological evidence—amulets, early icons, reliquary crosses, seals, the composition of the princes' coffins—has likewise proven to cut two ways in the scholarly discussion. Images of the princes on pectoral crosses [*enkolpia*] have been read as an indication that Jaroslav promoted a cult of Boris and Gleb among the common people by spreading word of their powers as healing saints [Lesjučevskij, 1946: 234]. Much the same evidence has been taken as a sign that, while Boris and Gleb were indeed revered as healers, their cult was confined to a small circle of noble relatives in the period before their canonization under Izjaslav in 1072 [Aleškovskij, 1972: 124-5]. A third position, based on considerations of baptismal names and ecclesiastical protocol, allows that the princes were probably venerated first by other princes and members of their clan and that their canonization took place after Jaroslav's death; the healing miracles are treated in terms of the documentation required for formal canonization, rather than as evidence of initial stages of worship [Poppe, 1966: 42-5; 1973: 21-22; 1981: 34].

The canonization date is yet another matter of dispute. Šaxmatov believes that it took place either in 1020 or 1026, the two dates closest to the murder on which the feast day of July 24 coincided with a Sunday, the customary day for canonization proceedings [1908: 58]. Other commentators set 1035 (the end of Metropolitan John I's prelacy) as the *terminus ad quem*, since John is identified as the author of the first office commemorating the saints. Sreznevskij's hypothesis that Metropolitan John II Prodromos (1076-1089) might have authored the office considerably extends the range of dates [1881: 31]. Lixačev gives precedence to ecclesiastical politics in his discussion of the problem. His hypothesis is based on the premise that Boris and Gleb were most probably canonized in connection with the establishment of a metropolitan see in Kiev, that is, around 1037 [1950: 65]. Karger suggests that a chronicle account of the disinterment of the saints' relics during the prelacy of Metropolitan George marks the "final and public recognition" of Boris' and Gleb's sainthood by the Byzantine Church hierarchy [1952: 82]. Karger's hypothesis has been accepted and extended by scholars with widely differing viewpoints on the nature and dissemination of the cult [see, for example, Ammann, 1955: 37; Il'in, 1957: 180-2; Poppe, 1965: 301-5; 1969: 369-72; 1973; 1981: 41-53].

Literary scholarship has been obliged to take a position on the historical issues, if only because the scenario one picks for the murder of Boris and Gleb and their subsequent canonization has a necessary connection to the production and dissemination of writings about their lives. The overriding preoccupation of literary scholars, however, has been to account for the fact that various texts were produced to fill apparently similar functions, and to categorize the texts in terms of perceived generic norms of the period and with reference to a projected medieval Russian literary genre-system.

The accounts of Boris' and Gleb's deeds present us with an unusually wide variety of literary texts, many of them dating from the pre-Mongol period. They include several offices (the first traditionally attributed to Metropolitan John I), a variety of readings for special services, thematic sermons, long and short biographies, and chronicle accounts of various periods. Paradoxically, the generalizations that have been drawn on the basis of this literary microcosm are primarily derived from a comparison of a few, controversial texts: the anonymous *S"kazanie i strast' i poxvala* ["Narration and Passion and Eulogy"], the *Čtenie o žitii i o pogublenii* ["Lection on the Life and Death"] attributed to the monk Nestor, and the Primary Chronicle entry for the year 1015.

One approach to explaining the generic anomaly of such texts as the *S"kazanie* has been to view them as essentially corrupted versions of texts which were originally produced with clear generic categories in mind, and which can be reconstructed by means of painstaking textual criticism. This approach is exemplified in the work of Müller, who in many ways continues the philological tradition associated with Šaxmatov before him. Müller's extensive studies on the cult texts are ultimately designed to provide us with reconstructions of hypothetical *Urtexts*: a heroic saga and a classic martyr's passion [1954-62; 1954; 1956^a; 1956^b; 1963]. If we accept his reconstructions we will also assume that the *Urtexts* were composed during the reign of Jaroslav with discrete secular and ecclesiastical functions in mind.

Čiževskij, who also subscribes to the notion that the texts were produced with discrete generic categories in mind, suggests that the anomalies perceived by the "reconstructionists" actually involve a failure to identify the precise genres of the texts. He solves this problem, again on the basis of what he sees as two central texts, by classifying the *S"kazanie* (hereafter, "Narration") as a martyr's passion and the *Čtenie* (hereafter "Lection") as a standard *vita* [1954: 108-111].

The counterarguments to this solution are likewise made with the core texts in mind. Most of the discussion has centered on the fact that, while the "Lection" might conceivably be a standard *vita*, there is some difficulty in representing the "Narration" as a classic *passio* [see, *inter alia*, the observations of Golubinskij, 1901-1910: I, 1, 746-9; Bugoslavskij, 1941: 320; Eremin, 1968: 71-21; Ingham, 1983: 230-33]. One's view of a given text as "standard" or "anomalous" inevitably reflects upon one's theory of the texts' probable genesis and interaction. Those who, like Bugoslavskij and Ingham, regard the "Narration" as erratic or nontraditional in its composition, for example, tend to conclude that it is a heterogeneous, transitional work. Those who believe that a standard *vita* had to have been composed initially, as Sobolevskij, Ajnalov and Golubinskij do, assume that the "Lection" was written first (perhaps from a lost Greek original), and suggest that the "Narration" is a later, poetic reworking of the basic material.

Although these and other disputes are conveniently described in either historical or philological terms, their solution is not so easily circumscribed. Our point of departure must be philological, because we are bound by the written texts at our disposal. All judgments on the veracity and significance of these sources are ultimately contingent upon our understanding of the conventions which mediate the recounting of actual events. The isolation of phrases and events dictated primarily or exclusively by considerations of propriety is a prerequisite for distinguishing decorum from documentation, and facts from commonplaces. For this reason, the methodological apparatus of the literary investigator is primary, and has far-reaching consequences in most other spheres of investigation as well.

The difficulty of arriving at a consensus, as I see it, stems from a methodology that attempts to accommodate itself to the premises of modern literary scholarship rather than to the viewpoint of the community that produced these texts. The first concession to modern notions of literature has been to isolate the cult texts which have a potentially aesthetic function from the corpus of texts recounting Boris' and Gleb's deeds. The second concession, which really follows from the first, has been to rely on abstract literary categories in identifying generic markers and anomalous features in the texts. The fact that the "Narration," the Primary Chronicle entry, and the "Lection" have been treated as the most significant texts, despite the evidence that works which are clearly not aesthetic in their function appear to have been of equal or greater importance for the community, has tended to discourage efforts to reconstruct such non-aesthetic functions. So, too, the certainty that medieval writers worked with an abstract conception of verbal categories and that all medieval texts belong to one or another definable genre has necessitated an abundance of commentary explaining away the numerous anomalies.

Taken *in toto*, the critical tradition illustrates how difficult it is to fit what should be standard texts into the categories that we believe represent the system of early Russian literature. The more we attempt to force the texts into pigeonholes defined by abstract verbal criteria, the more apparent it becomes that their underlying order is based on criteria that are not related to genre per se. Critics may view these narratives as actualizations of certain literary types, but that they deal with real princes who met their fate during a particular stage of Kiev's religious and cultural development is incontrovertible. This monograph is the result of my growing sense that the genesis of the texts and their forms are conditioned first and foremost by the writers' perception of real events, and that major textual developments are primarily a function of changing perceptions and social needs. For that very reason the patterns that emerge from the comparison of such texts with coeval writings appear to be a consequence of shared responses rather than of generic modeling. The texts connected with the cult of Boris and Gleb will here serve as a test case for determining the degree to which extra-literary factors engender and shape medieval Russian writings.

Early Russian Writing: Theory and Praxis

In his book on the principles of early Russian textual criticism Lixačev describes the physical process of writing in medieval Rus'. The bookman would sit on a low stool, his manuscript on his knees, the inkpot, quills and other writing implements on a small table by his side. He wrote on leaves of parchment or paper that were first folded into quires. It was the responsibility of the scribe to copy an original as faithfully as possible, although there seems always to have been leeway for editorial changes [Lixačev, 1983: 60].

When a writer was entrusted with the task of composing a text, he still followed some sort of guidelines. What was the nature of these guidelines? How did the early Russian writer compose a text? What rules and conventions constrained him? How much leeway did he have? The traditional response to such questions with respect to the pre-Petrine period has been to conceptualize the corpus as equivalent systemically to the belles-lettres of later periods. Most modern scholarship views this premise as fundamentally untenable, and recent contributions to genre studies reflect a shift away from this approach.

One of the first steps away from the traditional model was taken by Jagoditsch, who proposed that we distinguish medieval work-types [*Werkformen*] from modern literary types [*Kunstformen*]. Work-types are pragmatically oriented, according to this theory, and represent a more primitive literary system [1957/58: 121-22]. Lixačev adopts a similar posture. He treats a text's pragmatic function as equivalent to any other necessary or sufficient feature of a genre and, through his concept of literary etiquette, attempts to clarify the stylistic dimension of a text's social functions. Lixačev's observations that the medieval Slavic literary system is more chaotic than modern literary systems and marked by imprecise terminology and anomalous texts constitute an important point of departure for subsequent theoretical developments [1979: 55-79].[3]

Ingham's writings on genre theory continue to evolve away from the view that Old Russian literature constituted a belletristic genre-system. While his work on secular and sacred biography proceeds from the premise that the Kievans inherited a genre-system from Byzantium which they then modified and developed, he points out that East Slavic texts do not always correspond to well-established Byzantine literary categories and proposes new parameters for identifying their genres. In his study of Kievan lives of princes he addresses Jagoditsch's concept of work-types, suggesting that one must also consider a number of cultural factors (other than the ritual function of the *vita*) which give rise to hybrid genres, subtypes and *de facto* varieties. He also suggests that we must apply a more flexible concept of "system" to the medieval Russian literary corpus in order to describe it as a "literary system" [1983: 224-226].

In a recent forum on the problem of genres, Ingham writes that, although Old Russian writers did operate with genre categories, genres were "less well developed and less pervasive than in modern times" [1987[a]: 235]. He argues that the term is always relatively loosely defined and suggests, among other criteria, that we approach genre as "a social convention—a category in the minds of a historical community of writers and readers" [*ibid.*: 236]. Most such categories, he writes, constitute a group of texts which "bear a family resemblance to one another rather than a strictly systematic one" [*ibid.*]. The community of readers, he continues, most probably distinguished one genre from another by a complex of features such as structure, mode, subject-matter, style, commonplaces, implied functions and the like. No one of these may be deemed necessary, but it is the constellation that accounts for the genre. For Ingham a genre set can be described on the basis of shared features, titles and types of codices [*ibid.*: 237]. Works that cannot be so defined are "unique, reflecting no known productive type" [*ibid.*: 241]. Ingham also suggests that mode ("manner of representation") may have been a more important parameter for East Slavic writers than literary kind or pragmatic function [1987[b]].

In the last decade a number of important theoretical contributions to medieval genre theory have been made by a group of scholars affiliated with the Freie Universität of Berlin. Their views require the fullest elaboration here, for they are most closely related to the work of the *Formgeschichte* critics, which is my own point of departure [for precedents see Schmidt and Seemann, 1984]. In analyzing early Christian writings as the expression of a particular life style and world view, the *Formgeschichte* critics introduce the term *Sitz im Leben*, by which they mean "a typical situation or mode of behavior in the life of the community" [Bultmann, 1921: 4]. They view the form of the synoptic Gospel texts, among others, as originating in early Christian life itself, and urge that the models for such texts be sought, not in literature, but in the life and customs of the collective. The *Sitz im Leben*, writes Martin Dibelius, suggests to the critic what formal categories are possible or probable [1933: 7-8]. This theory has been refined by members of the Berlin Seminar for the Study of Medieval Slavic Literatures [Forschungsgruppe "Ältere slavische Literaturen"] and applied to the reconstruction of the system of early Slavic writing. The productivity of such an approach may be seen in their studies of early Russian military tales, pilgrimage accounts, and icon legends [see Schmidt, 1975; Seemann, 1976; Ebbinghaus, 1986, 1987]. This methodology also lends itself to the analysis of texts with unorthodox subjects and mixed functions such as, for example, the narratives recounting the life of the Tatar prince, St. Petr Ordynskij [Bamborschke *et. al.*, 1979]. Recent scholarship suggests that a *Formgeschichte* model could be applied to oral traditions [Birnbaum, 1985] and also used to chart the history of speakers' attitudes toward their native language [Worth, 1984].

Proponents of such a socio-cultural approach have been reluctant to abandon the concept of genres or genre-systems altogether. Instead, they have shifted the emphasis from form to communicative function. In a series of theses on the nature of medieval literary types and systems, Seemann characterizes medieval texts as "instruments" where pragmatic etiology and application are so closely bound that literary and extra-literary elements are indistinguishable [1984: 279]. According to this theory, frequently encountered situations and widespread customs, more often than not connected with Orthodox worship, give rise to well-attested categories which are the medieval equivalent of modern literary genres. They are best defined in terms of a communicative model incorporating the parameters of author, theme [*Gegenstand*], purpose, communicative situation, style, and response [*Wirkung*] [*ibid.*: 285]. So, for example, an exegetical sermon would be defined as a text authored by a member of the clergy who is empowered to instruct the community, based on the precedents of the Sermon on the Mount (as well as the Epistles and the writings of the Church Fathers), intended as an explication of theological dogma, to be delivered on any Sunday in a church for the enlightenment of the congregation [Seemann, 1987[a]: 249].

Seemann takes some care to define the communicative parameters of his medieval model with reference to modern generic parameters. The author of a medieval genre, he writes, is most often not identified as an individual, but derives his image from the genre itself. He may be represented as a person of considerable authority, as a witness, or simply as the sender of a message. The theme, as opposed to the kind of text, often inspires a work's title. Style is an important generic marker in the medieval period because, while modern literary style may often be a matter of taste, medieval genres require specific linguistic levels in connection with their subject and purpose [1984: 286-287].

In his seventeenth and final thesis, Seemann deals with the problem of anomalies in connection with his discussion of functional context [*Gebrauchskontext*]. A medieval text, he writes, can shift from one generic category to another without undergoing any concrete structural changes. Seemann views generic shift as an exceptional phenomenon, one which occurs primarily with texts originally composed to fulfill non-normative or non-institutionalized functions. It is a text's functional indeterminacy, then, that permits changes in its generic status [1984: 287-288].

The ultimate test of this or any theory of pre-Petrine writing is its ability to explain the interrelation of etiology and form in such a way that the exceptions are accommodated by the rule. Many texts that have survived do not fit into stable categories analogous to the categories of belletristic texts, regardless of the allowances that are made for their pragmatic functions. By the same token, texts with predictable institutional functions form systems that do not coincide with systems of verbal genres, and are shifted by their creators and users from one hypothetical generic category to another. Theories that deny these realities must ignore a substantial percentage of the corpus. I should like to present some examples in support of my observations before proposing what I believe is a more appropriate theoretical apparatus for describing the systemicity of medieval Slavic writings, and then applying that apparatus to the texts on Boris and Gleb.

Anomaly as Rule

In a recent study of medieval Bulgarian writing, W.-H. Schmidt suggests that early Slavic texts have a pragmatic plural functionality which is based on a religious concept of literature. In this connection, he continues, the controls that are placed upon a text will be increasingly stringent to the degree that it is bound to religious usage [1987: 190]. This premise would seem to follow from what we know about the strict controls exercised by the Church over all expressive media and behavior connected to Orthodox worship. Members of the ecclesiastical hierarchy, and parishioners as well, were conscious of the most minute deviations from liturgical tradition. The widespread social disturbances caused by opposition to Patriarch Nikon's reforms in the seventeenth century find parallels throughout the medieval period.

Though controls aimed at preserving liturgical protocol and decorum in various kinds of writing are unquestionably implemented by the community, it would be a mistake to equate those controls with generic prescriptions or to assume that they ensure generic stability. In point of fact, they are primarily concerned with dogmatic criteria and tend to focus on the formulaic expression of dogma and religious sentiments. A set of formulaic expressions can fill a variety of religious functions without undergoing any formal structural changes. By the same token, when the appropriate formulas are present, the larger structure of a text may have no relevance to the text's ability to perform a given religious function. The most commonly encountered types of liturgical hymns provide an excellent example of where the community's priorities lay. Troparia, kontakia, and various kinds of versicles are composed to fill certain slots in the worship service, frequently in offices commemorating saints. Many of these hymns can be interchanged in their liturgical functions without the slightest textual alteration.

Their plural functionality is encouraged by two factors. The first is a negative one. Poets have traditionally taken great care to set forth the structural models and patterns that identify verse as belonging to a particular genre (sonnet, madrigal, ode, etc.). In order to transform a Lomonosovian ode into a Petrarchan sonnet, one would be obliged to make radical structural modifications. Liturgical hymns, on the other hand, are not required to conform to any sort of rhyme or stanzaic scheme. To be sure, they must be chanted and therefore fit into a melody, but the eight-tone melodic system is such that texts can readily be accommodated without structural changes. The liberal use of the *stopica*, for example, allows for syllables that are not allotted individual notes. This is one of several ways in which the Slavs ensured that a wide variety of texts could be fit to a limited stock of musical formulas which also filled a variety of liturgical slots [see Lenhoff, 1983].

The second factor that conditions the plural functionality of liturgical texts is the emphasis placed on *topoi*. There are *topoi* for addressing the Deity or expressing divine attributes, and others which are specific to the cult of saints, such as the comparison of a saint to a star. Such *topoi* can occur in many types of texts with varying functions because they reflect the dogma that a saint is one who aligns himself with the forces of light, one who mediates between men and God, and so on. In other words, the formula is necessary to define the subject (saints), but not a necessary or sufficient feature of a kind (hymn, *vita*, chronicle entry).

Genre-oriented critics would argue that these texts belong to a recognizable, common type (the hymn) with functionally distinctive subtypes. In the final analysis, however, the common typology derives from the typology of a series of socio-cultural systems as represented in the forms of Orthodox worship. For the medieval Slavic community, such texts are differentiated not according to their describable verbal features, but according to their place and function in any given worship service. The function takes precedence to the empirical features of the text. Moreover, as Ključevskij has shown in his study of medieval Russian saints' lives, the degree to which a single text serves in multiple functions depends upon the community that uses the text. In the northern areas or in villages that lacked large choirs and well-trained clergy, and had only a minimal selection of service books from which to draw, polyfunctionality was not a choice but a necessity [1871: 362-64].

In such a context, structural alterations almost always derive from the writer's conception of decorum or function rather than from a notion of stylistic elegance or generic norms (see below). Again, such attitudes are by no means unique to the medieval Slavs, but are characteristic of texts produced by communities that do not valorize an aesthetic function. A graphic example is provided by the Lord's Prayer, which has been historically assigned to a variety of genres. It is a document, but also a petition, and, for some, a poem of faith. It was adapted by Christ's followers for use in the laying on of hands, possibly at baptism, for morning and evening worship, and in the Eucharist [Chase, 1891: 13-14]. The process of adaptation dictated certain changes in the text of the Prayer: phrases were added and deleted, and the order of words or lines was changed. Such changes may disturb a modern reader for any number of reasons: because of a conviction that Scripture is inviolable or because of a conviction that art (for those who wish to view it as a poem) should remain in the condition that the artist viewed as its final shape. For the early Christian community, on the other hand, the potential of the Lord's Prayer to be adapted to a variety of situations was a great virtue because it was God's Word, but also because it allowed the ministers of that Word to spread the Gospel more efficiently. The priority for that community was clearly on religious function and the structural changes made in the prayer were governed by that priority. Changes in wording had nothing to do with an ideal verbal model, but reflected the immediate exigencies of Christian worship. The fact that a text like the Lord's Prayer can change genres without losing its textual identity stems from the fact that its textual identity is extra-generic, as well as extra-literary.

Further indication that this is also true of early Russian texts may be seen when we attempt to differentiate between the theoretically distinct genres of sermons and saints' lives. The Greeks, and later the Russians, sometimes composed special sermons in honor of a saint that were read on the saint's feast day. In his study of the *martyrion* as a literary genre, Delehaye singles out a series of *topoi* which were customarily employed by the writers of such sermons to praise the saints' life and deeds, and an identifiable model—the rhetorical *enkomion* [1921: 133-169]. On this basis, Delehaye concludes, the panegyric saint's eulogy represents a Christian literary genre which derives from the classical genre of the panegyric [*enkomion*].

A recent investigation of medieval Slavic panegyrics in praise of saints seeks to confirm that "encomiastic disposition" (i.e., the arrangement of themes on the model of Greek *enkomia*) both accounts for their form and distinguishes them from narrative saints' lives [Alissandratos, 1982: 1-2, 7-8]. Alissandratos notes, however, that in a number of cases the panegyrics praising saints are virtually identical to narrative saints' lives: the two "genres" can and do share themes and may arrange these themes in the same order [*ibid.*: 10; cf. Krumbacher, 1897: 181].

It is difficult to distinguish one genre from the other in terms of religious function, as Alissandratos proposes, because sermons on saints and saints' lives serve very similar functions in Orthodox worship. Both types of texts are primarily encomiastic, for both are composed to praise the deeds of a saint and to set them forth as examples of ideal Christian conduct. Nor, in such a case, can one distinguish the two on the basis of their mode of presentation, a possibility elaborated by Ingham. One may agree that, in principle, a narrative mode entails chronological ordering while a panegyric mode gives preference to categorical ordering [1987[b]: 179-181], but in the case of the medieval Slavic panegyric the problem remains, for the encomiastic disposition cancels out the features that distinguish a panegyric from a narrative: the combination of themes follows a temporally structured sequence. The communicative situation is of little help here, since both panegyric and narrative might be read by an individual in private or declaimed aloud in a variety of circumstances (as an optional part of the worship service for the saint's day, for example, or during the course of a communal meal in a monastery refectory).

None of the approaches that have been applied to medieval Russian writings is able to account systematically for the phenomena outlined above. The plural functionality of medieval texts, their cross-generic nomenclature and structure, their open-ended form, and the ubiquity of anomalies are factors that must be ignored, trivialized, or treated as "exceptions to the rule" if the approaches are to retain their validity. Jagoditsch does not address the issues of plural functionality or exceptional texts [*Unikate*]. Lixačev relegates exceptions to situations where the rules of literary etiquette are suspended or to periods where etiquette has begun to degenerate [1979: 96-102]. Ingham's family-resemblance approach appears at first glance to be more accommodating. It seeks out flexible sets of similar features which characterize "productive" types (i.e., kinds of texts which were "imitated and generally accepted"), whose anomalies and/or instability are treated as unmarked. "Isolated" works, whose productivity cannot be assessed are viewed as *potential models for a genre* [1987^a: 241]. But "family resemblances" cannot account for cases where texts that have been relegated to different genres exhibit structural and functional equivalences (e.g., the sermon on a saint's life and a saint's *vita*). Nor can they account for cases where works with virtually no formal or thematic similarities are placed within the same category by the medieval community (e.g., the *Slovo o Merkurii Smolenskom* and the *Slovo o polku Igoreve*). The Berlin School attributes departures from generic canons and instances where a single text shifts from one category to another to plural functionality, but relegates this phenomenon to the status of an exception. Here, anomalous features can be attributed to a particular *Sitz im Leben*, but only *outside* a postulated hierarchy of genres [Seemann, 1987^a: 248-250; 1987^b: 216-220]. In other words, no single theory can account for the synchronic generation of works that appear to fit generic models and also for works that defy them.

The failure of "field" theories to accomplish this task is attributable to a common assumption that the medieval community possessed a generic literary consciousness. That such a consciousness cannot be taken for granted is evident when categories of medieval Russian writing are approached as sets which display "family resemblances." Wittgenstein's notion of family resemblance as a "complicated network of similarities overlapping and criss-crossing: sometimes overall similarities, sometimes similarities of detail" [1967: 32e] is based on an analogy to a biological relationship which produces perceptible common features. In his *Philosophische Untersuchungen* Wittgenstein proposes this analogy as a basis for exploring the nature of certain commonly recognized categories (a game, a color, a particular shape). When there is no actual genetic relationship, therefore, the analogy rests upon the tacit consensus that a particular kind exists. Without this consensus, the analogy has no force.

A number of theorists have applied the family resemblance approach to modern literary genres such as satire which, while universally recognized, are troublesome to define. Here, the primary difficulty is to clarify the nature of an acknowledged, productive textual category [Fowler, 1982: 41]. No such consensus can be made, however, with reference to the medieval Slavic written corpus where the absence of critical treatises, together with unstable morphology and inconsistent nomenclature, place the very existence of a generic consciousness at issue and make concrete generic categories a matter of inference.

The evidence supporting such inferences is surprisingly thin. In a recently published forum on the genre problem in Old Russian literature, for example, Seemann suggests that a pragmatic generic consciousness is manifested in "the compiling of similar texts in manuscript codices . . . [as well as] by an ordering [of the contents] according to church year, chronological sequence, the alphabet, and the like" [1987^a: 248]. Only a small percentage of codices are limited to texts that we would identify as members of a single generic set, however, and even within these codices the medieval nomenclature for the set's members is inconsistent. The fact that medieval editors arranged texts in alphabetical or chronological sets does not demonstrate an awareness of literary kinds. To the contrary, it would seem to suggest that extra-literary categories were given priority [Lenhoff, 1987^a: 262].

In the same forum, Ingham cites as an example of genre consciousness a phrase from the Kiev Cave Patericon, "sie že vpisanno est' v žitii svjatago otca našego Antonia." The author of these words, as Ingham rightly observes, is using the term *žitie* to refer both to the subject matter of St. Antonij's biography and to a specific written source (a no longer extant text). That, however, is really as far as we can go on the basis of the text. To claim that the medieval author is also referring to "a written source *of a particular kind*" [italics mine], i.e. that the word *žitie* here signifies a *genre* rather than the name of a specific historical document [Ingham, 1987^a: 239], is to betray a modern literary bias unsupported by the evidence cited. Because the available data fails to support the conclusion that the medieval community perceived sets of texts as "families" or reached a kind of consensus on categories of writing in the Kievan period, the precondition for the Wittgensteinian analogy, and for all other generically oriented approaches, remains unfulfilled.

Protogenres

In a literary system such as our own, which makes a fundamental distinction between writing and belles-lettres, there is an underlying, intrinsic, literary hierarchy. Any given text is composed and defined in relation to other texts of its generic class and to its generic model. This "lateral" relationship connects texts and genres within systems that are primarily literary in their function. In this way we recognize, conceptualize and compose a novel as opposed to, say, a short story, a classical tragedy as opposed to a one-act play, or a sonnet rather than an epigrammatic couplet. In this way, too, we *consciously* defy or modify recognized genres.

Medieval Russian texts seem to fall into parallel categories, but categories like "saint's life" or "prologue entry" are conceptualized and composed with very different criteria in mind. We can differentiate between such types as though they were exclusively verbal categories, but in the medieval period they have a relationship which overrides verbal categorizations. I have called this relationship "vertical." In a vertically organized corpus, the genesis of a text and the shape that it assumes is dictated from above, as it were, by extra-literary cultural systems and subsystems. It is based on the premise that when a bookman composed a text, the format into which he fit his testimony and the very phrases through which the testimony was communicated were determined by the function that the text was designed to perform. This function, in turn, reflected the hierarchies, needs and rules of one or more socio-cultural systems, which set certain specifications for the verbal instruments that they required. Such specifications could be minute and exhaustive, but often they did not cover broad areas that would be essential to the lateral specifications of a modern belletristic genre.

The term "genre" cannot express the nature of this writing process because it belongs by definition to a system of laterally related verbal artifacts, produced and defined primarily in relation to each other. What we are dealing with here are what I have called "protogenres." I define a protogenre as a category that we impose upon a set of similar verbal responses to the demands of one or more cultural system or subsystem. Implied in this term are, first and foremost, the real cultural imperatives (i.e., the vertical bonds) that produce and shape such texts. At the same time it reflects the need of the modern critic to seek some analogy with the laterally defined texts that dominate the modern tradition. Finally, it permits us to mark real genetic links between medieval types and subsequent literary genres that develop from them.

Many protogeneric categories that we perceive appear to have been interchangeable for the community (for example, a saint's eulogy and a saint's *vita*). Other protogeneric kinds were probably recognized as discrete types. The degree and nature of such distinctions depend on the constellation of vertical bonds that shape the text. When these vertical bonds coincide the distinction will be blurred or inconsistent. The community does not differentiate texts designated as *povest'* from those designated as *skazanie*, for instance. By the same token the texts of short hymns labeled "troparion," "kontakion" or "sticheron" are not consistently distinguished in structure or function for the Eastern Slavs as they were for the Greeks.

When the sets of vertical bonds have very little overlap, on the other hand, the distinction between kinds will be more consistent. The medieval reader would never have confused a saint's *vita* with a troparion praising that saint.

Liturgical texts such as the troparion manifest greater formal similarities to each other than texts such as a *vita* or a sermon because they are produced for a specific, limited function: as components of a service. The protocol of worship constitutes the primary vertical bond that places constraints on the length of the hymn and on its language. The service itself is a verbal structure that also requires "lateral" comparisons to be made between hymns. The composition of liturgical texts must, therefore, be regarded as in some sense anomalous for medieval writing because here the cultural imperatives include the form and style of existing texts—e.g. the aesthetics of the service require that hymns filling particular slots be approximately the same length as other hymns performing that function, and that they be written in Church Slavonic. As a rule, then, vertical bonding dominates, but in this limited sphere we can see the beginning of "generic" consciousness.

Given that the medieval community did not conceptualize written categories in primarily lateral terms, and that the texts were composed to meet a range of needs which vary in their specificity and the network of vertical bonds that shape them, many texts do not fit into a protogeneric set. The shapes they take and the functions they fulfill may not permit inclusion in a group of texts that simulates a literary genre. This does not make them anomalies; it merely means that their *Sitz im Leben* has shaped them with reference to a less frequently encountered combination of vertical bonds. Such texts almost always fit into extra-literary systemic categories with the exception of instances where a writer is describing something utterly alien to his world—Afanasij Nikitin's diary of his journey to India, for example—and has neither the verbal tools to convey what he sees nor the background to conceptualize it fully himself. We can best understand how the process works via some concrete examples. Since the cult of the saints is the single most important institution that shapes the texts recounting the acts of Boris and Gleb, I shall draw my examples with reference to the biographies of saints.

The Loci of the Saint's Life

A *vita* has traditionally been represented as a tri-partite literary structure inherited from classical biography [Loparev, 1910: 15-36]. Within each part is a chain of *topoi* arranged to achieve an underlying structural symmetry. The function and message of the genre prescribe a lofty style and an impersonal, elevated point of view on the part of the biographer [see, *inter alia*, Čiževskij, 1954: 109; Dmitriev, 1973: 8-12]. This generic model, though by and large accepted in the criticism, fails to cover many of the lives of important East Slavic saints. Ingham has suggested that we modify the model to allow for formal subgenres and *de facto* varieties. Subgenres are alternate types or combinations of types that can fulfill the same function as the *vita* proper. *De facto* varieties are lives which diverge from the model either because they must reflect the heterogeneous nature of the individual saint's deeds or because they incorporate special features of a particular type of saint, such as a hermit or a monk [Ingham, 1983: 227].

A protogeneric approach to this problem would begin from exactly the reverse position. The evidence suggests that the tri-partite structure, the sequence of *topoi* and the symmetry of the whole are secondary or tertiary concerns for most hagiographers, while the saint's typology within the cult and individual events of his or her real biography seem to always be central to the shaping of a *vita*. If we proceed from the premises of the Orthodox cult of saints, rather than with a laterally defined verbal model, we arrive at the following criteria. A *vita* is an account of events in the life of a person who imitates the example of Christ to a degree regarded as in some way exceptional. The events of the subject's real life are selected and combined so as to demonstrate that he or she is worthy of veneration. The protagonist's deeds place him or her within a division or subdivision of saints which is schematized in the General Menaion.

It is understood that because the acts of a saint are real events in the life of an individual and because a person's candidacy for this class is often signalled by miracles, there are going to be instances when a person whose behavior is not typical of a saint is nevertheless presented as being worthy of veneration. The lives of such saints may fail to fit into any single previously attested category. Such variants are intrinsic to the very evolution of the cult which began with the veneration of martyrs and then gradually expanded to include prophets, hierarchs, ascetics, and many other categories and subcategories of saints "made perfect in faith."

Insofar as the protogeneric model recognizes the saint's *vita* as the product of a continuously varying interaction between the coordinates of the cult of saints and the biographical loci of an individual, it is at once stable and open-ended. The cult of saints is the stabilizing system that structures individual texts in a similar enough fashion that they make up a protogeneric set. But the other vertical bonds that shape any single text must be plotted. A monk plots the verticals on the basis of the material that he has at hand before beginning the actual process of composition (although one must allow for instances when the verticals are plotted as the bookman works). The investigator must work from an inverse perspective, deducing the verticals from the clues in the manuscript.

In a masterfully executed biography such as the life of Constantine-Cyril the Philosopher, we are immediately referred by the title to the specific category in the Orthodox cult of saints to which the subject belongs—the category of apostle. Lest there be any confusion about what a saint is, and the sort of life that qualifies a person as an "apostle-saint," the writer begins his account with a capsule summary of the dogmatic principles of the cult and a review of the historical types. He concludes his introductory remarks with a brief statement of the function of his text: to set before the reader the example of a man who, like the apostle Paul, has said, "Be ye followers of me, even as I am of Christ" [I Cor. 11: 1; Kantor, 1983: 25-7].

The account of Constantine's childhood reflects his general status as a potential member of the choir of the saints in episodes such as the incident when a falcon eludes him during a hunting expedition. This marks him as one who is destined to follow things that are not of this world. His dream of choosing a beautiful woman named Sophia from among all other women in Thessalonica to be his wife has that same general function, but also prefigures his later life as an apostle whose service to the Church centers around the teaching of the Divine Wisdom. This function, rather than any sort of secular biographical motives, clearly inspires the lengthy account of Constantine's instruction in the Imperial City. He masters the arts of rhetoric, but also strives for mastery of the arts of the spirit.

Constantine's adult life is structured as a series of confrontations, mediated by brief periods of withdrawal to a monastery, in which he defends the truth of the Christian faith against heretics and worldly men, and teaches others to do likewise. He summarizes the essence of his service to Christ in his final prayer to God to deliver the faithful

> ... from the godless and heathen malice of those speaking blasphemy against Thee, and destroy the trilingual heresy belief. Increase Thy church to a multitude, gather all together in unanimity, and make a chosen people of those who are of one mind in Thy true faith and just confession. And inspire in their hearts the Word of Thy Son, for it is Thy gift. If Thou hast accepted us, unworthy ones, to preach the Gospel of Thy Christ, then those who are striving for good deeds and doing what pleases Thee, whom Thou hast given to me, I return to Thee as Thine [Kantor, 1983: 79].

The same network of vertical bonds that shapes the structure of a *vita* informs its language. A writer is always obliged to draw on the verbal resources available to him, which naturally include the various norms and conventions of the literary (and occasionally non-literary) language. This language is mastered, not as an abstract grammatical system, but from exposure to a set of texts. The writer is, moreover, encouraged to borrow words, phrases, commonplaces and passages from this set of texts by the medieval pedagogical system which emphasizes *auctoritas* [see Picchio, 1984[b]: 7]. To some extent, then, he had to have been aware of the conventions of "types" of writing [Ingham, 1983: 226]. But Constantine's life, a text with an unusually pronounced metalinguistic subtext, suggests that this awareness, too, was protogeneric. The author of the life is always conscious of the fact that his medium is the language of the Slavic Scriptures and liturgy. The emphasis here is properly placed on Scripture and liturgy rather than on language, and it is an emphasis that is intrinsic to the narrative's subject: a man who brought the message of Christianity to the Slavs in their own tongue. The real factor of Constantine's birthplace enabled him to communicate in this lingua franca. His readiness to translate Scripture into Church Slavonic was a function of the Orthodox doctrine that such texts can and should be taught in languages other than Hebrew, Greek or Latin. Constantine's life was recorded in Church Slavonic because it is addressed to a community that used this language as its written medium. He is, at the same time, acutely aware of the fact that the medium is able to convey such a message because Constantine and his brother Methodius extended the vocabulary to accommodate concepts hitherto expressible only in the three "sacred" tongues.

Not all the materials relating to the lives of potential saints, however, suffice for such a harmonious fusion of form, function and message. The life of St. Adrian Pošexonskij, for example, begins *in medias res* with the appearance of a mysterious monk named Bestuž who, knowing of Adrian's wish to found a monastery, leads him to a special place in the forest [Adrian, 1873: no. 4, 25]. The life of Mixail Klopskij is another example of a story that begins in the middle because the biographer had no way of knowing events that occurred before Mixail was discovered on the eve of St. John's day in a cell of the Holy Trinity Monastery, copying the Acts of the Apostles by candlelight [Dmitriev, 1958: 141]. The *vita* of Ioann and Loggin Jarengskie begins after the saints' death, with an account of how the two drowned men have begun to appear to villagers in their dreams, asking that their remains be moved to a church, and working miracles [Dmitriev, 1973: 214].

So, too, the language of saints' lives and the narrative viewpoint is very much dependent upon the *Sitz im Leben* of the saint (i.e., where he or she appears, to whom, and under what circumstances) and of the biographer, because more often than not the initial account is produced in the place where the cult first forms. The language and viewpoint of a hierarch's biographer is naturally going to be loftier and less personal than those of a provincial monk who is recording the testimony of villagers about miracles that they have witnessed in connection with a local figure. The differences are particularly striking in the Kievan period, where the writers are often hard pressed to master elementary verbal skills, and we see a wide degree of variance between texts produced in isolated monasteries or northern areas and texts produced in Kiev or Smolensk, which were cultural centers.

As time goes on, in connection with the formation of a more centralized

Muscovite state, the composers of saints' lives begin to standardize their texts stylistically and formally, subordinating the traditional vertical bonding to bonds that are increasingly lateral in nature. We may see this during the period of the so-called Second South Slavic influence and in some works edited by Metropolitan Makarij and his circle. Outside of such circles, however, vertical bonding remains the norm into the seventeenth century. A prime example of this is the life of Ul'janija Osor'ina. Its eccentricity is frequently conceptualized as an expression of a movement forward: i.e., from abstract, conventionalized religious biography to realistic secular biography. I think, however, that it is more properly classed as a kind of atavism. The biographer's experience in the chancery and social station profoundly influences the form and style of a life whose composition is motivated by the witnessing of traditional signs of sainthood: uncorrupted relics. This is precisely the sort of text that one would expect to be produced in the period before the medieval Russians were able to conceive of types of writing apart from types of saints or their veneration. What accounts for the atavism is, clearly, the "unconventional" status of the author, who, in his own way, is as new to the business of biography as were the early monks in Kievan scriptoria.

Plotting the Matrices of the Cult Texts

In the Kievan period, which will be the primary focus of this investigation, saints' lives were recounted in a variety of interrelated protogeneric forms, ranging from the bare minimum of hymns that had to be included in a service to long narrations and eulogies. The sort of models suggested by genre theoreticians to differentiate these forms are too simple to account for their etiology or shape. Even when we analyze the briefest of hymns composed for a saint's office, the coordinates of the vertical bonding may be highly specific and complex.

Rather than draw a general schema, then, we should take certain broad oppositions as guidelines for the investigation of texts where vertical bonding dominates or excludes lateral bonding:
   a) texts produced to meet the needs of institutions versus texts produced to meet private or transitory needs;
   b) texts produced to meet the needs of a certain class or profession versus texts that cross class or professional barriers;
   c) texts with strongly expressed temporal or spatial loci versus texts which are meant to transcend a specific point in time and space;
   d) messages that are medium-specific versus messages that may be actualized in a variety of media;
   e) messages that may be openly expressed versus messages that must be encoded or suppressed.

These guidelines are not meant to be all-inclusive, but merely to suggest some of the most important preliminaries for ascertaining the socio-cultural coordinates of a work.

In seeking to trace the process by which the text is modeled, we may have recourse to a variety of indices which will be suggested by our preliminary identification of the texts' *Sitz im Leben*. For texts related to the institutions of Orthodoxy, for example, such indices include service books, ecclesiastical codices enumerating various points of the religious canon, and authoritative commentary on doctrine or ritual. When a text's function is not confined to any ecclesiastical institution, we may need to consult legal codices, diplomatic protocols, annalistic records or even eye-witness reports. Such sources enable us to reconstruct the operative socio-cultural systems of the period and the matrix of vertical bonds with relative precision, and, on that basis, to explain why any given group of texts form a protogenre or do not.

Such, then, is the methodological apparatus that I shall apply to the texts produced in connection with the cult of martyred princes Boris and Gleb. The texts constitute an ideal test case not only because of their broad range, but because a number of problems raised in connection with them can be solved by identifying their socio-cultural analogues and exploring the vertical connections between the texts and the cult itself. I shall begin my analysis with a discussion of the *Sitz im Leben*, reconstructing the probable response of the Kievan community to the murder of the princes and the canonization process. In keeping with this approach the ensuing discussion of the texts produced and shaped by the cult will be ordered, not by chronology (which in any case is virtually impossible to establish), but by the nature of their relationship to the saints' veneration. The hymns which are indispensable or customary for a saint's office will be discussed first, followed by analyses of more loosely structured, optional cult texts with edifying or witness functions (homilies, biographies). The final chapter is devoted to the most heterogeneous of documents which treat the murder of Boris and Gleb as one event in the history of a Christian principality: the various entries compiled by regional chroniclers. In a few instances the conclusions reached in this process will coincide with those of scholars who have chosen a more traditional approach. My intent is not to question the legitimate achievements of the longstanding and copious research tradition connected with the cult of Boris and Gleb, but to present the answers in terms that are more consistent with the realities of literary production and dissemination in the pre-Petrine period.

2

THE KIEVAN CULT

> В лѣто 6552. И выгребоша 2 князя, Ярополка и Ольга, сына Святославля, и крестиша кости ею, и положиша я въ церкви святыя Богородица. . . .[1]
>
> Прииди, Господи, и освяти воду сию Духомъ Твоимъ Святымъ и огнемъ. . . .[2]

Kievan Rus' was converted to Christianity only a few decades before the murder of Boris and Gleb, yet the earliest accounts of the event and its aftermath place the community's response well within the norms of Christian conduct. Given the relatively brief exposure of the population to Orthodoxy, however, and the natural reluctance to abandon pagan traditions, it is likely that some descriptions of people's actions and motives have as much to do with the narrator's wish to portray what should have happened as with the facts of the matter. To acknowledge that the Kievans could not have entirely grasped or absorbed Orthodox Christianity at so early a date in their history is by no means to deny the existence of a cult involving the veneration of the murdered princes. It does suggest, however, that we should examine a possible pagan context for the cult, one which might account for the unexpectedly strong reaction to manifestations of the princes' saintliness by Prince Jaroslav and by the community of Vyšgorod. In the following chapter I shall argue that the circumstances of the brothers' murder and the recovery of their remains were interpretable according to either the pre-Christian or the Christian cultural code, and that this overlap elicited genuine veneration for the brothers which was accepted by the clergy as Christian veneration.

The Syncretic Response

Jaroslav's personal attitude toward the death of his brothers[3] is the first issue that must be addressed if we hope to understand how Boris and Gleb initially came to be venerated. Both the Laurentian Chronicle account and the "Narration" depict Jaroslav as the guardian of his brothers: he warns Gleb of Svjatopolk's plot, drives Svjatopolk, their murderer, into the wilderness, orders that Gleb's remains be recovered and supervises the canonization proceedings. A number of historians have doubted the purity of

Jaroslav's motives and suggested that the initial cult was promoted by the prince to serve his own political interests.

The most radical interpretation was proposed by Il'in in his much-discussed study on the chronicle entry for 1015 [1957]. Il'in argues that Jaroslav had his two brothers murdered by Varangian mercenaries, blamed the murder on Svjatopolk, and eventually promoted a cult of Boris and Gleb, modeled on the cult of the Bohemian sovereign-saint Wenceslas, in order to conceal his own guilt in the matter. This theory is based, in part, on Il'in's certainty that the earliest accounts of Boris and Gleb are modeled on the *vita* of Wenceslas (see Chapters Four and Five below), and, in part, on a comparison with non-Russian sources that supplement the chronicle accounts. A crucial link in his reasoning is provided by the *þáttr* (short saga-like tale) of Eymundr, son of Hringr, which has survived in the Icelandic *Flateyarbók*, a manuscript dated between 1387 and 1395.[4]

Eymundr, a king's son, flees his native Norway and travels to Rus', hoping to be hired as a mercenary by one of three warring princes. The three princes are identified as the sons of the late King Valdimar: Burislafr, the senior prince, has received the largest patrimony and rules in Kænugarðr (Kiev); Jarislafr rules in Holmgarðr (Novgorod); and Vartilafr rules Palteskja (Polock). Eymundr and his men are indeed taken on by Jarislafr, with the encouragement of his wife Ingigerðr. With Eymundr's help, Jarislafr's army defeats Burislafr's. Burislafr returns again and is again repelled by Jarislafr and his mercenaries. Eymundr advises Jarislafr that the conflict will never be resolved so long as Burislafr remains alive, and asks whether Jarislafr would like him to murder Burislafr. Jarislafr replies: "I will not incite people to do battle against Burislafr, nor will I hold them guilty if he is killed." Eymundr's men then murder Burislafr in his tent and bring his head back to Jarislafr. Jarislafr's reaction is to reproach the Varangians for their hasty deed and to charge them with burying Burislafr. When he asks about witnesses, Eymundr answers that Burislafr's army is in disarray and has probably fled. The Varangians bury the dead prince. The author of the tale concludes this episode with the note:

> Many people knew of the burial. The entire land came under Jarislafr's rule and swore fealty to him, and he became the king of that principality which was ruled before by two men [Rydzevskaja, 1978: 100].

There is no precise way to establish the identities of the three princes. Jarislafr is generally acknowledged to be a portrait of Jaroslav. Burislafr has been identified with Svjatopolk, since he is depicted as occupying the Kievan throne [cf. Hruševʹsky, 1895: 111, note 1; Ljaščenko, 1926: 1066, 1072; Cross, 1929: 186; Cook, 1986: 69]. Il'in identifies Burislafr with both Svjatopolk and Boris, arguing that the names display a sound coincidence and that Boris' fate most closely corresponds to the fate of Burislafr [1957:

160-169 and *passim*]. Pritsak suggests that there may be *two* different Burislafrs. He identifies the first Burislafr as representing both Svjatopolk and Bolesław; the second Burislafr, according to this theory, represents both Boris and Gleb [1985: 873]. Cross identifies Vartilafr with Jaroslav's nephew, Prince Brjačeslav Izjaslavovič of Polock.

A number of contradictions between the saga account and other documents have been noted. Boris' and Gleb's murders occurred in the year 1015. In the *Eymundar Þáttr*, however, Jaroslav is depicted as married to Ingigerðr, an event which occurred in 1019 [*Heimskringla*: Chapter 93, p. 342]. Brjačeslav attacked Jaroslav in 1021 [PSRL, 1926: 146] long after the murders of the princes. The description of the warring princes likewise most closely corresponds to the entries in the chronicles describing the strife following the princes' death between Jaroslav, Svjatopolk, and Svjatopolk's ally (and father-in-law) Bolesław Chrobry of Poland. Yet, as Cross points out, unless we identify Burislafr as a distortion of Bolesław, there is no mention of their alliance, which was well attested in other documents, and no mention of Jaroslav's contemplated exile [1929: 187].

The chronological discrepancies and omissions in the tale's version, which lead Cross to conclude that the *Eymundar Þáttr* is no more than a "confused reminiscence of the actual course of events" [1929: 187], and the need to telescope two central characters in the murder into the figure of Burislafr, identifying the living ruler with Svjatopolk and the headless corpse with Boris, speak against Il'in's reconstruction. There is no positive evidence of such a crime although the Primary Chronicle is filled with records of fratricide and internecine slaughter (Vladimir's murder of Jaropolk, for example). These factors, together with the heavy fictional element of such tales, have led most scholars to dismiss the theory that Jaroslav murdered at least one brother as contrived and implausible.[5] Accordingly, I shall proceed on the assumption that Svjatopolk was the murderer, as all of the Russian sources suggest.

Blood Revenge and Ancestor Worship

According to the Laurentian Chronicle, Jaroslav is told of the crime by a messenger from his sister Predslava, who warns him to be on his guard against Svjatopolk.[6] His decision to gather an army and march against his "brother" is the natural result of his concern to defend himself and his wish to take over the Kievan throne. Jaroslav's retainers rally to the call, showing themselves ready to let bygones be bygones (see Chapter Five). Two subsequent speeches uttered by Jaroslav *justifying* his action, however, stand in marked contrast with what one would expect of a Kievan prince in an epoch where internecine strife was the rule. Much of the rationale for his actions may be attributed to the Judaeo-Christian ethics of the chronicler. At the same time, by reading between the lines of these speeches and correlating what is expressed here with other sources, we can reconstruct the syncretic socio-cultural context of Jaroslav's response to the murders.

Jaroslav speaks as he is preparing for the first of three battles against Svjatopolk at Ljubeč. The prince calls on God to bear witness that

> "Не я почахъ избивати братью, но онъ; да будеть отместьникъ Богъ крове братья моея, зане без вины пролья кровь Борисову и Глѣбову праведною. Еда и мнѣ си[ц]е же створить? Но суди ми, Господи, по правдѣ, да скончается злоба грѣшнаго"[PSRL, 1926: 141].[7]

Jaroslav's second speech is uttered before the final battle against Svjatopolk on the River Al'ta:

> Ярославъ ста на мѣстѣ, идеже оубиша Бориса, въздѣвъ руцѣ на небо, рече: «Кровь брата моего вопьеть к тобѣ, Владыко! Мьсти от крове праведнаго сего, якоже мьстилъ еси крове Авелевы, положивъ на Каинѣ стенанье и трясенье;--тако положи и на семь». Помоливъся, и рекъ: «Брата моя! Аще еста и тѣломь [отошла] отсюда, но молитвою помозѣта ми на противнаго сего убиицю и гордаго» [ibid.: 144].[8]

The standard reading of these passages has been from a Christian perspective, as the Christian chronicler, no doubt, intended them to be read. Svjatopolk, who has violated the Lord's commandments in the spirit of Cain, has become accursed by men and God. In the scriptural passage Cain, though a fugitive, is marked so that no man will dare to kill him: his punishment will be inflicted by the Lord alone. Jaroslav's argument is slightly different: he makes himself out to be the Lord's instrument, implying that if he punishes Svjatopolk it is because the Lord allows him to be His agent. In the same spirit, the chronicler tells us, Jaroslav does not take it upon himself to kill his brother: he defeats him in battle, forcing Svjatopolk to flee the country. In his flight and exile, Svjatopolk is *divinely* punished. A *demon* causes his limbs to weaken so that he cannot sit on his horse and must be carried about on a litter. The demon then causes him to be afflicted with delusions of persecution that drive him from place to place until at last he expires. His fate and death are portrayed as divine judgment in the following terms:

> Егоже по правдѣ, яко неправедну, суду нашедшю на нь, по отшествии сего свѣта прияша мукы, оканьнаго. Показоваше явѣ посланая пагубная рана, въ смерть немилостивно въгна, и по смерти вѣчно мучимъ есть связанъ. Есть же могыла его в пустыни и до сего дне. Исходить же от нея смрадъ золъ. Се же Богъ показа на наказанье княземъ русьскымъ, да аще сии еще сице же створять [се слышавше, ту же казнь приимуть; но и больши сее, понеже, вѣдая се, сътворять] такоже зло оубииство. 7 бо мьстии прия Каинъ, оубивъ Авеля, а Ламехъ 70. Понеже бѣ Каинъ не вѣдыи мьщенья прияти от Бога, а Ламехъ, вѣдый казнь, бывши на прародителю его, створи оубииство [PSRL, 1926: 145].[9]

On one level, the recurring references to *měst"* and *krov'* draw analogies to the situation in the biblical tale of Cain, as Ingham discusses in his insightful study of the martyred prince [1984: 41-2]]. But, as often is the case, there are concrete references to the Kievan political situation encoded in the text. And one need not seek far to discover a native precedent for this sort of retribution. By ancient Russian custom, Jaroslav is entitled to exact blood revenge for the murder of his brother. The first code of Russian law, *Pravda Russkaja*, begins with the following article:

> 1. Оубиеть моужь моужа, то мьстѣть братж брата, любо сынови ѿтца, а любо ѿтцю сына, любо братоучада, любо сестриню сынови; аще не боудет(ь) кто мьстѧ, то 40 гривенъ за головоу . . . [Grekov, 1940-1963: 79].[10]

Blood revenge has been characterized as the leading means of dealing with homicide in Rus' up to the beginning of the thirteenth century [Kaiser, 1980: 62-64]. Jaroslav's *Pravda* is regarded as an effort to reform such practices. In contrast to the expanded *Pravda* that attempts to abolish blood revenge altogether, however, the article in question is generally seen as more modest in its goals, aiming only to limit the right of blood revenge and to offer an alternative. That Jaroslav would view the murder of Boris and Gleb as cases which merited vindication through this ancient practice should not surprise us, given their princely status and the realities of the struggle for the throne.

Jaroslav's repeated reference to "guilt" also sheds some light on his probable attitude toward the fate of Boris and Gleb. Their failure to resist their murderers has been seen as submission to a senior member of the clan and interpreted as the sort of behavior that would be cultivated, or at least approved [Fedotov, 1931: 22-23; Lixačev, 1954: 87-88; Poppe, 1973: 20-21; Ingham, 1973: 12; Maczko, 1975: 72]. But Jaroslav, like Vladimir before him, finds it perfectly acceptable for a junior prince to challenge a senior prince when the latter has crossed the boundaries of acceptable conduct. Svjatopolk's act of fratricide places him in such a position and, indeed, compels vengeance. If Jaroslav's reaction is justifiable in the eyes of the clan (and it is clearly within the limits of the law), Boris and Gleb might also have been expected to resist, all the more so because their attackers were neither brothers nor princes but hired assassins. Passive resistance of this sort could not have been viewed as a princely virtue because it would compromise a prince's ability to rule: it was, rather, the virtue of a saint and is foregrounded in texts reflecting later stages of the cult. Beginning with the second redaction of the paremia readings, for example, the motif of blood revenge is gradually overshadowed by the motif of the righteous victim [Soboleva, 1975: 116-117]. In this case, the conflict between princely and saintly virtues is so pronounced that Jaroslav could not promote Boris and Gleb as model *princes* without placing his own (entirely princely) behavior in a very unfavorable light.

There is another reason why Jaroslav would promote Boris' and Gleb's veneration, however, and it emerges in his extraordinary prayer to his dead brothers quoted above [PSRL, 1926: 144]. Commentators generally construe this prayer as a typically Christian petition. Yet the prince is praying to persons who at the time of the utterance have no status as saints, and who are therefore in no position to render assistance, at least from an ecclesiastical standpoint. We may be dealing here with a textual anachronism, but Jaroslav's behavior is quite explicable in non-Christian terms: he is invoking the help of his dead relatives by virtue of kinship, a practice characteristic of pagan Slavic ancestor worship.

Other entries in the Laurentian Chronicle suggest that princes continued to pray to their fathers and their grandfathers for help in overcoming some difficulty long after the baptism of Rus'. Among the princes mentioned as engaging in this practice are Mixalko, the son of Jurij Dolgorukij, Konstantin Vsevolodovič and Mixail of Tver' [Komarovič, 1960: 87-89]. None of their prayers are actually written out in the Chronicle entries—and given the biases and format of the yearly entries, one would not expect otherwise. Jaroslav's words are noteworthy because they express sentiments normally reported in summary. They testify to a sincere—and very pagan—bond to his murdered brothers. This bond would stem from ties of blood, strengthened by the belief that one's dead relatives had supernatural powers to aid or harm the living. Whatever political reasons Jaroslav may have had for pursuing Svjatopolk and taking blood revenge, then, a compelling motivation for the act of revenge and an important component in his own acts of "veneration" was the status of Boris and Gleb as kinsmen and their potential power to act on their brother's behalf.[11]

The Fire Miracles

Many sources testify that the ancient Slavs worshipped fire. Travelers describe rituals, sacrifices and the burning of the dead to ensure their ascent to paradise [Fraehn, 1823: 11-21, 102, 104-5; Niederle, 1924: 76-86]. The widely disseminated royal statute known as the *Ustav Vladimira* expressly forbids the Kievans to "molit'sja pod" ovinom" (i.e., to pray to the spirits in the *ovin*, a barn-like structure in which a fire is built to dry sheaves of grain) [Ščapov, 1976: 23]. A fourteenth-century copy of the *Slovo Xristoljubca* contains a list of East Slavic gods and reports that, among other deities, the Slavs prayed to Svarožič, the fire god ("ogněvě moljat'sja zovušče ego Svarožičem") [Tixonravov, 1862: 89]. Sermons attributed to St. Gregory of Nazianzus and St. John Chrysostom, as well as the writings of Kirill of Turov, contain similar references to pagan Slavic customs connected with fire worship.[12]

The Slavs, as well as other Indo-European peoples, identified fire with the soul of the departed. Afanas'ev writes that even in his day, fires appearing over graves due to phosphorescent fumes were taken for the souls of the deceased. Burning candles were reported by the inhabitants of a settlement in Tambov province on a site where the bodies of suicides, victims of strangling, or those who died of drink were buried. Other informants told of burning candles appearing over the graves of innocent men who had been hanged, until a funeral wake was held for them [1865-1869: III, 197; see also Xaruzina, 1906; Moszyński, 1934-1939: II,1, 501-2; Tokarev, 1957: 70 and *passim*]. According to Czech legend, when an unrepentant sinner died he or she was condemned to wander the earth forever: these wandering souls appeared in the form of fiery pillars or as humans with eyes and tongues of fire [Afanas'ev, 1865-1869: III, 198-99]. The Russians also believed that the souls of the dead who for some reason had not been permitted to enter the heavenly kingdom wandered through the countryside in one or another fiery form, leading travelers astray. Such a fire is known in Russian as *bludjaščij ogon'* (*ignis fatuus*, will-o'-the-wisp) [Afanas'ev, 1865-1869: III, 198-99].

The strong resemblance of the first posthumous miracles to the apparitions described above could be dismissed as coincidental were it not for the medieval witnesses testifying to the antiquity of such beliefs. This testimony, together with the fact that Boris' and Gleb's canonization came so swiftly after the conversion to Christianity (i.e., as early as 1020 and no later than 1072), suggests that the community response to the reported visions, like Jaroslav's response to the unavenged murder of his kinsmen, may have been at least partially attributable to syncretism.

The Laurentian Chronicle entry, as well as the two earliest narrative lives, testify that Boris' body was recovered and buried near the Church of St. Basil at Vyšgorod. The precise location is not specified in any sources, and no archeological investigations have been able to identify the site. Gleb's body remained lost somewhere in the wilderness along the River Smjadyn'. According to the "Narration":

> И сему убо святууму лежащю дълго время, [Господь] не остави въ невѣдѣнии и небрежении, отинудь пребыти неврежену, нъ показа: овогда бо видѣша стълпъ огньнъ, овогда свѣщѣ горущѣ, и пакы пѣния ангельская слышааху мимоходящии же путьмь гостие, ини же, ловы дѣюще и пасуще, си же видяще и слышаще [Abramovič, 1916: 43-44].[13]

The "Lection" gives the following account:

> Повелѣ же христолюбивый князь изискати тѣло святого Глѣба, его же много искавше и не обрѣтоша. По лѣтѣ же единомъ ходяще ловци обрѣтоша тѣло святого лежаще цѣло, ни звѣремъ, ни птицамъ прикоснувъшимся его. Абие шедъ въ градъ, възвѣстиша старѣйшинѣ граду. Он же, шедъ съ отроки, видѣвъ же святого, свѣтящася яко молнии, и ужасенъ бывъ старѣйщина; повелѣ слугамъ своимъ на мѣстѣ томъ

стрещи святого тѣла, дондеже посла възвѣстити христолюбцю Ярославу
. . . [*ibid.*: 14].[14]

Once the corpse had been located, Jaroslav's men brought it back to the Vyšgorod Church of St. Basil, where it was interred beside the body of Boris. Subsequently candles and fiery pillars were observed over the new grave sites. People came in increasing numbers to pay their respects to the dead princes, but there were still some who doubted. These doubters, too, were privy to miraculous signs, though of a more ominous character. In the most dramatic incident flames burst from the grave, burning the feet of a Varangian soldier who had inadvertently stepped on the holy site. A few days after the Varangian was burned, reports the author of the "Narration," the Church of St. Basil caught fire:

> И течааху людие на позоръ, и горяше церкы отъ вьрха, и все изнесоша иконы и съсуды, и ничьто же не съгорѣ, тъкъмо церкы едина. Повѣдаша же Ярославу о всемь семь. И призъвавъ митрополита Иоана, съказааше ему все о святою мученику, брату своею. И бысть преужасьнъ и въ усьмьнении, таче и въ дьрзновении и въ радости и къ Богу [*ibid.*: 53].[15]

The "Lection" devotes somewhat more space to the account, which it attributes to the devil's displeasure at seeing people visit the holy grave. The devil's agent is a careless sexton who is in such a hurry to get home that he leaves a candle burning in the church. Nestor adds:

> И весе, мню я, Божиимъ попущениемь сему быти. Убо тои худѣ сущи, обетшанѣ древомъ, дабы же ина церкы пакы възгражена была на томъ мѣстѣ во имя святою и блаженою страстотерпцю Бориса и Глѣба. . . . Иже во храмѣ свѣтильнице--си суть угодници Божии, иже не лѣпо бѣ такыма свѣтильникома скровенома быти подъ землею, нъ на суцѣ мѣстѣ положенома быти, да свѣтита всѣмъ, иже во храмѣ [*ibid.*: 16].[16]

The aforementioned miracles were the catalysts which provoked the official disinterment of the princes' bodies. In terms of their typology, the signs (candles, angelic chanting, fiery pillars) have many parallels in ancient and Kievan Christian literature. Similar miracles may be found in Nestor's biography of St. Feodosij of the Caves and in the Patericon of the Kiev Cave Monastery. Burning candles appear on the grave of the Czech saint Ludmila, as Jakobson pointed out [1944, 1976: 47; cf. Il'in, 1957: 60] and also by the graves of the Norwegian sovereign-saint Olaf Haraldsson [*Heimskringla*: Chapter 238, p. 523], Bojarynja Morozova and Ul'janija Osor'ina, among other saints. So, too, the punishment of the Varangian recalls incidents in saints' lives and pilgrimage accounts where unbelievers are killed or severely burned by flames that burst forth from a holy relic or grave. Ivan III's insistence on the disinterment of St. Varlaam's remains during a visit to the monastery at Xutyn' elicits a burst of dense black smoke [Dmitriev, 1973: 55-6]. The Greek pilgrim Phocas (late 12th century) recounts a closer parallel which he heard from his guides at St. George's Monastery in Palestine:

> The Catholic bishop presently assigned to the city attempted to open the mouth of [St. George's] grave. Prying up the boards, they found a large crypt in whose depths the saint's grave was located. When they made bold to open the grave itself, a blast of fire came out at them. One was almost turned into cinders. The other died instantly [Troickij, 1889: 27].

Fires or natural disasters frequently necessitated the translation of a saint's relics from one repository to another—a ritual that was often entered into the church calendar and commemorated as a separate feast day. The "Lection" representation of this fire as a sign that the princes should be reburied in a manner befitting saints is a standard Christian reading of the disaster as a miraculous event. The accompanying scriptural reference to letting one's light shine before all men [Matt. 5: 14-15] is commonly encountered in East Slavic saints' biographies in connection with the description of a disinterment or translation ceremony. At the same time, this miracle, like the preceding miracles, is amenable to "pagan" readings because it is connected with a manifestation of divinely provoked fire. Later miracles attributed to the relics of Boris and Gleb, in contrast, echo the more typical miracles associated with Christian saints, consisting almost exclusively of healing.

A certain section of the Kievan population (most notably the higher ranking clergy) must have interpreted the fiery miracles as evidence of Boris' and Gleb's sainthood. It is of some interest, therefore, that trustworthy, educated witnesses are not singled out for mention. On the contrary, the hagiographers record the testimony of hunters, shepherds and merchants. These are the sort of witnesses who would have taken the fiery pillars sighted over the graves of Boris and Gleb as a message that the souls of the brothers had not gone to heaven but were still forced to wander the earth for some as yet undetermined reason. The burning of the Varangian soldier and the burning of St. Basil's church could have confirmed such superstitious fears and served as an impetus for a hasty disinterment and reburial.

The likening of Gleb's glowing corpse to a flash of lightning recalls biblical descriptions of angels [Dan. 10: 6; Matt. 28: 3], although it is not typical of the light imagery associated in hagiography with such situations.[17] At the same time it suggests a connection to the pagan thunder-god Perun. The connection is confirmed in a variety of proverbs that link Boris and Gleb with the hagiographical incarnation of Perun, the Prophet Elijah [cf. Afanas'ev, 1865-1869: I, 469-79; Dal', 1862: II, 315]. Associations of this nature may have heightened the reaction to the fiery omens.[18]

The fact that the first posthumous miracles observed at the graves of the murdered princes correspond to supernatural manifestations associated with pagan Slavic beliefs and that they are reported by people who belong neither to the educated upper classes nor to the clergy is especially significant in assessing the earliest stages of the cult. Though the saints eventually became dynastic patrons with a special relationship to the princely and boyar classes, the written sources suggest that such was not the case at the onset of the cult. Rather, Boris and Gleb are here portrayed as the objects of genuine, popular veneration—very much in keeping with the syncretism of Russian religious practices of the time.

The Christian Response

The Laurentian Chronicle entry of 1015 focuses on the circumstances of Boris' and Gleb's murder (see Chapter Five). We must turn to the "Narration" and the "Lection" accounts to follow the process by which the princes were officially recognized by the Church as saints. Both sources describe how the *de facto* veneration for the princes led to an official investigation by Metropolitan John. The saints' remains were disinterred and found to be miraculously preserved. They were left above ground in a special chapel until additional miracles were documented. At that point, the metropolitan ordered a church to be consecrated in the princes' honor and designated a day for their formal commemoration [Abramovič, 1916: 18, 54-55]. Later, on a number of occasions, the relics were officially translated: Boris' remains were placed in a new stone sarcophagus (1072), and both sarcophagi were moved from an old church to a new one (1072, 1115) [*ibid*.: 21-22, 55-56, 64-66].

Several scholars have questioned the testimony of these sources that Boris and Gleb were glorified in Jaroslav's lifetime. They believe that formal canonization took place in 1072 during a ceremony which is identified in the "Narration," "Lection" and chronicle accounts as a translation (*perenesenie*), and was commemorated as a separate holiday with a special (optional) service. The fact that the 1072 ceremony is uniformly represented in medieval documents as a translation, together with the absence of any documentation to the contrary, places the burden of proof on those who claim a later date for the canonization. The arguments mustered to support the redating rest primarily on negative evidence, and in some cases on a misunderstanding of the meaning of canonization for the early Church, but have been widely accepted in the scholarship. They are best answered through a step-by-step reconstruction of the canonization process, which will permit us to correlate the accounts of Boris' and Gleb's veneration with other accounts of cults in Kievan, North, and Northeast Rus'.

Boris' and Gleb's Burial

Boris' remains were initially buried in a wooden coffin. This has been perceived as a violation of a "rule" that East Slavic saints had to be buried in stone or silver coffins [cf. Poppe, 1969: 374-375; Aleškovskij, 1971: 85 and 1972, 123; Xorošev, 1986: 20]. The evidence for deducing such a rule is the testimony of a Prolog *vita* that Leontij of Rostov's remains were placed in a stone sarcophagus, information that was confirmed by members of a Soviet archaeological expedition [cf. Voronin, 1963: 27-28]. The *vita* itself does not represent the burial of the saint in a stone sarcophagus as a matter of protocol, but merely as a matter of fact [Filippovskij, 1982: 126]. Archaeological evidence and accounts of other saints' lives confirm that the decision to translate a saint's relics to a stone or silver coffin was elective in East Slavic practice of the period. Wealthy patrons periodically expressed the desire to honor a saint by decorating or replacing the old coffin. On occasion a fire, natural catastrophe or simple deterioration required that a saint's remains be translated to a new coffin. The initial burial materials depended upon a number of factors, among them the social status of the saint (a prince or bishop would naturally receive a more elaborate coffin than an ascetic monk or a fool-in-Christ) and the materials available to the coffinmakers.

Boris' burial in a wooden coffin represents a departure from the norm quite apart from the question of his canonization, however, for Kievan princes and nobles were customarily buried in marble sarcophagi [Karger, 1958: 472]. How are we to account for this anomaly? The theory that Boris' burial in a wooden coffin reflects pagan practices [Sciacca, 1985] is contradicted by archaeological and manuscript evidence of similar practices in Byzantine monasteries [Abrahamse, 1984: 131]. In areas such as Northeast Rus' Christian princes who had been tonsured were routinely buried in monasteries in wooden coffins because of the difficulty in obtaining or working with stone. Boris' initial burial in the wooden coffin after his murder, then, probably testifies to his ambiguous social status. The reason he was not buried with honors after his murder can only be that he was the enemy of Svjatopolk, at the time grand prince of Kiev. Gleb's body, on the other hand, was recovered after Jaroslav had taken control of the principality, and it is not surprising that he would have been given the standard treatment: burial in a stone coffin.

More difficult to explain than the initial circumstances of the princes' burials is Jaroslav's failure to rebury Boris in a stone coffin. He could have done so, regardless of whether Boris was canonized, precisely because Boris was a prince. Aleškovskij believes that the apparent preference shown for the younger brother Gleb indirectly confirms his own hypothesis that Gleb was initially more highly venerated than Boris [1972: 104-125]. The lack of commentary on the discrepancy in the coffins casts some doubt on this theory, as does the fact that both brothers were laid side by side in a new grave by the Church of St. Basil.

It is likely that Boris' remains were initially kept in their original casket because the faithful valorized it for its healing powers or for its associations (the physical traces of his blood, the identification of humble material with the humility of the saint), much as one would prize a relic. We can find ample precedents for such beliefs in the East Slavic tradition where not only the sarcophagi but also the birchbark shrouds of saints such as Nikita of Perejaslavl' [see BAN 31.6.22: f. 11ᵛ] or Prince Andrej of Smolensk are reported to have healed those who touched the artifact or a piece of it [Smirnov, 1908: 64]. By 1072, as we shall discuss below, Boris' wooden casket was ostentatiously upgraded by Izjaslav to a stone sarcophagus, in conjunction with the translation of relics to a new church built by the prince. In 1102, the coffins of both Boris and Gleb were covered with gilded silver casings by Vladimir Monomax [Abramovič, 1916: 63], who also had their remains translated to a new church in 1115 [*ibid.*: 64-66; PSRL, 1908: 280-282].

The Miraculous Evidence
According to the "Narrative of the Miracles" appended to the "Narration," Jaroslav reported the miraculous manifestations discussed above (the fiery apparitions, the burning of the Varangian, the fire in the Church of St. Basil) to Metropolitan John. The metropolitan is described as skeptical about the alleged miracles, a reaction which has been ascribed to his official status as *advocatus diaboli* [Müller, 1962: 43], but may also have been due to the syncretic nature of the cult, as we have seen. In any case, he initiated the necessary process of verification. Accompanied by Prince Jaroslav and the clergy from the cathedral, he visited the grave site, where a small chapel had been erected. The metropolitan celebrated a requiem for the dead brothers,[19] and on the following morning the bodies of the princes were exhumed. The most detailed account is given in the "Narration":

> Наставъшю же дьни, иде архиепископъ Иоанъ съ крьсты, идеже лежаста святою телеси пречьстнѣи, и сътворивъ молитву, повелѣ откопати пьрьсть, сущюю надъ гръбъмь святою. Копающемъ же, и исхожааше благая воня отъ гробу ею святою, и отъкопавъше, изнесоша я отъ земли. И приступивъ, митрополитъ Иоанъ съ презвутеры, съ страхъмь и любъвию, отькры гроба святою. Ти видѣша чюдо преславно: телеси святою никакоя же ѣзвы имущи, нъ присно все цѣло, и лици бяста свѣтлѣ акы ангела, яко дивитися и архиепископу зѣло, и всѣмь людьмъ испльньшемъся благоухания многа. И вънесъше въ ту храмину, яже бяше поставлена на мѣстѣ погорѣвъшия цьркве, и поставиша я надъ землею, на деснѣи странѣ [Abramovič, 1916: 53-4; cf. 17].[20]

Following the disinterment, two posthumous miracles are reported. The first involves a lame boy, identified as the servant of the town's senior official. Except for a few details which are not relevant for our purposes, the accounts are quite close in the "Lection" and the "Narration." In the former we read:

> Старѣйшина бо града того имѣ отрокъ хромъ: бяше бо нога его скорчена и суха, акы трость, ни понѣ малы ея чюяше, нъ бѣ яко мертва. Не могы ходити, древяную ногу подъдѣлавъ, хожаше. То, пришедъ, моляшеся у ракы святою и пребываше день и нощь, моляшеся. И въ едину нощь предъстаста ему святая страстотерпьца Христова Борисъ и Глѣбъ, глаголюща ему: «что яко тако вопиеши к нама?» Оному же ногу простирающю, исцѣления просящю. Скорая же врача и цѣлителя, имше же за сухую ногу и трижда прекрестивша, цѣлую створиста. Видѣвъ же с нима и отрока, иже бѣ палъ на блаженемь Борисѣ, свѣщю несюща предъ святыма. Таче въспрянувъша ему, и к тому не требующю древяныя ногы, нъ воскочи и, скоро текый, приде на мѣсто, идеже стояста рацѣ святою, и припадая к нима, моляшеся съ слезами, и всѣмъ исповѣда, яже створиста съ нимъ святая милость [Abramovič, 1916: 17-18].[21]

Soon after this miraculous cure, a second one is witnessed at the site. A blind man prays to Boris and Gleb, then falls to the earth before their coffins, touches his eyes to the coffin and recovers his sight [*ibid.*: 18; cf. 54]. Upon learning of the two miraculous cures, writes Nestor:

> Архиепископъ ... ужасенъ сы бысть, и свѣтъ же благый помысливъ въ умѣ, глаголя къ христолюбцю: «лѣпо ли бы намъ, благовѣрный царю, церковь имя ею възградити и уставити день, воньже праздновати има» [*ibid.*: 18, 54-55].[22]

Proponents of the 1072 canonization date have challenged the reliability of this version on a number of counts. Their arguments are based on two premises: first, that three miracles were required for the Orthodox Church to recognize an individual's status as a saint, and, second, that this requirement was fulfilled only in 1072 in Boris' and Gleb's case. Neither premise is supported by the sources.

The assertion that three miracles of a certain type were required for canonization is based on a passage from ms. 153 of the Synodal collection which Ključevskij [1871: 423-424] cites as a rule "known" in Old Rus' stipulating that before a person could be canonized his or her relics had to be verified according to the following criteria:

> Аще гдѣ мощи явятся въ земли, то не створят 3 чюдеса: глухъ да прослышитъ, нѣмъ проглаголетъ, слѣпъ да прозритъ; и аще сотворитъ чюдеса, то отъ Бога и отъ св. Апостолъ; аще ли не сотворять тѣхъ чюдесъ, то не приимите ихъ [Gorskij and Nevostruev, 1855-1917: vol. II, otdel 2, čast' 2, 283 (f. 296ᵛ)].[23]

Vasil'ev, who also cites the passage from Ključevskij's account, goes farther and asserts that this rule was not only "known" but consistently applied from the inception of the canonization process [1893: 125-126]. Among other examples illustrating how "consistently" the rule was applied;

he cites the case of Boris and Gleb, whose canonization he, like Ključevskij, dates in Metropolitan John's prelacy. Clearly, both of these historians, as Golubinskij after them, emphasize the importance of miraculous testimony *per se*, rather than the quantity or type of miracles. Their broad understanding of the "rule" is dictated by two facts which are well attested in their historical surveys of East Slavic canonization:

1) Many early East Slavic saints whose veneration is commonly acknowledged to predate the Councils of 1547 and 1549 do not meet the criteria specified here;
2) No other extant pre-sixteenth century sources establish such criteria as binding.

Poppe's complex argumentation, built on a literal interpretation of this "rule," involves a number of other contradictory and/or unsubstantiated conclusions. A major contradiction involves the miraculous healing of a lame parishioner which was registered *after* Metropolitan John ordered a church to be built in honor of the princes (i.e., too late to count for that canonization process), but long before the alleged "true" canonization of 1072. The identification of this miracle as the third, necessary proof of sanctity is especially problematic if one takes the aforecited "rule" literally because it does not fulfill the stipulations that a deaf person hear and a mute speak.

A second problem is the considerable delay in the Church's decision to act on the miraculous evidence. Poppe's assertion that the miracles were not *reported* until the eve of the ceremony of 1072 [1973: 17] finds no corroboration in any of the extant sources. Such a delay would be highly irregular. Normally, miraculous cures are recorded on the spot (some of the unedited protocols are appended to manuscript copies of saints' lives). Moreover, the miracles performed by Boris and Gleb are represented as having been publicly witnessed and/or affecting prominent persons in Vyšgorod. If these records were ignored, lost or suppressed for two decades after Jaroslav's death and then brought to the attention of the prince's sons, one would expect to find some reference to the circumstances or, at the very least, a note documenting the delay.

The problems that arose in observing, verifying and weighing the evidence of miracles are discussed in Golubinskij's 1903 history of canonization in Russia. He notes that monasteries, where there was a natural interest in identifying potential saints, assigned monks to watch for and record miracles by the graves of revered ascetics. Although most saints venerated in the pre-Mongol period manifest thaumaturgic powers, however, it remained a matter of individual judgment as to when the number and quality of recorded miracles merited formal recognition [266, 278-83].

The Protocol of Canonization
Neither the "Narration" or the "Lection" explicitly state that Boris and

Gleb were canonized in a given year. This is the norm for saints' lives. Before the Church councils of 1547 and 1549 we seldom find documentary sources registering official canonizations. That fact must be deduced from a variety of sources, including church calendars [святцы], oblique references in other texts to churches, icons, and acts of veneration and the like. Evidence of early canonization is rarely as forthright as in the case of Boris and Gleb, however: their *vita*, as we have seen, specifies that in the reign of Jaroslav and the prelacy of Metropolitan John, a church was named for them and a date of commemoration established. Such honors are conferred only on persons whose sanctity is officially acknowledged.

Il'in attempts to reconcile the report about the church with his theory of a later canonization by arguing that the church *could* have been dedicated to St. Basil (Vladimir's patron saint) [1957: 155]. Poppe suggests that it could have been named for the patron saints of Boris and Gleb (Romanus the Melodist and King David) [1973: 18-19]. Either possibility remains a mere conjecture, however. Poppe also contends that the reference to the feast day of July 24 is a later interpolation, suggesting, instead, that Boris and Gleb were originally commemorated in May on the date of the ceremony of 1072. There is no solid evidence which would support such a conclusion but a good deal which would refute it.

Saints' feast days are customarily set on the anniversary of the subject's death when the date is known. The earliest calendars that mention the feast day are in Gospels dating from 1096-1117 [Žukovskaja, 1983: 275, f. 202^b, lines 8-11], 1164 and 1270 [Vasil'ev, 1893: 66]. All list July 24, the date of Boris' death, as the official holiday. A group of later sources (*synaxaria*, Gospels, the *vitae*, and other liturgical books dating from the thirteenth century) mention, in addition to July 24, September 5 (the date on which Gleb is believed to have been murdered), and May 2 (the date given in the Laurentian Chronicle for the translation of the saints' relics during the prelacy of Metropolitan George). Other calendars and lives give May 20 (the date of the translation in the Hypatian Chronicle and Uspenskij Sbornik copy of the "Narrative of Miracles"), August 11 (the date when the relics were allegedly translated in 1191 from Vyšgorod to Smolensk on the Smjadin'), and August 12 (a date sometimes identified as the day of Gleb's murder) [Golubinskij, 1903: 49].

In her study of the evolution of Menaion texts dedicated to Boris and Gleb, Soboleva observes that the May 2 service is not included in many Menaia, a fact which she explains by its status as a *local* feast day [1979^a: 6]. Oblique confirmation of the primacy of July 24 is provided by the Typikon of 1641. The entry listing May 2 as the feast of the translation of Boris' and Gleb's remains is crossed out with a note on the margins that the service for Boris and Gleb is sung on July 24, but that at the discretion of the local superior the May 2 feast day may also be celebrated [Nikol'skij,

1896: 19]. This distinction between local and national or all-church veneration, often overlooked, is of primary importance for an understanding of the Kievan cult of Boris and Gleb. Too often the cult (and the sources) are treated synchronically without regard for the stages and development of veneration. In order to clarify what stage is represented by the description in the "Narration" and the "Lection" a brief digression on the East Slavic attitude toward formal glorification will be necessary.

For the Kievan and Russian Churches, as Golubinskij explains, the degrees of veneration are in a certain sense territorial: the most restricted cases involve the commemoration of a saint's memory at the site of his or her relics. Such veneration can lead to local canonization with the approval of the appropriate authorities, at the very least the local bishop. The second degree of veneration involves canonization and commemoration within the boundaries of an eparchy, while the third degree involves the territory of an entire nation or church. Each successive degree of veneration demands additional documentation of the candidate's worthiness for sainthood. The nature of this documentation depends on the category to which he or she belongs. Hierarchs, for example, or saints such as Constantine and Helena, who are "equal to the Apostles," need not show evidence of thaumaturgic powers, nor need their remains be uncorrupted. Since Boris and Gleb fit neither of these categories and died in a civil war, evidence of thaumaturgic powers was crucial in order to warrant their canonization. A third brother who died under similar circumstances was not canonized, apparently because there was no evidence of miracles [Golubinskij, 1903: 40-41, 265].

The account of Metropolitan John's investigation and ruling described in the "Narration" and the "Lection" clearly depicts the transition from a preliminary stage (unofficial, local veneration) to an intermediate stage of the brothers' cult: i.e., the approval of the bishop (here the metropolitan) and commemoration within the boundaries of an eparchy. The description of the 1072 translation, in contrast (see below), illustrates well-established and official veneration. The metropolitan's decision to authorize canonization, as it is represented here, is entirely consistent with the East Slavic tradition and in no way exceptional.

As in any such situation, Christian protocol is tempered by specific cultural norms that arise from the clerics' experience. Thus, while the decision to investigate the princes' claims to sainthood is initiated by the fire miracles, the decision to authorize commemoration (by setting a date and building a church) depends on two other types of miracles that were subsequently registered. The crucial factor seems to have been the discovery that the princes' remains were uncorrupted.[24] The two healing miracles that followed this discovery served as additional corroboration because they conformed to a variety of authoritative scriptural precedents. The third miracle observed by the congregation during the service that itself constituted the official glorification of the saints, though not necessary evidence, is interpreted as confirmation of the metropolitan's judgment.

Some of the strongest negative evidence cited by Poppe and Aleškovskij speaks against the canonization under Metropolitan John *only* if we assume that the cult was initially confined to noble circles and extended beyond the boundaries of Vyšgorod. The premise that it was a local cult which had adherents in variegated social circles and gradually spread gives us another, no less valid, reading of this negative evidence. The fact that princely families apparently did not name male children in honor of Boris and Gleb until the 1070s, for example, may be seen as confirmation that the princes were venerated initially by the lower classes for their healing powers, and that their status as princely patrons was a later development, a course of evolution for which compelling evidence is found in the liturgical tradition.[25] This would also explain why Metropolitan Ilarion does not mention the canonization of Boris and Gleb as a precedent for canonization of Vladimir in his "Sermon on Law and Grace" or praise the princes as intercessors for the land of Rus', and why the Novgorodian Ostromir's Gospel Book (1056-1057) fails to include Boris' and Gleb's feast day in its calendar of saints.

The Veneration of the Princes' Relics

Following Jaroslav's death in 1054, the relics of the murdered brothers are periodically mentioned in chronicle entries as being adorned or relocated at the order of princes. These accounts, given in expanded (sometimes censured) versions of the posthumous miracles appended to the "Narration" and the "Lection," indicate that Jaroslav's sons and grandsons came to regard Boris and Gleb as charismatic patrons. During this stage of the cult, in contrast to later stages when Boris and Gleb were venerated as intercessors for the Land of Rus', powers to bring good fortune and health for an individual ruler and his domain are ascribed to the physical relics. The princes seem to vie for possession of the saints' remains, building new churches to house them and attempting to outdo each other in donating silver and gold ornaments for the sarcophagi. Not coincidentally, the first two translations occur in connection with a struggle for the throne of Kiev.[26]

According to the "Narrative of Miracles," the occasion for the first translation is the deterioration of the church built by Jaroslav to commemorate the saints, and the decision of Jaroslav's son, Izjaslav, to build a new church. An additional factor may have been Izjaslav's status in the bitter internecine warfare of that period. After having been driven into exile by Vseslav Brjačeslavovič of Polock, Izjaslav reconquered Kiev. The Laurentian Chronicle reports that he reclaimed his throne on May 2 of 1069. The coincidence of this date with the date of the translation (as given in the Laurentian Chronicle) and its close temporal proximity to the official ceremony may indicate Izjaslav's desire to thank SS Boris and Gleb as ostensible patrons for his recent victory, and to ensure continuing good fortune.[27]

The earliest copy of the "Narrative of Miracles" describes the proceedings as follows:

> О пренесении святою мученику. Бысть же въ время перенесению святыима мученикома Романа и Давида. И съвъкупивъшеся вься братия: Изяславъ, Святославъ, Всеволодъ, митрополитъ Георгий Кыевьскый, другый--Неофитъ Чьрниговьскый, и епископи Петръ Переяславьскый и Никита Бѣлогородьскый и Михаилъ Гургевьскый, и игумени Феодосий Печерьскый и Софроний святааго Михаила и Германъ святааго Спаса, и прочии вьси игумени: и створиша праздьникъ свѣтьло. И възьмъше на рама князи, предъидущемъ преподъбныимъ чьрноризьцемъ съ свѣщами, а по нихъ диякони, таче и прозвутери, и по сихъ митрополита и епискупи, и по нихъ съ ракою идяаху. И принесъше въ цьрьковь, поставиша, и отъвьрзъше раку, и испълнися цьрькы благоухания и вонѣ пречюдьны, и вьси видѣвъше прославиша Бога. И митрополита обиде ужасъ, бяше бо и не твьрдо вѣруя къ святыма, и падъ ниць, просяше прощения. И цѣловавъ мощи, въложиша въ раку камяну [Abramovič, 1916: 55-56].[28]

The opening of Boris' wooden coffin and his reburial in a stone sarcophagus, together with the miraculous evidence that his remains are still uncorrupted, have been interpreted as evidence that this ceremony, though identified as a translation, is actually the true, official canonization of Boris and Gleb [cf. Ammann, 1955: 37, Poppe, 1969: 373-5; Aleškovskij, 1971: 85; Xorošev, 1986: 19-20]. The argument rests on two interconnected assumptions:

1) that a second disinterment would be highly irregular;
2) that a hierarch of Metropolitan George's stature could not have expressed doubts in the sanctity of canonized saints without committing blasphemy.

The first of these premises is incorrect and the second requires careful qualification.

Medieval descriptions of translation ceremonies and acts describing occasions when a saint's coffin was opened for other reasons show that, practically speaking, there was no limit as to the number of times that bodily remains could be examined when it was deemed necessary or advisable.[29] An official disinterment could be ordered before or after a formal canonization for a variety of reasons. According to the earliest surviving *vita* of St. Ol'ga, for example, Prince Vladimir arranged to have the saint's relics exhumed and buried in a church even though she was not at the time recognized as a saint (she was probably canonized in the fourteenth century) [Serebrjanskij, 1915: appendix, 6-12]. The "Pamjat' i poxvala Vladimiru" describes Ol'ga's coffin as having a small window through which the uncorrupted remains could be viewed [*ibid.*: 13].

There are records of disinterments following formal canonization, as well, usually because of doubts about the authenticity of the relics. St. Anna Kašinskaja is an interesting case in point. She was formally glorified in 1650, at which time her feast day was entered in the official calendar. Twenty-seven years later her feast day was struck from the calendar when an investigation established that her personal life failed to correspond to her vita; that her miracles may have been falsified; and that her supposedly uncorrupted relics had decayed. The impetus for the investigation appears to have been a combination of legitimate doubts and the fact that her hand had been preserved in a gesture of blessing that was suspiciously close to the *dvoeperstie* of the Old Believers and had been used by schismatics to justify their practice [Golubinskij, 1903: 164-66].

While Metropolitan George had the canonical right, and indeed a certain obligation, to investigate claims about false miracles, no source represents the hierarch's doubts as the grounds for an official investigation of Boris' and Gleb's sanctity. There is no mention of a complaint or request for a disinterment at all. In contrast to the account of the first disinterment, where all present are awaiting a verdict and Metropolitan John formally indicates that the requisite evidence has been verified, Metropolitan George is the only person who expresses any doubts about the state of the relics. When confronted with the miraculous evidence that his doubts are unwarranted, he is struck with terror and prostrates himself before the relics of the saint.

The East Slavic canonization process does not, of course, require high-ranking hierarchs to throw themselves on the ground and formally apologize to a saint for doubting his or her status. The only requirement is a thorough investigation of each case. There is not the slightest precedent for a metropolitan serving as a devil's advocate. These considerations, together with the clear distinctions made by the sources in their identification of the first and second disinterments suggest that there is no reason to seek veiled references to canonization in this account. It is no more or less than what it is purported to be: an official relocation of the sarcophagi to a new church built by the reigning prince.

Precisely because the ceremony is a translation rather than a canonization, and the princes' sanctity is already proven to the satisfaction of the Church, the metropolitan's doubts are perceived by the narrator as a potentially punishable transgression. A number of parallel instances in East Slavic hagiographical literature come to mind. The priest Konstantin opens the coffin of Prince Fedor of Jaroslavl' and dares to pull at the saint's robe, an act of desecration for which he is paralyzed. Archbishop Trifon of Rostov, who also doubts the prince's miraculous powers, suffers the same fate [Makarij, 1869: 1258-1259]. When Vasilij Skvorcov, the keeper of the

Church of the Mother of God in Jaroslavl', opens the coffins of the holy princes Konstantin and Vasilij, daring to touch their relics, he is thrown against a pillar and struck with a terrible illness until he repents for his sin [Vasilij and Konstantin, 1874: 332-332]. Similar cases where hierarchs, priests or laymen "test" the powers of a saint are generally recounted in the miracles appended to *vitae* which, in fact, is where this incident is placed in the "Narration" and the "Lection." All teach that God swiftly punishes those who yield to the devilish temptation and desecrate the relics of the saints. Such precedents explain the metropolitan's fear when his doubts are exposed as groundless and motivate his swift act of contrition.

Confirmation that Boris and Gleb's veneration was well established by 1072 is given in the following account of how the princes gather around the coffins to kiss the relics of the saints. The Uspenskij Sbornik copy describes, almost as a matter of course, how Metropolitan George blessed Izjaslav and Vsevolod with the hand of St. Gleb, and how Svjatoslav

> ... дрьжащю святааго руку, прилагааше къ вреду, имьже боляше на шии, и къ очима, и къ темени, и по семь положи руку въ гробѣ [Abramovič, 1916: 56].[30]

During the ensuing liturgy Svjatoslav complains that something is piercing his head. A retainer identified as B'rn lifts the prince's cap and discovers the fingernail of St. Gleb lodged in Svjatoslav's head. He removes the nail and gives it to the prince, who gives thanks to God for what he evidently perceives as a gift or a good sign from the saint. Oblique confirmation of Svjatoslav's belief in Gleb's patronage may be seen in his subsequent efforts to build a church in honor of the saints and in his choice of the name Gleb for his son.[31]

Later developments of the cult are reflected in the two other earliest records of this incident, both of them preserved in fourteenth-century copies. The copy appended to Nestor's "Lection" in the Sil'vestrovskij Sbornik eliminates the account of how Gleb's coffin could not be moved and describes Metropolitan George's actions in the following sequence: he kisses the hand of Boris, applies it to his eyes and heart, and subsequently blesses Izjaslav, Svjatoslav and Vsevolod, in that order [Abramovič, 1916: 22]. Aleškovskij attributes this account to twelfth-century editorial interference because of the apparent preference accorded to Boris [1972: 119]. The incident with Gleb's nail is summarized in passing and characterized as a blessing [*na blagoslovenie*] bestowed upon Svjatoslav by the saint.[32]

In the very next year after the translation ceremony, Svjatoslav and Vsevolod forced Izjaslav to abandon the Kievan throne. The Laurentian Chronicle attributes this coup to Svjatoslav. During his brief reign, Svjatoslav began building a church to Boris and Gleb but, according to the "Narrative of

Miracles," died before the project could be finished [Abramovič, 1916: 60]. Vsevolod, who succeeded him as Grand Prince of Kiev in 1076, is said to have actually completed the church. On the very night of its completion, however, the roof caved in and the structure was reduced to ruins.

The subsequent ruler, Svjatopolk Izjaslavovič, is not regarded favorably by the editor of the "Narrative," who worked in the reign of Svjatopolk's rival Vladimir Vsevolodovič Monomax.[33] In one version of a much debated miracle (see the discussion in Chapter Four) two men imprisoned unjustly by Svjatopolk are miraculously freed by the saints. Svjatopolk's patronage of them is portrayed as dubious (like his rule of Kiev). He establishes a feast day commemorating a subsequently documented healing miracle and he is credited with wanting to build a church on the site of Jaroslav's old wooden structure. By his own admission, however, he does not dare to move the relics from place to place [Abramovič, 1916: 60-62]. Later, after Oleg Svjatoslavovič has restored the church built by his father, Svjatopolk repeatedly refuses to permit the translation because the church was built by another prince [*ibid.*: 64].

The narrator interprets this as a temporary prohibition dictated by "God's plan and the will of the holy martyrs" [*ibid.*: 62-63]. The final segment of the posthumous miracles links the translation of the relics to the fortunes of Vladimir Monomax. While Svjatopolk ruled in Kiev, Vladimir governed in Perejaslavl'. Although the two principalities were very distant, Vladimir paid unusual attention to the saints' relics in Vyšgorod. In 1102, having conceived the desire to adorn the saints' sarcophagi with silver and gold, the narrator writes, Vladimir

> ... пришьдъ нощь, премѣри гроба; расклепавъ же дъскы сребрьныя и позолотивъ, и пакы тако же пришьдъ нощию и обложивъ, окова чюдодѣиная и достохвальная святая гроба страстотрьпьцю Христову мученику Бориса и Глѣба, и тако же нощь отъиде [*ibid.*: 63].[34]

Vladimir Monomax's ascension to the throne permitted the triumphant translation of the princes' relics from the old church built by Izjaslav to the newly restored church completed by Oleg Svjatoslavovič. The description in the "Narrative of Miracles" depicts a glittering assembly of princes and prelates. Apart from the members of Vladimir Monomax's family, the princes David and Oleg Svjatoslavoviči of Černigov, together with their families and retainers, were invited to take part. The celebrants included Metropolitan Nikifor, and Bishops Feotikst of Černigov, Lazar of Perejaslavl', Mina of Polock, together with the abbots of leading monasteries. So many people had assembled, writes the narrator, that not even the city walls were free. On May 2, a Sunday morning, after celebrating Matins in both of the churches, the saints' sarcophagi were loaded onto separate sledges specially crafted for the occasion. Boris' coffin was taken first, accompanied by Vladimir and the clergy:

> И идяху, влекуще ужи же великыими, тѣснящеся и гнетуще, вельможѣ и все болярьство. Бяше же устроенъ върьмь по обѣма сторонама, удуже волочаху чьстьнѣи рацѣ, и не бяше льзѣ ни ити, ни повлещи отъ мъножьства людии. Тъгда Володимиръ повелѣ метати людьмъ кунами же, и скорою, и паволокы. И узьрѣвъше, людие тамо обратишася, а друзии, то оставивъше, къ святыима ракама течаху, да быша достоини были прикоснутися [*ibid.*: 65].[35]

Gleb's coffin followed, escorted by David of Černigov and a procession of clergy and the faithful, chanting "Lord, have mercy." Boris' coffin passed easily through the church. Gleb's coffin, exactly as at the first translation, refused to move. Then, writes the narrator, there was a most wondrous miracle:

> Яко потягоша силою, ужа претьргняхуся, велика суща зѣло, яко одва можааше мужь обияти обѣма рукама, и тако единою вся претьргняхуся, а людьмъ зовущемъ: «курелеисонъ». И бяше множьство много по всему граду и по стѣнамъ, и по забороломъ городьнымъ, аки изо пчелъ, и въсхожаше гласъ народа отъ всѣхъ: «Господи, помилуи!», яко и громъ. И тако одъва възмогоша отъ утрьняя до литургия превести сущии цьркви [*ibid.*: 65-66].[36]

Vladimir Monomax's reign marks the zenith of the Kievan cult, as well as the beginning of its spread beyond the borders of Kiev and Vyšgorod. In the twelfth and thirteenth centuries the chronicles report that churches were built commemorating Boris and Gleb on the sites of their murders (the Al'ta River and Smolensk on the Smjadin' river), as well as in Černigov, Turov, Grodno, Novgorod, Kidekša (Suzdal') and Rostov. The relics of the princes evidently were lost when the Vyšgorod church was burned by Batu's armies, but their powers of intercession continued to be invoked by the princes of Rus', who increasingly viewed Boris and Gleb as military patrons.[37] We can trace the evolution of the cult, not only in the proliferation of churches, but also in surviving artifacts, icons, manuscripts preserving local legends, and in the official texts produced to meet the needs of their commemoration.[38] By the sixteenth century Boris' and Gleb's names were entered into the *Book of Degrees of the Imperial Genealogy* [*Stepennaja kniga*], and the martyred princes joined the ranks of saints invoked as patrons of the Muscovite prince. It is the Muscovite cult, rather than the Kievan cult, that shaped the post-medieval image of Boris and Gleb as saints with a special concern for the empire ruled by their "descendants."

* * *

All of the available evidence suggests that the Kievan cult was not forcibly encouraged by Jaroslav, but developed gradually according to the following sequence. In all likelihood Svjatopolk murdered Boris and Gleb, whom he viewed as potential contenders for the Kievan throne. After a series of battles, Jaroslav drove Svjatopolk from the land, avenging his murdered brothers and claiming the throne for himself. In keeping with the obligation to provide a fitting burial for his kinsmen, Jaroslav ordered that Gleb's body be buried beside the body of Boris at the Vyšgorod Church of St. Basil. The location of Gleb's corpse, which had been abandoned in the wilderness, was allegedly determined by miraculous signs attested to by local witnesses. Additional miracles were witnessed at the new burial site. Jaroslav informed Metropolitan John, who presided over a formal disinterment of the bodies. The corpses were found to be uncorrupted and, for that reason, were not reburied below ground. Two miraculous healings, recorded at the grave site, were judged to be sufficient evidence for canonization. The date of Boris' death (July 24) was designated for the saints' commemoration. Thereafter service hymns were composed, an icon was painted, and the first church named for Boris and Gleb was built. Boris' and Gleb's graves became a site of pilgrimage for the faithful and a touchstone of power for the Kievan princes. Each successive prince built (or attempted to build) a church in the saints' honor. The saints' relics were translated on two occasions to new churches in the Vyšgorod area. Their cult gradually spread into outlying areas of Rus' and they came to be identified, not primarily as healing saints or as saints who brought luck to a particular principality, but as patrons of imperial power.

3

RITUAL COMMEMORATION

> Купьно ловяще пьрвѣе въ дубровѣ питающаяся и видяще свѣтъ отъ твоего лица яви сияющь, «чьто се видѣнне,--другъ къ другу глаголаху,--придѣте, видимъ преславьное видѣние». Видѣвъше же чудо, проповѣдаша всѣмъ. . . . [1]

> Правдивая страстотерпца, и истинная евангелия Христова послушателя, цѣломудренный Романе съ незлобивымъ Давидомъ, не сопротивъ стаста врагу сущу брату, убивающему тѣлеса ваша, душамъ же коснутися не могущу: да плачется убо злый властолюбецъ, вы же радующеся съ лики ангельскими, предстояще Святѣй Троицѣ, молитеся о державѣ сродниковъ вашихъ, богоугодный быти, и сыновомъ Россійскимъ спастися. . . . [2]

The princes' murder, and the miraculous events that led to their official recognition as saints, inspired written monuments that vary widely in scope and specificity. We shall begin our investigation with the writings that were subject to the most demanding specifications, the hymns composed for ritual commemoration, and then proceed to progressively less strictured writings, ending with the most idiosyncratic documents, the chronicle entries. In each case we shall be seeking the vertical bonds that connect a text with its real analogues in order to trace the relationship between that text's locus in the community's life and its form. As a rule the most highly structured cultural systems place the most extensive restrictions upon the texts produced to meet their needs. But within each system there are subsystems and hierarchies that vary in their requirements. Certain liturgical forms, for example, are designed to accommodate variations in structure or theme in accordance with the church calendar and the rank of the celebrants. Another factor is the relative specificity of a text's function. Texts with a broadly edifying function or texts that are not obligatory from a liturgical standpoint tend to tolerate a wider spectrum of structural variation.

I should stress that the sort of latitude we observe in some texts is by no means guaranteed. It is a potential laxity that may arise from a text's *Sitz im Leben*. Under some conditions, as we shall see, texts which ought to have virtually no latitude take on uncharacteristically free forms. Conversely, texts that are by nature loosely structured may assume highly conventionalized forms. Such exceptions are difficult to predict, but they can almost always be accounted for when we identify the set of specifications that apply in the given situation and trace the coordinates of the verbal artifact back to the life, customs and institutions of the community whose needs it serves.

The Saints' Office [ἀκαλουθία, служба]

Few East Slavic saints have inspired so longstanding and extensive a liturgical tradition as Boris and Gleb. Hymns written in their honor predate the services to other Kievan saints by over a hundred years. The Archeographic Commission's catalog of Church Slavonic codices in Soviet archives dating from the eleventh to the thirteenth centuries lists hymns commemorating the princes in eighteen manuscripts, among them a parchment Menaion and a Typikon-Kontakarion from the late eleventh or early twelfth century.[3] By the mid-twelfth century there were at least two redactions of the full office—one attributed to Kievan Metropolitan John (1020-1035 or 1076-1089) and a second to Novgorod Bishop Arkadij (1156-1163) [text in Abramovič, 1916: 136-150]. Additional verses honoring the saints which did not become part of the mainstream liturgical tradition have survived as well.[4] A third office, which represents an intermediate stage in the liturgical tradition, has come down to us in the Ivaniči Menaia of 1547-79 [text in Bugoslavskij, 1900: 53-70]. A fourth, dating from the fifteenth century, is essentially the same as the office in the printed Menaion of 1628 under July 24 [Abramovič, 1916: XXI, 150-167]. Services and hymns for the May 2 feast day, which remained largely a local holiday, and for September 5, the day of Gleb's death, initially formed a separate tradition, but gradually contaminated the July 24 commemorative office [ibid.: 168-76].

Metropolitan John's Office

Metropolitan John's office is not only the earliest extant service for Boris and Gleb, but one of only a few surviving copies of a pre-thirteenth-century service to East Slavic saints. Nevertheless, there is evidence that we may be reading a text which, itself, is a supplement to the original hymns employed for the commemoration of the murdered princes around the time of their canonization. In order to clarify this issue, we should briefly review the norms for saints' offices in the medieval period. Once we have set the "first" service in diachronic, comparative perspective, we can discuss its composition, the imagery and interrelation of individual hymns, and the relation of Metropolitan John's office to subsequent services honoring Boris and Gleb.

Institutional commemoration of an Orthodox saint requires the composition of special hymns of praise. These hymns are incorporated into the cycle of services in combinations that vary according to the day of the week, the coincidence with other holidays, the rank of the celebrant, and a number of factors specified in the Typikon.[5] An office must include stichera for Vespers and a single or combined kanon for Matins (see below). The stichera are distinguished according to the way in which they are performed and their place in the ritual. Stichera on "Lord, I cry unto thee" [Psalm 140] are inserted between the last verses of the Vesper psalms, for example, while stichera aposticha are sung in the second half of Vespers after the entrance, and so on. Following the stichera (or sometimes at the very beginning of the recorded office) we would expect to find the saint's troparion. The troparion is one of the most important hymns because it sums up the central theme of the saint's day and because it is sung not only during Vespers, but also in Matins, the Liturgy, and the Hours.

The central hymn of the Matins service is the kanon, which consists of nine odes, each based on a specified biblical canticle. An ode is made up of three or more stanzas, also known as troparia. The initial stanza, called the heirmos, establishes the thematic interplay with the biblical canticle and, in the Greek tradition, serves as a metrical model. After the third ode of the kanon we sometimes find a hymn which is known in Greek as καθισμα and in Church Slavonic as сѣдаленъ. After the sixth ode of the kanon we almost always find two short hymns known as the kontakion and the oikos.[6]

Initially in the Byzantine tradition liturgical hymns were recorded according to hymnographic categories. Prior to the thirteenth century in Greek manuscripts one finds codices which contain one or several types of hymns (the criteria being, in part, a matter of function and, in part, a matter of the style in which the hymn was chanted). The Heirmologion contained the opening heirmoi for the kanons; the Tropologion contained troparia; the Kontakarion contained kontakia and oikoi for Orthodox saints; the Kanonarion contained kanons, the Psaltikon contained kontakia, hypakoai (an equivalent to the Church Slavonic sedalen), and other ornamental chants for the soloist; the Asmatikon contained parts sung by the choir (sometimes the two codices were combined); and the Service Menaion contained both stichera and kanons for each office [Wellesz, 1961: 129-145]. In the thirteenth century, however, the composition of Greek liturgical books underwent a radical change, which is related to reforms in the system of musical notation. At this time hymns began to be recorded primarily according to their order in the service, although not consistently.[7]

Church Slavonic hymnographic codices copied before the fourteenth century generally reflect the first type of ordering although, as we shall see below, a number of East Slavic parchment codices mix categories that were separated in Greek liturgical books. Subsequent liturgical books reflect one or a combination of both organizing principles. Fifteenth-century codices where one would expect to find offices recorded in proper order are highly varied in their composition. Hymns are "missing," doubled, and recorded in an order that may change from copy to copy. Services honoring certain saints contain several alternate troparia, kontakia or kanons; others lack central hymns. Still others consist of two or three core hymns that summarize the essence of the saint's feast day. Hymns initially contained in special codices may be recorded in a Psalter, Trefologion (here the entire office is frequently included) or in a miscellany.

The mechanisms of this variance have only begun to be systematically investigated. The length and complexity of an East Slavic saint's office in the pre-Petrine period was determined by current liturgical and notational norms. It also depended upon his or her status in the community where a given text was used. We can see this by comparing liturgical codices from provincial monasteries with codices from central cloisters such as the Kiev Cave Monastery or the Trinity-Sergius Laura. Major saints, such as Leontij of Rostov or Sergij of Radonež, whose veneration crosses regional boundaries, are universally commemorated by full, elaborate offices. Other saints, such as Nikita of Perejaslavl' or Vasilij and Konstantin of Jaroslavl', are represented by a full office in their native regions but only by selected hymns (if at all) in codices originating in other eparchies.

Each case must be investigated on its own grounds, but there are a few broad rules of thumb which can guide us in diachronic studies. Liturgical writers were conservative: they preferred to copy the text that was available to them mechanically for fear of inadvertently omitting information or corrupting the text. The most common changes, other than mistakes, are the addition of phrases and epithets which enhance the expression of praise to the saint [Golubovskij, 1900: 135]. When a saint's service was combined with another service or condensed to meet the needs of a given locality, entire hymns could be deleted. Conversely, services were expanded by inserting newly composed hymns—probably a sign of growing veneration or to promote a particular cult.

A number of commonly encountered indicators tell us that a service has been expanded, rather than composed as an integrated whole. The most obvious clue that something of this sort has occurred comes when we find alternate hymns of the same category with rubrics identifying the doubles as "another" [другыи, инь"] troparion, kontakion or kanon. Odes three through nine of the printed kanon for St. Pafnutyj of Borovsk (d. May 1, 1477), for example, contain two groups of heirmoi and troparia: the second heirmos of each ode is preceded by the rubric инъ. Manuscript rubrics identify the author of one kanon as Pafnutyj's disciple, the elder Innokentij, and the author of the second kanon as a monk from Pafnutyj's cloister [GBL, f. 304, no. 791; f. 113, no. 382]. Innokentij's kanon corresponds to his life of Pafnutyj, which contains a detailed eyewitness description of the hegumen's last days; the second kanon contains phrases and details corresponding to a later, extended *vita* of Pafnutyj attributed to Vassian Sanin [Ključevskij, 1871: 207-208].

Sometimes the doubles are not labeled as such but turn up in unexpected places in the service. On occasion, one finds alternate hymns to a saint in a different section of a codex. An interesting case in point is a mid-fifteenth century Service Menaion for the month of May [GPB, sob. Titov, no. 3798] which contains a full, extended office for St. Leontij of Rostov on ff. 174ʳ through 197. Folio 260 gives a second oikos which it labels "другой." The first oikos [f. 194] praises the saint as an apostle for the Orthodox faith, exactly as he is praised in the earliest Prolog *vita* [text in Filippovskij, 1982: 125-6]. The second oikos praises Leontij as a miracle-working saint whose relics heal the sick. This information corresponds to later redactions of Leontij's *vita* which give accounts of posthumous healings [text in Titov, 1893: 1-35].

All of the above doublets represent hymnographic strata attributable to diachronic developments in the individual saint's cult. It is important to differentiate between insertions which mark historical stages of veneration and insertions which reflect changing trends in liturgical composition. Beginning in the fifteenth century, for example, hymnographers insert additional theotokia and stichera in accordance with the new Typikon [Odincov, 1881: 52]. Post-medieval services often contain a new kontakion and oikos after the third ode of the saint's kanon. Both types of stratification are evident in the services for Boris and Gleb, beginning with the office attributed to Metropolitan John.

Three codices are of particular importance in analyzing the evolution of Metropolitan John's office and its relation to other redactions. The oldest is an eleventh or twelfth-century Menaion with services for the second half of July [CGADA, f. 381, no. 121]. A second codex, known as the Tipografskij Ustav [State Tret'jakov Gallery, K-5349], dates from the late eleventh or early twelfth centuries and is actually a combination "Typikon and Kontakarion. It contains part of a kontakion followed by an oikos [text in Dostál and Rothe, 1976-: vol. V, p. 112]. The fullest copy, which Abramovič takes as the basis for his edition, is located in a twelfth-century Service Menaion [CGADA, f. 381, no. 122] for the month of July. Other twelfth century liturgical codices contain either selected stichera to the saints or combinations of stichera, the kontakion (with or without oikos). The Blagoveščenskij Kontakarion [GPB, Q.p.1.32], dating from the late twelfth to the early thirteenth century, contains two kontakia for the saints [text in Dostál and Rothe, 1976-: vol. 5, pp. 110, 114].

Let us first consider the two earliest manuscripts containing the fullest version of Metropolitan John's office (CGADA, f. 381, nos 121 and 122). Both copies mix up elements from Vespers and Matins services, which suggests that neither derives from an archetype of a single service. Rather, the offices given here were most probably copied from components contained in separate, specialized codices or from several previously recorded offices. In the case of Menaion 121, one might suppose that the kanon for Matins is given first because it was copied from a Kanonarion.[8] The remainder of the service, which begins with the stichera for Vespers, contains some of the hymns that, according to post-fifteenth century norms, would be included in the kanon—the sedalen and the kontakion—but lacks an oikos.

Menaion no. 122 contains the following hymns in the indicated order: a sedalen, a kontakion, an oikos, three stichera on the praises, three stichera on "Lord, I cry unto thee," three stichera aposticha, and a kanon [Abramovič, 1916: XX]. It is fuller than Menaion no. 121 but, as several scholars have remarked, lacks a troparion. This is not without precedent. The early offices for St. Feodosij of the Caves (d. 1074), for example, also lack a troparion [text in Golubinskij, 1901-1910: vol. I, part 2, 513-17].[9] The first three hymns which open the office would be part of the saint's kanon according to post-fifteenth-century liturgical norms (which is where they are located in the final redaction of the service published by Abramovič as no. I, 4 [1916: 150-167]). Many of the early manuscripts used as variants for Abramovič's edition retain this order. The remainder of the service follows the post-fifteenth-century liturgical norm.

While the composition of both early codices bears witness to the pre-thirteenth-century practice of ordering by hymnographic categories, it also reflects the *Sitz im Leben* of the early cult. Initially that cult was limited to a few parishes in a single eparchy of a newly-converted nation. Boris' and Gleb's feast day coincided with that of St. Christine of Tyre. For the Church as an institution Christine was the more important saint. This "ranking" would have determined the number of hymns that were initially necessary for the observance of Boris' and Gleb's feast day. When services for more than one saint have to be combined, the celebrant has the option of either combining full services, or allowing elements from one service to take precedence over the other. The latter is more common. In such cases the celebrant selects a varying number of hymns which he considers sufficient for the commemoration of the lesser saint and integrates them with the central services.

In the case of Boris and Gleb, we can deduce which hymns were composed for earliest stages of institutional commemoration with a reasonable degree of certainty by comparing the two fullest offices, taking into account the specialized codices. Both Menaia 121 and 122 contain a sedalen and a kontakion which form a single liturgical set (in terms of their placement and historically), and both record these hymns in an order which departs from the fifteenth-century norm (where they would be placed within the kanon). Their order and separation from the kanon to Boris and Gleb suggests that they may have been originally composed for insertion in the kanon to St. Christine. The manuscript convoy, the diachronic development of the office, and individual hymns (which become progressively more specific and elaborate) indirectly confirm the likelihood of this hypothesis. The service in Menaion no. 121 follows a service to St. Christine which does have the kanon in the proper order [Mur'janov, 1981: 269-270]. This is also the case with Menaion no 122, which I was able to examine personally. Comparison of thirty manuscript offices commemorating the martyred princes indicates that, as the cult spread, Boris' and Gleb's office gradually took precedence to the office for St. Christine, eventually displacing it altogether in sixteenth-century Menaia [Soboleva, 1981: 98].

The three opening hymns are the simplest and most abstract of all the hymns in Metropolitan John's service. The sedalen is by far the most generalized:

Сѣдаленъ гласъ 1, подобенъ: Ликъ ангельскыи.
Измлада Христа възлюбивъши купьно, брата честнаа, и жизнь не старостьную възлюбивъши, славьная, цѣломудрие изволиста и пощение отъ страстии душегубьныихъ: тѣмь, съ поспѣшениемь Божию благодать приимъша, ицѣляета болящая [Abramovič, 1916: 136].[10]

Boris and Gleb are not even mentioned by name or identified as princes. The brothers are praised as righteous men who lived a chaste life and, for that reason, were granted the power to heal after death. This hymn is similar to the troparion given in the General Menaion for the category of unmercenary and wonderworking saints. Although no Greek source has as yet been identified, the fact that it opens the saints' service without mentioning the saints by name suggests that it is probably a translation of a Greek hymn rather than an original composition.

The kontakion that follows provides a few more specific references to the princes:

Кондакъ гласъ 3, подобенъ: Дѣва днесь.
Въсия днесь преславьная память ваю, мученика Христова Романе и Давыде, съзывающи насъ къ похвалению Христа, Бога нашего. Тѣмь и притѣкающе къ рацѣ ваю, исцѣления дары приемлемъ: вы--божествьная врача еста![11]

Here Boris and Gleb are referred to by their Christian names: Romanus and David. But, again, the names seem to have been added to hymns originally composed in praise of other saints. Two plausible originals have been identified by Keller. Most of the kontakion, he notes, is virtually identical to a Greek sticheron praising the martyred saint Procopius. The closing line is borrowed from a hymn to SS Cyrus and John [Keller, 1973: 67-69].

The oikos comes the closest to the saints' historical biography, but it is also none too close:

Икосъ, подобенъ: Едема Вифл[еемъ].
Разумьное житие съвьршая, преблажене, цесарьскыимь вѣньцемь отъ уности украшенъ, пребогатыи Романе: власть велия бысть своему оте-

чьству и веси твари. Тѣмь, видя твои успѣхъ, Христосъ Богъ судомь Своимь на мучение призъва тя и крѣпость ти подавъ съ небесе, да побѣдиши врага съ Давыдомь мужьскы, съ братомь си, пострадавъшимь и живъшимь съ тобою. [12]

Here, although we learn that Boris and Gleb were of royal birth, the reference to the crown of the Caesar is anachronistic: the princes take their place in the imperial genealogy of the Muscovite Caesars only much later, in the fifteenth century. Their death is represented as the response of willing martyrs to Christ's call, just as their struggle with Svjatopolk is represented as a fight against mankind's enemy (i.e., Satan). The lack of specificity derives, in great measure, from the fact that the hymn is a "reworked translation" of the third oikos for SS Cyrus and John [Keller, 1973: 70-71].

The nine stichera that follow develop the image of the brothers as chaste martyrs who followed Christ's teachings and the example of St. Stephen, protomartyr, by sacrificing themselves for the faith. The images of the martyr's crown and the heavenly kingdom recur, as they do in all services for this category of saint. Some concrete Greek models have been identified, and we may assume that most of these hymns were likewise reworkings of Greek originals. A good portion of the text of the sticheron aposticha "Kyimi poxval'nymi" in the second tone [Abramovič, 1916: 137-138] is a literal translation of a Greek sticheron for the feast of SS Peter and Paul, and the syllable counts are identical [Velimirovič, 1967: 131-132]. The sticheron aposticha immediately precedent to the kanon [Abramovič, 1916: 138], though identified as an original melody [*samoglasno*] is a literal translation of a sticheron used in Greek Menaia for the offices of SS Demetrius, George, and Nicetas, and in Slavic Menaia for the office of St. Procopius [Velimirovič, 1967: 136]. There are two instances where the abstract, conventionalized verses take local interests into account. One sticheron aposticha praises the brothers as "zemlja rus'skyja udobrenie" and a sticheron on the praises refers to them as Boris and Gleb rather than Romanus and David.

All saints' cults have strong bonds to a given locality. Had a Kievan or Vyšgorodian cleric composed this service, one could have expected him to mention the precise city where the brothers' relics worked wonders for the faithful. We do see this in the local services composed for the translation of the relics: their hymns were gradually incorporated into the July 24 service for the feast day proper. One could interpret the reference to the Land of Rus' as a sign of burgeoning nationalism, but that would be anachronistic and stands in clear contradiction to the abstract tone maintained in the early hymns. Most probably the epithet reflects the viewpoint of a composer who was working in the Greek language and identified with the eparchy as a whole rather than with any single part. The reference to the saints as Boris and Gleb, which is echoed in the title of several redactions, could not have been made by a Greek monk writing in the initial years of the cult before Boris and Gleb became accepted as Christian names. The title and sticheron praising Boris and Gleb are clearly the work of native writers who were most comfortable with the prince's worldly names. It is impossible to say whether the sticheron was composed in Greek and then corrupted by a Kievan copyist or whether it is an original Church Slavonic composition. I would be inclined to attribute the nomenclature to a scribal error because the hymn itself is highly abstract and disappears from later services, where it is replaced by hymns with increasingly specific details.

The rubric for the saints' kanon indicates that it was translated from a Greek original which had the acrostich "Si Davydu pesen' prinošu Romanu" [138; Spasskij, 1951: 80]. The phrase given in the rubric ["imějai po glavam" gr'čskii stix"], as Hannick rightly observes, is peculiar, but entirely comprehensible [1973: 162]. Only eight odes are given, which is typical (the second odes were almost always eliminated from later Byzantine and Slavic kanons).[13] Each ode has a designated heirmos. Mur'janov [1981: 269] has discovered that the heirmoi for Boris' and Gleb's kanon are identical to the heirmoi for the martyr's kanon in a twelfth or thirteenth-century General Menaion [Cod. slav. 37 of the Austrian National Library; cf. Birkfellner (1973: 321-4)]. After each heirmos, there are three stanzas [troparia] followed by a hymn to the Mother of God [theotokion].

A kanon could contain from three to fifteen troparia per ode, followed by theotokia. Boris' and Gleb's first kanon sticks to the minimum number, however, and takes only modest advantage of the form's hymnographic possibilities to provide us with a few more particulars about Boris' and Gleb's life. The fourth ode of this kanon, for example, stresses the youth and innocence of the murdered brothers [*ibid.*: 139-140]. The fifth ode denounces Svjatopolk as a second Cain and contrasts his wicked behavior to the example of the martyrs [*ibid.*: 140]. The sixth ode describes how Boris was pierced with a spear as he prayed to the Lord. The eighth ode relates how Gleb's body was left in the fields to be devoured by birds and beasts, how it was guarded by angels, and how passers-by witnessed miraculous signs on the site [*ibid.*: 142-3]. The ninth ode relates how the Varangian who inadvertently defiled the brothers' grave was singed with fire, and how the sick and lame men were healed when they touched the sarcophagi containing the martyrs' relics [*ibid.*: 143]. Nowhere in the kanon are the brothers identified as princes, however, or praised as patrons of their land. Nor is there any mention of Jaroslav.

If we compare the image of Boris and Gleb conveyed by this service with the picture of the initial cult described in the preceding chapter we see a clear opposition between syncretic and non-syncretic veneration which is entirely natural under the circumstances. Indeed, it would be naive to suppose that Boris' and Gleb's violent death was seen by the broad population as a martyrdom in the Christian sense of the word. The same events assessed by the population at least partially in terms of pagan Slavic ancestor worship are represented in the earliest hymns within a purely Christian perspective because the Greek monk who composed the verses was operating with Orthodox historical and poetic models.

These models, rather than dictating the form or contents of the hymns, provide the hymnographer with a series of general patterns comparable to the sketches in a composite picture book. The composer matches the life and deeds of the saint in question to increasingly specialized hagiographical categories and prototypes. The composite image, in turn, inspires what Leclercq calls "reminiscences"—phrases and quotations evoked by parallel associations between the individual saint and other saints with coinciding images [1962: 209-217]. The phrases must then be matched to melodic phrases making up one of eight tones in which all Orthodox services are chanted.

Inevitably the historical persona praised in the hymn is overshadowed by the wonderworking saint, who, like all intermediaries in an "I-Thou" relationship with divine persons, must be addressed in a formalized manner. The conventionality of the hymns is, in part, a reflection of the conventions of cultic veneration and the subsystems that define the typology of the saints. All saints have certain common characteristics for which they are venerated. Their lives in some way make them images of Christ, recalling his precepts, his passion, and thereby inspiring the worshiper to his praises. Saints also function as channels of communication between the worshiper and the Divinity: they convey prayers to God and they help to answer prayers through their own divinely-granted powers of intercession.

Boris' and Gleb's untimely murder suggests in this context the category of μάρτυς in opposition to the category of ὁμολογητής, a type of saint who does not sacrifice his or her life.[14] This inspires the comparisons of Boris and Gleb to St. Procopius and St. Stephen, protomartyr. The decision to borrow from a hymn to SS Cyrus and John is inspired by other common attributes: like Boris and Gleb, these saints appear in tandem and perform miracles of healing.[15]

Conventionality is likewise demanded by the liturgical setting into which the hymns are inserted. Short hymns tend to be repeated, migrating from one service to another and filling a variety of liturgical slots, especially when the celebrants have only a few hymns at their disposal. They must be brief enough and sufficiently general in their themes to fit more than one context. At the same time, liturgical protocol requires that the service proper be either sung or chanted in one of eight specified tones. Within each tone there are melodic phrases and model hymns [αὐτόμελα]. Both the kontakion and the oikos for Boris and Gleb are identified as подобны [προσόμοια] that have to be sung to the melodies of two model hymns taken from the Christmas cycle: "Today a Virgin," and "Bethlehem hath opened Eden." They need not correspond syllable for syllable to the notes of the automelon, but there is a limit on the degree of variation. The sixth phrase of St. Procopius' sticheron was too long for the sixth phrase of "Today a Virgin" whereas the last phrase of SS Cyrus and John's oikos did fit the melodic model [Keller, 1973: 69]. The constellation of typological reminiscences, functional considerations and melodic structure may have encouraged the composer to continue "citing" from the service for SS Cyrus and John in the oikos for Boris and Gleb.

The Novgorod Sticherarion Office

A second version of Boris' and Gleb's office is contained in a Sticherarion [GPB, Sof. 384]. On f. 99 there is an inscription noting that the scribe began the book in June and finished it on September 13 on the eve of the Elevation of the Cross, during the prelacy of the Novgorod bishop Arkadij [*Svodnyj katalog*, 1984: 95-96; Golubovskij, 1900: 128]. According to the First Novgorod Chronicle, Arkadij was chosen as bishop in the summer of 1156 [NPL, 1950: 216]. In 1158 he journeyed to Kiev to be consecrated, and returned to Novgorod on September 13 of 1158 [*ibid.*: 216-217], that is, exactly on the day that the book was finished. Golubovskij, who first noted this coincidence, hypothesizes that Arkadij obtained a copy of Metropolitan John's service, together with other manuscripts during his stay in Kiev. The service may have been reworked in Kiev, he continues, and then copied, and brought back to Novgorod on September 13, or simply dated to coincide with Arkadij's journey [1900: 139-40]. He believes that it was probably first used to commemorate Boris' and Gleb's feast day in July of 1159.

The Sticherarion hymns are based on those in Metropolitan John's office but are by no means identical to them. The three stichera on the praises, for example, are not included. This version begins with the first two stichera aposticha from Metropolitan John's office, and adds nine other hymns. Four praise the brothers in general terms, developing the analogy between the martyrs' death and the death of Christ (the piercing with the spear, the slaying of the lamb). In the last five hymns, the writer calls upon the brothers by name, asking directly for their intercession [Abramovič, 1916: 144-146].

The new stichera are syntactically more complex than the earlier hymns. They are also marked by emotionally-charged epithets condemning the envious fratricide, Svjatopolk, and his evil servants. Here Boris and Gleb are not only praised as chaste martyrs and innocent lambs, but as princes who use their thaumaturgic powers to heal the sick, help those in misfortune, and free prisoners [*ibid.*: 145]. For the first time, they are asked to intercede for their native land. The references to Rus' also increase here: Boris and Gleb are called "lightbearing stars" of Rus', and enlighteners of the Russian land [*ibid.*]. The hymn that precedes the kanon summarizes the events of the passion and calls upon the newly christened Kievans to come and commemorate the princes' feast:

> Придѣте, новокрьщении русьстии сьбори, и видимъ како без вины судъ приемлеть мученикъ Борисъ, завистию братьнею: копиемь тѣло его прободоша и кръви пролитие сътвориша отъ наважения диявола; Глѣбии же отъ тогоже брата Святополъка ножьмь зарѣзанъ бысть и межю дъвѣма колодами съкровенъ, нъ сия вѣньчастася, а онъ бес памяти погыбе. Сия же Христа Бога молита о съпасении душь нашихъ [*ibid.*: 146].[16]

The kanon that follows (despite the fact that a Sticherarion is only supposed to contain stichera!) is, by and large, copied from the kanon attributed to Metropolitan John, with some notable exceptions. One or more stanzas of every ode have been eliminated and replaced with alternate stanzas. In the alternate stanzas of the first, fourth, fifth, sixth and eighth odes, the hymnographer expresses contrition and asks for absolution of his sins. The phrases are conventional, but they are so unexpected in this context that they seem like intimate personal revelations. In the first ode, for example, the third stanza reads:

> Отъпустъ дажь ми, Христе, грѣховъ моихъ зълыихъ, въ зълыихъ дѣлѣхъ осквърньшася, да быхъ възмоглъ бес порока прославити доблею твоею мученику [*ibid.*: 146].[17]

The third stanza of ode seven is borrowed from the May 2 service commemorating the translation of the martyrs' relics and contains a specific reference to Vyšgorod:

> Чюдесы ваю кыпитъ Вышеградъ пречьстьныи, яко рѣкы, исцѣления отъ гроба истачаета: немощьныя ицѣляета и печальныя утѣшаета: благословл(енъ) [*ibid.*: 148].[18]

Ode nine ties in the theme of personal contrition with the motifs developed in the additional stichera. After the first stanza, which is copied from Metropolitan John's kanon, the hymnographer adds two stanzas, asking Boris and Gleb (whom he addresses by their princely names) to pray for the forgiveness of his transgressions and for deliverance from his enemy. Following the fourth stanza, likewise copied from the original kanon, are three stichera vividly evoking the scene of Boris' murder. The first reads as follows:

> Егда на поли Льтьстьмь стояще, къняже Борисе, напрасно приступиша оружьници незнаеми, посълани отъ брата твоего Святопълка, видя же приставьникъ твои копие, на прободение устроено, нападе на пърси твои, въпия: обаче оли мене прободъше, толи мои господинъ, еже и сътвориша

беззаконьнии, прободъше исквозѣ того, тя продобоша, къняже [*ibid.*:149].[19]

The second is identical to the first sticheron in Menaion no. 121 [text in Mur'janov, 1981: 274-275], which is one of three that are not in Metropolitan John's service.

The closing hymn calls upon the Kievans to:

> Придѣте, вьси вѣрьнии събори русьстии, да похвалимъ добра къназя Бориса и Глѣба, яко отьчею любъвию даръ въсприимъша, а колики воя земля русьскыя въ руку дьржаща, непротивящася брату, оноя славы възирающа; тѣмьже увязостася вѣньцьмь отъ Христа Бога и Спаса душамъ нашимъ [*ibid.*: 150].[20]

Apart from the penitential ring of the kanon, the Novgorodian copy illustrates a marked change in the cult of Boris and Gleb. Their passion is evoked with greater pathos. At the same time, their connection to Kiev and their status as princes is beginning to come to the foreground. The oscillation between their baptismal names (Romanus and David) and their princely names increases here, which suggests that the new stichera were written in Church Slavonic by natives. It seems improbable, however, that this service was reworked by Bishop Arkadij or one of his retinue, copied in the span of three months, and then brought back to Novgorod. The fact that one of the "new" stichera matches a sticheron in Menaion no. 121—one which is not in Metropolitan John's office—and the attention paid to Kievan concerns would seem to indicate that we are dealing with a Kievan revision of the service attributed to Metropolitan John. It reflects an intermediary stage in the cult when Boris and Gleb were acknowledged as patrons of the Kievan princes but had not yet been accorded the highest degree of veneration. During his stay in Kiev, which extended from June to September, Bishop Arkadij probably attended a service to Boris and Gleb which was far more extensive than the service currently used in Novgorod (Metropolitan John's office). It is most likely that he ordered a copy rather than a revision of the Kievan service, along with other texts in the Sticherarion, which he brought back to Novgorod. Shortly thereafter, in the spring of 1167, the first Novgorodian church consecrated to the princes was erected [NPL, 1950: 219; Golubovskij, 1900: 137].

The Ivaniči Menaion Office

A further development of the services may be seen in the office preserved in a July Service Menaion dated 1547 from the Galician village of Ivaniči. The manuscript and convoy are described at length in G. K. Bugoslavskij's preface to the text [1900: 29-70]. A detailed comparison of this office with Metropolitan John's office and the Sticherarion office of 1156-63 is given in the same journal by Golubovskij [1900: 125-166]. The Ivaniči service incorporates the entire service attributed to Metropolitan John, and shares five hymns in common with the Sticherarion office.

Golubovskij believes that the archetype of the Ivaniči service predates the Sticherarion office. The impetus for composing a new, more elaborate office, according to his theory, was the commemoration of a church newly-built in the princes' honor and the solemn translation of their relics in Vyšgorod in the year 1115 [cf. PSRL, 1928: 290-291]. The theory that the Ivaniči service was written prior to the Sticherarion service is supported by a comparison of a sticheron contained in both the Novgorodian and Ivaniči offices, but not in Metropolitan John's service. The texts are virtually identical, but the Ivaniči Menaion hymn contains an extra phrase: "s"suda č'st'naja presvjataago Douxa javistasa" ["Ye were the vessels of the honorable, most holy Spirit" (Abramovič, 1916: 145, lines 10-11)]. The Ivaniči version also describes the brothers as keeping the *pravověrnaja* instead of the *pravoslavnaja* faith [*ibid.*: line 21]. Proceeding from the premise that a liturgical composer would never strike out an epithet from a hymn, Golubovskij concludes that the Ivaniči version of this particular text was written before the version contained in the Sticherarion, a generalization which he extends to the respective offices.

While it is entirely likely that new hymns were written for the celebration of 1115, there is no allusion to the event in the Ivaniči Menaion that would justify dating the office back to the twelfth century. On the textual level, the differences between the Ivaniči hymn and the version in the Sticherarion are insufficient to establish any kind of priority. The phrase praising Boris and Gleb as vessels of the Holy Spirit could easily have been inadvertently omitted by a copyist rather than intentionally expanded. By the same token it is impossible to determine whether a copyist deliberately substituted the synonymous *pravověrnaja* for *pravoslavnaja* [both are calques from the Greek ὀρθόδοξος] or vice versa. Several additional considerations further undermine Golubovskij's hypothesis. As we have seen, it is by no means certain that the service in the Sticherarion was composed by a Novgorodian writer, if only because that service introduces so many references which concern Kiev. Nor is Golubovskij able to explain the rationale that would lead a Novgorodian to copy five hymns from a long elaborate Kievan service, add more original hymns of his own composition, and then scale the final product down to a service for a minor feast when a simpler Kievan service was on hand.

A more plausible explanation of the relation between the offices suggests itself, namely, that the Sticherarion service was composed before the Ivaniči service at a stage when Boris' and Gleb's cult was spreading from the South to Northeast Rus' and from the lower or middle to the upper classes, but was nevertheless still viewed as a minor feast day. The archetype of the Ivaniči Menaion service, as Bugoslavskij rightly observes, must have been commissioned at a later date when the holiday shifted into the middle [*srednij*] category of feast with Polyeleos. The most likely period where one would expect such a change would be in the fourteenth century, when the Studite Rule was replaced by the Rules of Athos and Jerusalem, which required longer, more solemn services for the commemoration of saints' days. At this point Boris' and Gleb's cult had not completely overwhelmed the cult of St. Christine, but was important enough to displace her feast day from July 24 to July 23, so that it no longer coincided with the commemoration of the prince-martyrs [G. K. Bugoslavskij, 1900: 32-34, 39].

Comparison of the Sticherarion and Ivaniči offices confirms that the new redaction of Boris' and Gleb's service was commissioned primarily to conform with changing liturgical norms. Metropolitan John's office, which served as the basis, was reordered and supplemented with additional hymns. Five hymns that we also find in the Sticherarion service were added, together with many new stichera, to make up a full Great Vespers and Matins service. The final office contains sixty-five hymns in the following order. Great Vespers begins with six stichera on "Lord, I cry unto thee" [Psalm 140]. The first two date back to Metropolitan John's office, where they are identified as stichera aposticha, and the third is first found in the Novgorod Sticherarion. The following three stichera (numbered IV, V, and VI in G. K. Bugoslavskij's edition) are new. Sticheron seven is also found in the Novgorod Sticherarion [Abramovič, 1916: 145, lines 8-22]. The copyist then gives the paremia readings for the feast (see below). The rest of the Vespers service, which is entirely new, consists of: three new stichera on the Litiia (followed by two theotokia); four more new stichera aposticha; a troparion to the saints (followed by two theotokia); two sedalens (interspersed with theotokia); and a final sticheron.

The saints' kanon is virtually identical to the kanon from Metropolitan John's office, except that the kontakion and oikos are inserted after the sixth ode. The kanon is followed by a new photagogikon and a theotokion. Three stichera on the praises, identical to those found in Metropolitan John's office, and a closing sticheron identical to one found in the Sticherarion office [Abramovič, 1916: 146, lines 3-8] conclude the service.

While the Ivaniči office contains almost a third more hymns than the preceding two offices, the new verses do not alter the main themes associated with the princes' veneration in the Sticherarion office. Boris and Gleb are praised as fervent intercessors for the land of Rus', as princes above all other princes, as divine physicians, and as martyrs for the Orthodox faith. A few more civic references are added: the sixth hymn, for example, asks the princes to protect their city and Church from enemy invasions and addresses them as the pious descendants of the blessed Vladimir [Bugoslavskij, 1900: 54]. No new information about the cult is conveyed here, however, and the penitential leitmotifs of the Sticherarion kanon disappear entirely.

The Fifteenth-Century Office

The final stage of institutional commemoration is exemplified by the service published by Abramovič on the basis of a fifteenth-century manuscript from the Novgorod Sofijskaja biblioteka [1916: 150-167]. It begins with a new service for Little Vespers (four stichera of the day and four stichera aposticha) followed by a service for Great Vespers which differs both in order and in contents from that in preceding offices. Three new stichera on "Lord, I cry unto thee" precede the stichera numbered I-III in the Ivaniči Menaion office, followed by an additional sticheron. The paremia readings have also been replaced with standard readings from the Old Testament (Genesis, Isaiah, and the Wisdom of Solomon). New stichera on the Litiia replace the stichera composed for the Ivaniči service. The four stichera aposticha that follow contain phrases from the stichera aposticha in the Ivaniči Menaion but, given the tendency of liturgical composers to work around standard epithets, must count as new compositions. The troparion to the saints is new, as are the two sedalens.

The Matins service calls for three kanons: one for the Mother of God, and two for the saints. The first kanon for the saints, which consists of a single ode, is new. The second kanon is based on the one contained in Metropolitan John's office and the Ivaniči office, but additional heirmoi and troparia have been added. The photagogikon is new, and two of the subsequent stichera on the praises differ from those in the Ivaniči Menaion, as does the closing hymn.

This office, which is virtually identical to the services in the printed Menaion of 1628 [Bugoslavskij, 1900: 42-3], projects an image of the martyred princes as patrons of imperial power. We sense this in the opening stichera for Little Vespers, where Boris and Gleb's "all-holy" memory is described as illuminating the lands of Rus', and the congregation is called to praise these newly-revealed saints of the imperial line [Abramovič, 1916: 150]. While in the earliest services, the majority of the prayers were directed to healing and purification, the motif of guarding the fatherland takes precedence here. This theme also dominates in the new stichera on "Lord, I call to Thee" that initiate Great Vespers:

> Блажено отчьство ваше и градъ, вь немже вьспитастеся, и честнии храмъ, телеса ваше вьсприемше, яко вѣнцемь царствиа обложися: хранителя благоприетна и оружника, враги устрашающе и далече нѣгде отчьства своего отгонеща, Романе славне и Давыде пречюдне, молите спастися душамь нашимь [*ibid*.: 151-2].[21]

While in the Ivaniči service Vladimir was identified as the most blessed ancestor of the princes, he is here extolled as a "worthy autocrat . . . who has submitted to the purple cloak of Christ and has enlightened his people" [*ibid.*: 152]. So, too, the troparion to the saints praises them as a heavenly rain nurturing their fatherland and asks them to guard the citizens and protect them from the enemies of their princes [*ibid.*: 155]. The solemnity of the service is enhanced by the sheer number and variety of hymns and by rhetorically-charged, compound epithets which reflect the so-called Second South Slavic influence. In the fourth sticheron aposticha for Little Vespers, for example, the saints are addressed as "consecrated duo," "luminescent warriors" and "divine guides" [*ibid.*: 150]. The closing hymn for Little Vespers describes the tombs where the "honorable and consecrated bodies of the most praised pair" have been laid to rest [151]. Svjatopolk is condemned, not only as an accursed Cain, but as a *bogomerzky bratonenavistnik* ["brother-hater who is hateful to God," *ibid.*: 152]. This elevated, emotional tone is characteristic of all the hymns that have been added to the final redaction of the princes' service.

The hymn of praise that closes the Matins service sums up the essence of veneration for the princes in the late fifteenth century and to the present day:

> Днесь празнолюбнихь сьбори, сьшедшеся радостнимь лицемь и чисти душею, духовне ликь сьставльше, не вь кимвалѣхь иудеискы, нь вь сьрушенихь сердцехь похваляюще Христа, истиннаго Бога нашего, прославляющаго святиа своа, добляго Романа сь Давыдомь, ихже ныня многоцѣльбную и чюдотворную раку обьстоеще, любезно облобизаемь, глаголюще: Радуитеся, иже Христови заповѣди по образу сьблюдше; радуитася, яко Христово смирение вьсприемше, никако же противистася врагу и брату, немилистивно убивающому телеса ваша; радуитася, иже люди своя кь истиннѣи вѣрѣ наставльше и ныня сьхраняюще не оставляите, Романе пречюдне и незлобиви Давыде, отчьству си прѣсвѣтли свѣтилници и молитвеници дрьзновенни о душахь нашихь [*ibid.*: 166-167].[22]

The Homiletic Tradition

So far we have confined our discussion to hymns prescribed for the ritual commemoration of saints. There are a variety of texts which, though related to the service, are not mandatory for a service. Lying as they do on the periphery of liturgical veneration, they need not (though they may) reflect the degree of ordering that characterizes mandatory components of a highly ordered system. For the Slavs, in contrast to the Greeks, the decision to exploit that potential latitude has little or nothing to so with verbal conventions or genre. The most important factor seems to be a desire that the text in question inform or edify in apposition to the liturgical context. The vertical connection between a primary edifying function and the verbal structure that incarnates this function is exemplified in several types of texts that were composed to supplement the earliest services.

The Eulogies

In both Byzantine and medieval Russian liturgical practice, a eulogy could be read during or following a service on the saint's feast day [Krumbacher, 1897: 181]; it could also be composed for reading and anthologized in a variety of codices. Some eulogies follow a series of *topoi* or motifs inherited from the classical *enkomion*,[23] but little or none of these encomiastic patterns are evident in the two panegyrics for Boris and Gleb that have been preserved.

Both surviving eulogies commemorate the second translation of the saints' relics in 1115. The princes' relics had been translated in 1072 to a wooden church built in Vyšgorod by Izjaslav Jaroslavovič as described in the Laurentian and Hypatian Chronicle entries for that year. According to the "Narration" a new stone church, begun by Svjatoslav Jaroslavovič (d. 1076) and finished by his brother Vsevolod, collapsed and was left in ruins. Oleg Svjatoslavovič had a stone church erected and requested permission to have Boris' and Gleb's relics translated there, but was refused by Svjatopolk Izjaslavovič, the reigning Grand Prince of Kiev, "because he [Svjatopolk] had not built that church" [Uspenskij Sbornik, 1971: 69]. Svjatopolk's successor, Vladimir Monomax, gave permission for the translation, which took place in Vyšgorod on May 1 and 2 in the year 1115 [*ibid.*: 70-71; cf. PSRL, 1926-1928: vol. 1, vyp. 2, pp. 290-291; NPL, 1950: 204].

One of the eulogies, the *Slovo poxval'no svjatoju mučeniku Borisa i Gleba* ["Panegyric for the Holy Martyrs Boris and Gleb"], was composed for the *Velikie Minei Četii* of Metropolitan Makarij [Abramovič, 1916: XIX]. It represents the extreme of conventionalization which we associate with the work of Makarij's circle, but which is intensified because the eulogy is conceptualized as a component of a liturgical setting. The text resembles an amplified hymn that divides neatly into two parts with complementary themes. The first part is a pastiche of liturgical phrases summarizing the reasons for the saints' veneration which is only slightly more extended than the core hymns. The second part is composed of equally formulaic apostrophes to the saints, praising them and asking for their intercession:

> О, брата честная, свѣтозарная чюдесъ луча испущающа по всеи земли .... заступаета и храняета въ мирѣ, въ здравии родъ своихъ благовѣрныя князи наши, моляща Бога, зане нынѣ почиваета, святая и славная страстотерпца Христова, заступника всѣмъ христианомъ. О, брата честная и красная, блаженная княже Борисе и Глѣбе, свѣтилѣ пресвѣтлии, вѣнценосца святая, бисера прекрасная, имуща много дръзновение къ Богу! [Abramovič, 1916: 126].[24]

Though the epithets are more numerous than those in the core hymns due to the proportionately greater edifying function of the eulogy, it does not undertake to communicate even the limited historical information that is incorporated in the saints' kanon.

The second extant sermon, *Poxvala i mučenie svjatyx" mučenik" Borisa i Glěba* ["The Eulogy and Martyrdom of the Holy Martyrs Boris and Gleb"], illustrates the degree of deconventionalization permitted in a text composed for the purposes of religious edification. The work has survived in several copies, the earliest dating from the fifteenth century.[25] It is more than twice the length of the *Slovo poxval'no*, though it commemorates the same event. In addition to its commemorative frame (the translation of the relics is briefly mentioned at the very beginning and end of the text), the eulogy delivers a stern rebuke to all men who fail to love their brothers. Boris' and Gleb's lives serve as the point of departure for this sermon urging peace and reconciliation. Their self-sacrifice is contrasted to the ruthlessness of Svjatopolk, who was willing to slaughter his kinsmen for the sake of power:

> Слышите, братие, како по дъяволю дѣиству и окаянныи Святополкъ вражду имѣ, противяшеся своеи братии старѣишеи, рать възводяще поганыхъ на свою братию; сия же святыя вражды не имѣста, въ скоро минующемъ семъ житии вся та претерпѣша и вѣнець отъ Христа прияша [*ibid*: 128].[26]

In two copies the preacher actually addresses the senior princes of Rus':

> Слышите, князи противящеся старѣишеи братьи и рать воздвижуще и поганыя на свою братию возводяще, не обличилъ ти есть Богъ на страшнѣмъ судищи. [Loparev, 1894: 15].[27]

The central portion of the sermon consists of two parables [притчи]. Parable one presents an example of a bad king from the Bible:

> Нѣкогда чающимъ Израильтяномъ рати Халъдѣйския на Иерусалимъ, и послаша къ фараону въ Египетьскыи, помощи просяще, дабы Халдѣи не плѣнили Иерусалима. И посла Богъ пророка ко Израильтяномъ, глаголя: «Понеже не уповасте на Бога, създавшаго выи, но надежю всю възложисте на Египтяны, Азъ же Халдѣянинъ отвожу отъ васъ, но отъ Египтянъ плѣнени будете: на нихже уповасте, отъ тѣхъ и погибнути выи», якоже и бысть [Abramovič, 1916: 128-29].[28]

Parable two presents a local example of a good king, Prince David Svjatoslavovič of Černigov (d. 1123), whose long, prosperous rule is attributed to his good relations with his brothers. David's saintly qualities are manifested as he lies dying in the cathedral that he has built in honor of Boris and Gleb. Under the mistaken impression that the prince has died, Bishop Feotikst begins to sing the funeral kanon:

> И внезапу разступися верхъ храминѣ, идеже князь лежить, и ту ужасошася вси людие, и влетѣ голубь бѣлъ, и сѣде князю на честныя его перси,

и сягну носомъ въ уста, князь же душу испусти, и голубь невидимъ бысть, и наполнися храмина благоухания [*ibid.*: 130].²⁹

The concluding section of the sermon draws together the morals, citing many additional scriptural parallels. It closes with what must be regarded as the only markedly liturgical passage, a picture of Boris and Gleb together with the archangels, the cherubim, seraphim, apostles, martyrs and hierarchs sitting at the foot of God's heavenly throne and singing the angelic hymn:

... «святъ Отець, святъ Сынъ, святъ Духъ въ единомъ Божествѣ въ безконечныя вѣки». [*ibid.*: 132].³⁰

The sermon is obviously conceptualized less as a means of offering praise than as an occasion to teach a lesson, and its concerns are reflected in its style and structure. In the introduction to his edition, Loparev notes that, measured by the homiletic norms of the nineteenth century, the sermon may seem curious and even deficient since relatively little time is spent discussing the theme or analytically justifying the moral premises of the argument. Rather, the center of the sermon is a historical anecdote about a prince (and one not even confirmed by any chronicle). Loparev attempts to vindicate this dubious compositional mode by suggesting that it may have had a Greek model: a twelfth-century homily delivered by Byzantine Archbishop Theophanes of Kerameos against the iconoclastic heresy [1894: 7-8]. But, of course, to structure a sermon around an anecdote is to reject or overlook the sort of lateral generic models that Loparev has in mind. The *Poxvala i mučenie*, like its alleged Greek prototype (and no evidence of any actual or potential contact is offered) is a text shaped primarily by a constellation of vertical bonds to a localizable situation.

The homily retains strong links to the city of Vyšgorod, where the relics were translated, of course, but even stronger bonds to the principality of Černigov because of the central role played by the anecdote about David.³¹ References are also made to David's sons Svjatoslav (d. 1143), Vladimir (d. 1151) and Izjaslav (d. 1161). An additional vertical bond may be traced to the evolving cult of Boris and Gleb. If, as the development of the offices, the archaeological evidence and records of baptismal names would indicate, the saints became princely patrons by the late twelfth century,³² it is not surprising that Boris' and Gleb's behavior would be set forth as a model for peaceful coexistence among rulers, and that the expression of these sentiments would be closer to an entry in the official princely annals than to a hymn of praise. I should note in passing that, though directed at princes, this behavioral model is Christian in provenance and character; it is not integral to the princely code of conduct as has been claimed (cf. the discussion of Jaroslav's "guilt" in Chapter Two and Lixačev [1954: 87-91]). Nor does it reflect the behavior of princes to each other which, to judge by the chronicles, was neither peaceable nor loving.

It is only when we seek to match sermons to rhetorical models that texts such as the *Poxvala i mučenie* must be viewed as "idiosyncratic." Seen in the larger context of medieval Russian writing, they reflect the influence of lateral, generic constraints. The writer of this text, like the writer of the ornate eulogy contained in the *Velikie Minei Četii*, is simply tailoring his composition to the needs of Church and parishioners. In the first case, this approach produces an analogical relationship between the eulogy and the core hymns of a saint's office. In the second case, the ritual commemoration is shaped, not only by analogy to institutions of worship, but also by analogy to historical documents maintained by the State.

The Paremia Readings

One final example should be mentioned in this connection. On feast days with Polyeleos or a Vigil, three readings from the Old Testament [παροιμία, паремии] can be inserted in the Great Vespers service after the prokeimenon [Nikol'skij, 1900: 222-223]. In the medieval period such readings were contained in special codices [Προφητολόγιον, Парамийник].

Since paremias are direct citations from Scripture, their contents (and by default their form) are entirely predetermined. The three readings designed for Boris' and Gleb's office in the Parimijnik of 1271 [GPB Q. 1. 177] forms a curious exception to this rule: they are labeled "Ot Bytija čtenija," but they are not taken from the book of Genesis. Sobolevskij was the first scholar to comment on the anomalous readings. His interpretation of the rubric as "iz bylogo, iz istorii" ["from the past, from history"] and his theory that the texts were based on some chronicle [1890: 797-780] has been widely accepted. The exact date of the paremias' composition remains open. Šaxmatov suggested that the paremias must have been composed in connection with the second translation of the relics between 1095 and 1116 [1908: 45-54]. Abramovič noted that the texts must have been written in Vyšgorod at some time before 1191, when the princes' relics were translated to the monastery named in their honor on the River Smjadin' in Smolensk [1916: XIX]. Soboleva, who examined 85 full and 9 incomplete texts, initially dated the earliest "Osobaja" redaction from 1036-1054 [1975: 119-120], but later stipulated only that it must have occurred before the translation of 1072 and that it predates the Primary Chronicle account. From 1072 to 1115, she writes, three new redactions appeared: the "Kratkaja" [text in Abramovič, 1916: 115-121]; the "Prostrannaja"; and the "Dopolnennaja" [Soboleva, 1981: 91].

The "Osobaja" redaction, which has survived in a single copy [GBL, Undol'skij Sob., no. 1277; text in Soboleva, 1975: 124-125], provides an excellent illustration of how local considerations could override generic conventions inherited from the Greeks. Rubrics identify each reading as "ot byt'ja." But the first paremia consists only of a note directing the celebrant to use the paremia from Proverbs 17: 17-18 which is prescribed for the fifth week of Lent. The second paremia relates how Jaroslav heard of his brothers' murders and gathered an army of Varangians to avenge them:

> ... яко же Авраам Лота деля с лица месть сътвори на враги, так Ярослав за братью свою на Святополка поиде, нарек Бога, глаголя: «Не аз начах братью избивати, се бо без вины кровь праведных пролья, да будеть месть ему, Бог въздая кровь за кровь брату моему, зане в страси Божии пожиста лета своя, ведуще яко нетлинным златом искушена быста сего временнаго житья, но от своего брата заколена быста, аки агнеца непорочьна и пречиста ко Христу приидоста» [*ibid.*: 124].[33]

The third paremia continues the story of Jaroslav's revenge, developing two main themes: first, that unavenged blood cries out to heaven, and second, that a land receives the prince it deserves (here, Svjatopolk). The reading concludes with an account of the clash between Jaroslav and Svjatopolk, which ends with Svjatopolk's flight, and the Jaroslav's ascension to the Kievan throne.

Soboleva's comparison of this redaction to three later redactions reveals how the anomalous paremias developed into standard Old Testament readings. Initially, the motif of blood revenge and the horrors of fratricide overshadowed all other themes. There were no direct citations from the Bible. The style of the "Osobaja" redaction is very close to the paratactic, laconic style of the early chronicles. The language and the viewpoint suggest that the "Osobaja" redaction was composed in the reign of Jaroslav or at least based on annals gathered at that time. Noting these features, Soboleva concludes that the readings are "no more than a justification of Jaroslav's actions, a eulogy to him" [1975: 117]. We ought not to lose sight of the fact that we may be dealing with a stratified text here, however, and that it most probably dates to a period when the feast day was a middle [*srednij*] holiday—long after Jaroslav had passed away.

I would reconstruct the process as follows. At some time before the Tatar invasion when Vyšgorod still housed the princes' relics, the initial service to Boris and Gleb was revised (as discussed earlier). Paremias were required for the Great Vespers service. The composer of the service evidently misunderstood the nature of a paremia reading. It may be that he regarded the Old Testament, not as Scripture, but as a profane annalistic document, one that could be augmented, edited or replaced at will in the interests of providing the fullest possible information. He therefore took a historical account (perhaps, as Soboleva suggests, the Vyšgorod annals) and copied it out with some revisions to fill this liturgical slot. I would guess that initially there was only one account without the rubric directing the reader to Proverbs 17 (which does not seem to relate to the following readings).

Once the annalistic text had been copied, the Old Russian respect for *auctoritas* ensured that it would be recopied. Successive editors initially adjusted the text to bring it closer to standard paremias. If my hypothesis is correct, the single annalistic reading was divided into two paremias. An opening paremia based loosely on Proverbs 17: 17-28 was worked into a sermon condemning internecine strife in fairly concrete terms.[34] The text of the "Osobaja" redaction was edited to de-emphasize the theme of blood revenge, as Soboleva shows, while opposition between the righteous Christian prince (Jaroslav) and the criminal (Svjatopolk) was strengthened [1975: 115-117]. The next redaction, which Soboleva calls "Prostrannaja" improvises around phrases from I John 3-4, developing the theme of brotherly love [*philadelphia*] and focusing on the opposition between the martyred princes (who did not oppose their brother) and the proud, defiant Svjatopolk [*ibid.*: 112-114]. Beginning in the fifteenth century, the paremia readings were replaced with standard selections from the Old Testament [Soboleva, 1979[b]: 28].

Judging from the manuscripts that have survived, the practice of composing paremias from annalistic notes was not customary in Kievan Rus'. The fact that these paremias were copied in so many liturgical codices before they were replaced by citations from the Old Testament indicates that they were viewed as acceptable alternates to readings from Scripture. I would go even farther and argue that the principle grounds for that acceptability are analogous to the grounds that led the ecclesiastical authorities to accept idiosyncrasies in texts associated with the liturgy that were optional and edifying in function. This, in turn, demonstrates how the *Sitz im Leben* of even the most normative liturgical text could override laterally prescribed verbal models.

4

TESTIMONIALS

> ... и видѣвъше третьее чюдо оужасошася и возрадовашася потом же. Житье се преподобнаго не предано быст писанию доселѣ. Аз же смѣреныи и охудыи рабъ оубояхся осуженья лѣниваго раба съскрывшаго талантъ господина своего ... се же в малѣ написахъ житье преподобнаго отца нашего Игнатия, епископа ростовьскаго. Богу нашему слава. ...[1]

> В лѣто 6944 ... во единомъ от монастыреи белозерских кириллов имянуемъ ... бѣ пребывая прежде реченный Саватие, его же выше намнѣнихомъ. А иже града или веси, или родителя его пребывания, многа бо лѣта прешла сут до писания сего, необрѣтохомъ нами, или коликими лѣты возраста своего тогда бѣ егда во образ иноческаго жития облечеся, но единоточию обрѣтохомъ от боголюбивых мужъ и бесѣдъ духовных от приходящих мних от острова того и сих стяжах в малѣ бесѣдами палими в пользу духовную хотящимъ спасения душамъ своим и сих ревновати по Бозѣ добродѣтелнаго жития. ...[2]

When an individual was considered for canonization, as we have seen, the local bishop initiated a formal investigation, gathering evidence of that person's saintliness and powers of intercession. The process of evidence-gathering involved the accumulation of oral and written testimony from people who had witnessed miracles connected with the individual. Their testimony provided the grounds for canonization, the material for the office, and the contents for a narrative of the saint's life and acts. In a highly abbreviated form, such a narrative could be read during the saint's office, but the composition of longer narrative lives was not part of the liturgical veneration of a saint. Saints' lives were, first and foremost, a kind of official dossier. They had a broad edifying function as well, and were customarily read at the monastery table or in private. If the original biography was found wanting by subsequent generations, as was frequently the case, it could be revised as required to correspond to new revelations of the saint's powers of intercession or changing notions of ritual decorum. It could also be revised for the sake of clarity or as a way of marking the commemoration of an important anniversary or event.

Composed as a record of an individual's acts and disseminated in a wide variety of contexts, saints' lives had a potential for thematic and formal variety far greater than that of texts conceived appositionally to the liturgy. As always, the actual degree of latitude exercised in each work depended upon the constellation of vertical bonds that shaped it. A story based on a person's life could be cast in a highly conventionalized form, fulfilling the needs of a hierarchically organized system with rigidly formulated demands. When the needs of more loosely organized cultural institutions had to be served, however, a correspondingly unstructured narrative could be produced from the same *fabula*. Two extended accounts of Boris' and Gleb's lives, the "Narration and Passion and Eulogy of the Holy Martyrs" and the "Lection on the Lives and Deaths of the Blessed Passion-Sufferers," illustrate the potential variation that we may find in verbal responses to intersecting, but discrete socio-cultural systems.

The "Narration"

The "Narration" had a far wider circulation than the "Lection." S. Bugoslavskij counted 172 copies, which he grouped into six redactions.[3] The earliest copy, contained in the Uspenskij Sbornik (late twelfth or early thirteenth century), concludes with the *Skazanie čjudes svjatoju strast'rp'cju xristovu Romana i Davyda* ["Narrative of the Miracles of Christ's Holy Martyrs Romanus and David"]. Bugoslavskij, who adjusted his initial hypothesis [1914: 134-135] to Šaxmatov's arguments [1916: LXXIII], believed that the "Narrative of the Miracles" was composed after the "Narration" proper by at least three writers. The first, who describes the translation of 1072 and the miracle of the withered hand, concluded his segment after 1089 (the date when Metropolitan John II decreed that the translation of St. Nicholas' relics to Bari be celebrated in Rus') and before 1105 (the consecration of Lazar' as bishop of Perejaslavl'). The second writer made his contribution between 1108 (when Svjatopolk' Izjaslavovič initiated a series of churches) and 1113 (the death of Svjatopolk Izjaslavovič). The third account can be dated between 1115 (the date when the princes' relics were translated by Vladimir Monomax) and 1118 (the death of Bishop Lazar' of Perejaslavl') [1928^a: XIII-XIV]. Bugoslavskij's reconstruction of the original "Narration," based on the Uspenskij Sbornik copy and the manuscripts belonging to the so-called Čudov redaction [1928^a: 138-154], ends with a prayer to the martyrs to intercede for the faithful [Uspenskij Sbornik, 1971: p. 58 (f. 18^a, line 15)].

Most of the evidence suggests that the Primary Chronicle account, itself based on earlier annalistic records of the princes' death, served as a source for the "Narration." A substantial portion of the "Narration" coincides with or strikingly resembles the tale of the princes' passion as it has been preserved in the Laurentian codex. These include entries from the years 977, 980, 1015, 1016, and 1019 describing the genealogy of Vladimir's twelve sons, Svjatopolk's negotiations with the murderers, parts of the murder scenes, and the narrative of Jaroslav's final revenge. Specific references in the "Narration" to concrete places, historical or scriptural figures, and (in the miracle accounts) the names of witnesses, confirm the "Narration's" debt to the chronicle.[4]

The precise time when the "Narration" was composed cannot be determined from dates given in the tale proper. If we agree that the narrative of the passion was composed before the narrative of the miracles, it would follow that the "Narration" proper was composed before the translation of the saints' relics in 1072. A further clue to the text's dating is its treatment of Jaroslav. An inordinate amount of attention is focused on the prince in passages which are not inspired by the martyrdom, and he is shown in a highly flattering light. While the Laurentian Chronicle portrays Jaroslav as a capricious, violent prince who is quick to anger and must sometimes be taught a lesson, the "Narration" depicts him as a wise leader who avenges his murdered brothers and serves as God's instrument for punishing the sinner Svjatopolk. This contrast leads Bugoslavskij to conclude that the author of the "Narration" consciously reworked the chronicle material into a panegyric to Jaroslav [1939; 1941; 320]. The preoccupation with the positive side of Jaroslav's image, according to Bugoslavskij, suggests that the "Narration" was probably commissioned during Jaroslav's reign over Kiev, some time between 1036, the period when he had consolidated his power [cf. PSRL, 1926: 150], and 1054, the date of his death. The motivation for ordering such a work is not difficult to deduce. Jaroslav would have done so, in part because he wanted to preserve the memory of his murdered brothers, and in part to assure that his relation to them would be painted in glowing colors.

Related to the issues of provenance and dating is the "Narration's" place within the categories of the literary-genre system imputed to Kievan literature. The text is commonly acknowledged as an anomaly that corresponds to no single literary category, combining features of historiography and hagiography. Many distinguished critics of medieval literature have attempted to accommodate it to their own theories. Čiževskij's hypothesis that the "Narration" was composed, not as a *vita*, but as a *martyrion*, has failed to stand the test of time [1954: 109-110]. Comparison of the text to ancient Greek *martyria* confirms what has been duly noted by other critics, namely, that while the "Narration" describes what is represented as a martyrdom and incorporates many elements of that hagiographical category, it is not a standard *martyrion*.

Müller has attempted to explain the anomaly by positing two hypothetical, generically distinct texts that he regards as the original sources for the "Narration:" a secular saga and a hagiographical *Urlegende*. The saga, he argues, can be reconstructed by isolating passages marked by paratactic syntax, *topoi* of folk and military tales, and an impartial, unemotional narrative viewpoint [Müller, 1954]. Passages from the *Urlegende*, in contrast, are marked by hypotactic syntax, characteristic hagiographical *topoi*, quotations from Scripture, and numerous Grecisms. Müller believes that the *Urlegende* was composed in Greek and subsequently translated into Church Slavonic [*ZSPh*, 25, 2, 1956; 27, 2, 1959].

For a variety of reasons, Müller's hypothesis is difficult to accept. The heterogeneous lexical and syntactic strata need not be explained in terms of generically pure originals, but may stem from a single source. The entry in the Primary Chronicle, itself containing numerous biblical citations and passages translated from Greek sources, could have been reworked by the author of the "Narration" to correspond more closely to a Christian martyrdom. The Grecisms, imprecise Church Slavonic calques and mistranslations that Müller cites as evidence of derivation from a lost Greek *martyrion* of Boris and Gleb have no necessary link to a specific text. We find them in many writings from the pre-Mongol period because the literary language initially developed in large part as a vehicle for the translation of Greek scriptural and liturgical texts [Uspenskij, 1983: 1-32 and *passim*].

From a literary perspective, Müller's arguments are based on mutually contradictory premises. If, on the one hand, Kievan writers followed the literary norms that were operative in Byzantium, then they would surely have been reluctant to mix two texts belonging to separate literary and ideological categories, regardless of what language they were originally written in. If they felt free to mix literary genres, on the other hand, then it becomes more difficult to explain how an original "pure" *martyrion* came to be composed. What we know of medieval Church practice indicates that there is no liturgical need for such a work.

Ingham pinpoints the fundamental problem of the "Narration" when he describes it as "a unique transitional work that illustrates, perhaps better than any other major composition, the characteristic interpenetration of historiography and hagiography in Kievan literature" [1983: 231]. Such, indeed, is the paradox: the interpenetration of historiography and hagiography is characteristic, as even a cursory examination of the chronicles reveals, and yet the "Narration" is a unique work, even against the background of this characteristic interpenetration. There are, quite simply, no hybrid native works on which the "Narration" could be modeled. The "Narration's" uniqueness is further underscored by the absence of works modeled after it.

But what of non-native precedents? One oft-cited model for this curious amalgam of hagiography and historiography is the legend of King Wenceslas. Jakobson was the first to point out the similarities between the Bohemian and Kievan legends of this martyred sovereign [1940, 1976]. Jakobson's hypothesis that Kievan hagiographers were guided by the Wenceslas legend in composing the "Narration" inspired a series of follow-up studies [Il'in, 1975; Ingham, 1965, 1973; Rogov, 1970; Florja, 1978; Freydank, 1983]. In

"The Martyred Prince and the Question of Slavic Cultural Continuity in the Early Middle Ages," Ingham, summarizing and developing his earlier work on the subject, concludes that while it is difficult to prove direct influence of the Bohemian legend on the Kievan "Narration," we can single out a set of basic cultural concepts common to both traditions. They include that of the prince as a righteous victim (one whose death places him in the category of Christ and the martyrs) and of the ideal ruler, who is a secular and religious role model [1983: 39-47].

For all these general areas of correspondence and the clear evidence that the Kievans themselves perceived an analogy between Wenceslas and the princes, what is most remarkable, in my view, is the difference between the Latin and Slavonic lives of Wenceslas[5] and the *vitae* of Boris and Gleb. The proportions of the Wenceslas lives do not correspond to those of the "Narration" (or the "Lection"). The introductions differ radically in subject matter, length and choice of *topoi*. Wenceslas' childhood is described at great length while the "Narration" lacks any account of the Kievan princes' childhood and the "Lection" devotes very little space to the subject. The conclusions vary to no less a degree. One can readily acknowledge Ingham's theory that the Wenceslas legends provided an example of "how to portray as a Christian martyr a secular prince who was not killed for the faith but for political reasons. . ." [1983: 45]. It is equally clear, however, that the borrowing of concepts such as that of the sovereign-martyr or the righteous victim was hardly limited to the texts in question, or to a particular category of texts. To borrow a passage, theme, or topic, in other words, was not equivalent to borrowing a literary structure. The accounts of Boris and Gleb vary so substantially in form, content, and style from the accounts of Wenceslas that one cannot account for the heterogeneity of the "Narration" in terms of these non-native models.

The heterogeneity of the "Narration" is attributable, I believe, not to the merging of normally discrete literary genres or to the emulation of West Slavic models, but to the fact that Kiev had no literary system per se. Literary kinds, as we have seen, were probably not distinguished as such, but rather in terms of the cultural systems they served. The "Narration" was produced in a recently converted society where a large proportion of the population still adhered to pre-Christian beliefs and customs, and the native clergy was only beginning to be instructed on the fine points of the faith. An inescapably syncretic point-of-view was further complicated by vertical bonds extending to the Kievan court, for the evidence suggests that the "Narration" was commissioned during the reign of Jaroslav, perhaps by the prince himself. This *Sitz im Leben*, rather than any conscious desire to create an artistic variation on a familiar norm, would have shaped what is in many respects a unique biography.

Two distinct cultural models are at work here. The first model, which is derived from pre-Christian kinship structures and East Slavic ancestor veneration, demands that Boris and Gleb be treated as members of Vladimir's dynasty, and that the account of their death be related in terms compatible with that status. The second model, which originates in the typology of Orthodox Christian saints, dictates that the princes' death be depicted in terms of martyrdom, i.e. as a feat of asceticism and sacrifice which earns them special powers of intercession. What appears in retrospect to be a mixing of the secular and the sacred, of historiography and hagiography, arises in the "Narration" because these two models, in certain respects diametrically opposed, must be combined. The textual manipulation required to do so can best be appreciated by comparing the demands placed on the Primary Chronicle in this regard with those placed on the "Narration." The chronicle account also focuses on the twin themes of martyrdom and succession, but the annalistic context permits the chronicler to ignore contradictions. His primary task is to document events that may relate to various cultural models and/or systems in chronological order, and he can shift point-of-view as required. For the author of the "Narration," in contrast, the events of 1015 and their aftermath are part of a broader monolithic tale whose central focus is the fate of Vladimir's sons. His solution to the problem of potentially conflicting cultural models is to shift the focus away from classic Christian martyrdom per se, concentrating rather on the historical reification of a moral premise: God punishes the wicked and causes the righteous to prosper. Although Boris' and Gleb's violent death resembles the passion of Christ and earns them martyrs' crowns, the slaughter is vindicated for the author of the "Narration" by the fact that a righteous prince ultimately ascends the throne.

The dynastic conflict, which makes up the *fabula* of the tale, is provided with a Christian context through citations or allusions to Christian precedents. The opening citation summarizes the moral of the story that is to follow: "Rod" pravyix" blagoslovit'sja, reče propok", i sěmja ix" v" blagoslovlenii budet'" [Abramovič, 1916: 27]. It is an amalgam of several biblical passages [Psalm 111: 2, Psalm 36: 26 and/or Isaiah 65: 23] which promise prosperity to the descendants of the Israelites and all who keep the Lord's commandments.[6]

The reference is concretized with a genealogy listing the twelve sons who represent Vladimir's clan. The number twelve and the first three names of the list coincide with the Laurentian Chronicle entry for the year 988, whereas the explanation of Svjatopolk's tainted genealogy and the following names were borrowed from an alternate list contained in the entries for 977 and 980 [Šaxmatov, 1908: 35-36]:

Сего мати преже бѣ чьрницею, гръкыни сущи, и поялъ ю бѣ Яропълкъ, братъ Володимирь, и ростригъ ю красоты дѣля лица ея, и зача отъ нея сего Святоплъка оканьнааго. Володимиръ же, поганъй еще, убивъ Ярополка и поятъ жену его, непраздьну сущю, отъ нея же родися сий оканьный Святопълкъ. И бысть отъ дъвою отцю и брату сущю, тѣмь же и не любляаше его Володимиръ, акы не отъ себе ему сущю [Abramovič, 1916; 27-28].[7]

In keeping with the dynastic orientation, Boris and Gleb are introduced, not as future saints, but as the youngest sons of Vladimir by a Bulgarian woman. The names of three sons—Stanislav, Pozvizd and Sudislav—are not given here, while Izjaslav's name is counted twice [Müller, *ZSPh* 27: 282]. The change in order and the combination of the two lists clarify the relations of the protagonists to one another. They also emphasize that Jaroslav, Boris, and Gleb are genealogically distinct from the accursed Svjatopolk, although they have the same father. This preoccupation with lineage is clearly related to the framing premise that "the seed of the righteous shall prosper." The names of other brothers, according to one theory, were deleted because they were either illegitimate or, in the case of Sudislav, were at war with Jaroslav, while the biblical number of twelve was retained for symbolic reasons [Müller, *ZSPh* 27: 284].

Once the basic grid of kinship has been defined, the narrator introduces a number of related dynastic themes, each supported by scriptural references. The initial theme concerns the relation between father and son. Vladimir, we learn, is struck by a grave illness which prevents him from marching against the Pecheneg nomads. He sends for Boris, who declares that he is ready to obey Vladimir's will. Boris' filial obedience is placed in its moral context with a citation from Proverbs 4: 3:

О таковыихъ бо рече Притъчьникъ: «сынъ быхъ отцю послушьливъ и любиимъ предъ лицьмь матере своея» [Abramovič, 1916: 28].[8]

When Vladimir dies, however, the Kievan throne must be taken over by one of his sons: at this point brotherly relations become a dynastic issue.[9] The Laurentian Chronicle reports the event, noting that Svjatopolk had his father's body wrapped in a rug and hauled away for burial at night. The account is followed by a long eulogy to Vladimir. The "Narration" depicts Vladimir's death and its aftermath in a series of scenes that set the virtuous behavior of Boris in dramatic contrast to the lawless behavior of Svjatopolk. The incident is portrayed via a lyrical monologue revealing Boris' feelings, rather than from the viewpoint of a third-person omniscient narrator. The prince learns of his father's death and of Svjatopolk's reaction from a messenger. Boris expresses his sorrow at his father's passing,[10] and regrets that he had not personally made the funeral arrangements. He wonders who might console him in his grief and his thoughts turn to Svjatopolk. It occurs to him that his brother may be contemplating his murder in order to secure the throne.

Svjatopolk, we learn, has indeed ascended the Kievan throne, and sent a messenger informing Boris that he wants to maintain good relations. The message is only a pretext, however, for Svjatopolk is in the power of the devil. In contrast to Boris, the model son and brother, Svjatopolk hopes to seize all power for himself. He is equated to Cain by virtue of his lawless behavior. As in the Laurentian Chronicle version, Svjatopolk contracts with Put'ša and his men from Vyšgorod to have Boris murdered in his tent [Abramovič, 1916: 32].

The prince's martyrdom is elucidated with reference to the dynastic code of behavior. The prerequisite for Boris' sainthood is kinship loyalty. He is ready to obey his older brother as he has obeyed his father. The dilemma that occasions his martyrdom is his knowledge that obedience may be fatal. His decision to return and to submit to his older brother without a struggle is the result of painful meditation on the subject of God's will. Three scriptural references suggest the following chain of reasoning: God wants men to love their brothers; those who obey this commandment and submit humbly to the proud will be granted grace everlasting and will prosper. By acknowledging Svjatopolk as his lord and father, and submitting to his authority, Boris is submitting to the will of God. If Svjatopolk sheds his blood, Boris reasons, and he does not defend himself, but continues to do what is right, he will become a martyr:

> Да аще кръвь мою пролѣеть и на убииство мое потъщиться, мученикъ буду Господу моему. Азъ бо не противлюся, зане пишеться: «Господь гърдыимъ противиться, съмѣренымъ же даеть благодать». Апостолъ же: «иже рече: «Бога люблю», а брата своего ненавидить,—лъжь есть». И пакы: «боязни въ любъви нѣсть, съвършеная любы вънъ измещеть страхъ». Тѣмь же что реку или чьто сътворю? Се да иду къ брату моему и реку: «ты ми буди отець, ты ми братъ и старѣй, чьто ми велиши, господи мой?» [Abramovič, 1916: 29-30].[11]

In contemplating his impending martyrdom, Boris thinks of three precedents: the martyrdom and passion of SS Nicetas, Wenceslas, and Barbara.[12] Each case involves a saint who was killed by a member of his or her family. He then says his evening prayers and attempts to fall asleep:

> И бяше сънъ его въ мънозѣ мысли и въ печали, крѣпъцѣ и тяжьцѣ и страшьнѣ, како предатися на страсть, како пострадати и течение съконьчати и вѣру съблюсти, яко да и щадимый вѣньць прииметь отъ рукы Вьседьржителевы [ibid.: 33].[13]

In the morning, as Matins is being served and Boris is reciting the morning kathisma of the Psalter, the assassins draw near. Boris chants the kanon, and then prays to an icon of the Savior, asking to be made worthy of the passion. As he hears the men approach his tent, he commends his soul to the Lord, and reaffirms that he is submitting to the Lord's will. His priest and retainer echo this motif, stressing the fact that Boris had the troops to fight back, but that he voluntarily submitted to the will of God and the will of his brother, saying:

> «Милый господине наю и драгый, колико благости испълненъ бысть, яко не въсхотѣ противитися любъве ради Христовы,--а колики вои държа въ руку своею» [*ibid.*: 35].[14]

The mercenaries stab him with lances, running through the body of his retainer Georgij first, and then prepare to finish him off. Boris begs for time to say a final prayer. He cites excerpts from the psalms and Scripture, summarizing the essence of his martyrdom, which he portrays as submission to his brother for Christ's sake:

> Призьри съ высоты святыя твоея, вижь болѣзнь сърдьца моего, юже прияхъ отъ съродьника моего, яко Тебе ради умьрщвляемъ есмь вьсь дьнь, въмѣниша мя яко овьна на снѣдь. Вѣси бо, Господи мой, яко не противлюся, ни въпрекы глаголю, а имый въ руку вься воя отьца моего и вься любимыя отьцемь моимь,--и ничьто же умыслихъ противу брату моему. Онъ же, елико въздвиже на мя, възмогъ: да аще бы ми врагъ поносилъ, претърпѣлъ убо быхъ; аше бы ненавидя мене вельречевалъ, укрылъ быхъ ся. Нъ Ты, Господи, вижь и суди межю мною и межю братьмь моимь, и не постави имъ, Господи, грѣха сего, нъ приими въ миръ душю мою. Аминь [*ibid.*: 36].[15]

Gleb's martyrdom is also inseparable from clan loyalties and conflicts. Jaroslav personally sends a messenger to warn the prince of the impending danger, thereby reinforcing his image as the righteous brother and defender of his clan. In a lyrical monologue, Gleb laments Boris' death, asking why it had to come, not from an enemy but from the princes' own brother, but he takes no action to save himself. Confronted by Svjatopolk's men, he protests his innocence and begs to be taken to their lord. When they refuse, he calls, first, upon his dead father to "incline thy ear and hear my voice" [cf. Psalm 85: 1], then upon heaven and earth [cf. Isaiah 1: 2], and finally upon his dead brother Boris to bear witness to the crime. These syncretic pleas to dead ancestors for aid in time of trouble are expressed in words borrowed from Scripture. They were evidently recognized by the author of the "Lection" as pagan, however, and deleted from that biography. Gleb then asks that the Lord grant him the courage to accept the same martyrdom and join his brother in the world to come. As the murderers prepare to slaughter him, Gleb cites a passage from the Bible in which the apostles predict that Christians will be slain by members of their own family:

> And ye shall be betrayed both by parents, and brethren, and kinsfolks, and friends; and some of you shall they cause to be put to death" [Luke 21: 16; cf. Abramovič, 1916: 42].[16]

The account of Gleb's passion concludes with the affirmation that the young prince entered into heaven and, joining his brother, received the martyr's crown [*ibid.*: 43].

Jaroslav, the fourth brother, who has nothing to do with the princes' martyrdom, nevertheless is highlighted in the "Narration" as the divine instrument for punishing the sinner and restoring the dynasty of the righteous to the throne. The account of his revenge is, again, prefaced by a series of citations from the psalms promising that sinners will be sent to hell and destroyed by God [Psalms 9: 17; 36: 14-15; 51: 1-5]. Here, as in the Primary Chronicle account, we follow Jaroslav's pursuit of Svjatopolk, which is set in its moral context by a second reference to the conflict between Cain and Abel. The prince asks the Lord to revenge the blood of Abel (Boris) and to punish the fratricide Cain (Svjatopolk).

The "Narration's" denouement, as in the Primary Chronicle, shows Svjatopolk's flight and death in the wasteland. The chronicle account portrays the punishment as an example to all princes who violate the law, citing Cain's punishment for killing Abel, and Lamech's punishment for a similar crime. The "Narration" adds a Christian precedent which Abramovič traces to the legend of St. Mercurius of Caesarea [1916: XIII] and Müller to the Chronicle of Hamartolus [*ZSPh* 30: 38]:

> ... да аще кто си сътворить, слыша таковая, си же прииметь и вящьша сихъ. Яко же Каинъ, не вѣдый мьсти прияти, и едину прия, а Ламехъ, зане вѣдѣвъ на Каинѣ, тѣмь же седмьдесятицею мьстися ему: така ти суть отъмьстия зълыимъ дѣлателемъ. Яко же бо Иулиянъ цесарь, иже мъногы кръви святыихъ мученикъ проливавъ, горькую и нечеловѣчьную съмьрть прия, невѣдомо отъ кого прободенъ бысть, копиемъ въ сьрдьце въдруженъ: тако и сь, бѣгая, не вѣдыйся отъ кого, зъластрастьну съмьрть прия. И оттолѣ крамола преста въ Русьскѣ земли, а Ярославъ прея вьсю волость Русьскую [Abramovič, 1916: 47-48].[17]

The equation of Svjatopolk with Julian the Apostate creates yet another link between this political act and a Christian martyrdom. It is Svjatopolk's punishment, however, and the assumption of power by Jaroslav, the righteous prince, that banish all discord in the Land of Rus'. This is the vindication of the princes' deaths and the happy ending to the story promised by the opening prophecy that "the generation of the righteous shall be blessed."

According to the "Narration," once Jaroslav has occupied the throne of Kiev he begins to inquire about his brothers' bodies and learns that miraculous signs have been observed. His order that presbyters locate Gleb's body and bring it back to Vyšgorod has a twofold motivation: the miracles indicate that Gleb may be a saint and, as Jaroslav himself puts it, "He is my brother" [*ibid.*: 48]. Thus, both the martyrdoms and their recognition by the Church are precipitated and conditioned by the dynastic model.

The "Lection"

The earliest copy of the "Lection" is found side by side with the anonymous "Narration" in the fourteenth-century Sil'vestrovskij Sbornik [CGADA, f. 381, no. 53 (described in Orlov, 1896: 1-13)]. This extended biography, identified in the text as the work of the monk Nestor, has survived in a good deal fewer copies than the "Narration." In the critical apparatus for his edition, S. Bugoslavskij cites variants from eighteen manuscripts, including a Prolog dated 1406, two late fifteenth-century codices from the Soloveckij Monastery collection, and a number of sixteenth-century Toržestvenniki and Menaia [1928[a]: 179-180].

The exact relation of the "Lection" to the "Narration" is still disputed. Šaxmatov originally believed that the "Lection" was a source for the "Narration" [1908: 34], a theory which he later retracted without accepting the opposite hypothesis, that the "Narration" was a source for the "Lection" [1916: LXVIII-LXXVII]. S. Bugoslavskij presents a convincing case for the claim that Nestor used the "Narration" as his point of departure. He points to the general narrative exposition, plot elements, and lyrical passages that coincide in the "Narration" and "Lection" but are missing from the chronicle entries. The same holds true for certain passages reflecting excerpts from services for Boris and Gleb. Both extended *vitae* cite a eulogy from an early office [Abramovič, 1916: 25-26. 49-51] which is entirely different from the eulogy in the Laurentian Chronicle entry [PSRL, 1926: 137-138]. The "Narration" cites names, places and other information which reflect local records. These specific references are abbreviated or abstracted, sometimes to the point of incomprehensibility, in the otherwise lucid "Lection" [1914: 139-142]. Most historians and literary scholars writing in the last three decades concur for these reasons that the "Narration" must have preceded the "Lection."[18]

In dating the text, scholars have relied upon the account of the posthumous miracles, which they believe was an integral part of the original composition. Šaxmatov set the *terminus a quo* in 1072, when the saints' relics were translated under Metropolitan George, and the *terminus ad quem* in 1088, the end of Nikon's term as hegumen of the Kiev Cave Monastery. The *terminus ad quem* is derived from Nestor's statement that he composed the biography of the murdered princes before the *vita* of St. Feodosij in which he speaks of Hegumen Nikon as though he were still alive [Uspenskij Sbornik, 1971: 71]. An additional clue comes in one of the miracles. A woman with a withered arm is said to have been cured on August 15, a Sunday. August 15 fell on Sunday in the years 1081 and 1087. Given the other data, Šaxmatov initially regarded the earliest date as the most probable time of the "Lection"'s composition [1908: 55-56;].[19] Nestor's rebuke to rebellious princes has suggested to some scholars that the "Lection" may have been written during the period between 1078 and 1085 when internecine wars initiated by the younger princes reached a high point [Loparev, 1894: 8-9; Abramovič, 1916: I-II; Poppe, 1965: 300-304].

S. Bugoslavskij points out that the references to a hegumen who is still living at the time when Feodosij's *vita* was being written, like the references to the princes in the "Lection" of Boris and Gleb, are very general and cannot be related to concrete historical persons [1914: 174-175]. He believes that one of the posthumous miracle accounts incorporated in the "Lection" provides a more accurate point of reference. This miracle describes how several prisoners were freed through the intervention of Boris and Gleb. The version appended to the "Narration" is set in the reign of Svjatopolk Izjaslavovič (d. 1113), who is accused by the author of neglecting the Church of Boris and Gleb in Vyšgorod and imprisoning two men without reason. When the prince hears how the men were miraculously freed by the saints, he resolves to mend his autocratic ways and makes plans to build a new church by the graves of the saints in Vyšgorod. The narrator tells us, however, that these plans were realized only later [Abramovič, 1916: 60-62]. This miracle, writes Bugoslavskij, was most probably written around 1108, when Svjatopolk began to devote more attention to church construction [1914: 131-135]. The version in the "Lection," which takes place during the reign of Jaroslav, is shorter, simpler and generalized. It takes place in "a certain town" where the senior official [*starejšina*] has condemned and imprisoned some men. When informed of the miraculous liberation of these prisoners, Jaroslav resolves to build a church on that site. The "Lection" version ends with the note that many other prisoners were freed by the saints in many other places [Abramovič, 1916: 20]. Bugoslavskij argues that the writer of the "Lection" deleted the unflattering references to Svjatopolk and reset the episode in the reign of Jaroslav for political reasons, since no monk of the Kiev Cave Monastery could speak so sharply about a royal patron during his reign [1914: 165-168].

None of the aforementioned arguments can be accepted in its entirety. We know that the *vita* of Feodosij was composed some time after 1074, the date of the saint's death. The fact that Nestor does not mention the translation of Feodosij's relics in 1091, however, would appear to preclude Bugoslavskij's theory that the *vita* was written in the early twelfth century.[20] Given the absence of any concrete proof that Nikon was still alive when Nestor wrote, the date 1088 cannot be taken as a *terminus ad quem* for the "Lection." The dating of the prisoner miracle is more problematic because its provenance is so complex, and the version in the "Narration" appears to be a corruption of at least two sources [Müller, *ZSPh* 23: 76; Ingham, 1965].[21] But even if the account was written during or after Svjatopolk's reign, it may have been added to the "Narrative of Miracles" by a subsequent editor. This possibility would not contradict the hypothesis that the posthumous miracles were part of Nestor's original in some form, since the earliest extant version of the miracles in the Uspenskij Sbornik postdates the "Lection's" composition, and this particular miracle seems to be an appendage (it is not assigned a number like the preceding miracles and comes at a seam in the exposition). I would, therefore, be inclined to date the "Lection" between 1072 and 1091, while not ruling out the possibility that it was written later, at some time before the translation of the relics in 1115.

Of the two narratives, the "Lection" is closest to the sort of Byzantine saints' lives that were composed in the eighth and ninth centuries. Golubinskij characterizes it as the first Russian attempt at producing a genuine *bios*. "The man who decided to transfer this verbal form from Greece," he writes, "naturally had to perceive his task in terms of imitating his models as closely as possible" [1901-1910: I, 1, 749]. Bugoslavskij theorizes that Nestor did not regard the anonymous "Narration" as a "genuine" *vita* appropriate for reading during a service or in the monastic cell, and therefore he initiated "a carefully considered reworking of the 'Narration' in the spirit of Byzantine ascetics' and martyrs' lives" [1941: 326]. Čiževskij [1948: 127] and Ingham [1983: 229] stress the institutional need for a *vita* which conformed to the conventions of the genre proper.

In assessing these arguments, we must be careful to distinguish what the Church required and in what forms its demands could be realized, on the one hand, and what the historical author's motivations were and how they might have been realized, on the other. There is no reason to assume that the Church as a formal institution required an extended *vita* for any liturgical reasons whatsoever. Commemoration of the princes' holiday at the time when Nestor wrote the "Lection" called for an office. A short Prolog-type legend could have been read during such a service, but never a full-length biography. This explains why we encounter full-length lives with relative infrequency in codices up to the mid-sixteenth century [Ključevskij, 1871: 358-359]. Nor is there reason to conclude that the institution of the Church, in the person of Nestor or his readership, regarded the "Narration" as improper or anomalous for generic reasons. Its wide circulation testifies that it fulfilled its edifying function to the satisfaction of the overwhelming majority of writers and readers, although it is neither a classical *martyrion* nor a full *vita*. Its retention in institutionally sanctioned Menaia confirms its acceptability.

Why was a second life written? Most new biographies of saints are commissioned when the existing life is perceived to be outdated. The additional information is generally appended mechanically onto the existing text, often with the addition of excerpts from liturgical eulogies or prayers to the saint. Leontij of Rostov's *vita* is fairly typical in this respect [text in Titov, 1893]. A second reason for commissioning a new version of a saint's biography is the "stylistic" enhancement of a *vita*. This process has been seen by literary critics primarily as one of adding elaborate, often redundant epithets, after the example of Byzantine or Athonian models. Comments made by hagiographers themselves emphasize their desire to narrate the events in the best sequence (*po rjadu*), clarify obscure places, and fill in "missing" parts [see Lenhoff, 1986].

The hagiographer supplements the existing life, first and foremost, on the basis of new information, as we may see from Paxomij Logofet's remarks about his work on St. Sergij of Radonež's *vita*:

> Сия же азъ смиреныи таха иеромонахъ Пахоме, пришедшоу ми во обитель святаго и видя чюдеса часто бывающая от ракы богоноснаго отца, паче же оувѣдѣвъ от самаго оученика блаженаго, иж мьнога лѣта паче же от самаго възраста юности живъша съ святыимъ, глаголю же Епифания, иж бѣше и духовникъ велицѣи лаврѣ всему братству. Вѣдыи блаженаго извѣстно иж и по ряду сказаше о рожении его и о възрасту и о чюдотворении, о житии же и о преставлении . . . [Tixonravov, 1892: appendix III, 59].[22]

When new data was not available, a hagiographer had the option of extrapolating events that he could assume to have taken place (that the saint distinguished himself from other children, for example, or read many holy books or gave alms to the needy) and of adding epithets that clarify the nature of the individual's sainthood. Among the commonplaces for martyrs are the image of an innocent lamb whose sacrifice imitates Christ, the metaphor of the martyr's crown, the repeated references to the miracles of healing [see Delehaye, 1927: 95-108; Ingham, 1984: 44]. These *topoi* are not linked to any generic model. They are clustered together with the greatest density in the hymns of a saint's service, but they naturally play a role in any account of his deeds and characteristics because they identify features that distinguish a particular type of saint.

In the specific case of the "Lection," both the presence of new information and the desire for reordering enter into the revisions. What appears to have determined the selection and arrangement of material, however, is more specifically related to the writer's *Sitz im Leben* than to the need for a *vita* that corresponded more closely to Byzantine literary canons. The historical context that shaped the "Narration" has changed considerably. After Jaroslav's death, the dynastic focus begins to lose its relevance for the cult of Boris and Gleb. Moreover, the "Lection" is aimed primarily at an audience for whom the premise that the "generation of the righteous shall prosper" cannot really apply: the celibate monks, addressed by the narrator as "brethren." This audience, whose members have chosen to withdraw from the secular community, has interests which encourage more ascetically-oriented literary motifs, foremost among them *imitatio Christi*. Boris' and Gleb's life and passion are portrayed as examples which illustrate this monastic ideal. Vladimir's and (to a lesser degree) Jaroslav's conduct also exemplify the ideal behavior of a Christian prince as perceived by a monk.

All of the additions and correspondences to the text of the "Narration," as well as the deletions and reordering of the *fabula*, are determined by the presumption of a monastic addressee and this dual homiletic function.

The introductory passages of the "Lection" project the typical image of a monk who, by definition, is unequal to the task of describing such perfect saints (*sermo humilis*), followed by a prayer for the wisdom to recount what the writer has learned about the lives and passion of the Kievan martyrs from "a certain Christ-loving man." The subsequent account of the Creation, the exile from Eden, Christ's passion and the baptism of Rus' that follows, however, reflects the author's homiletic intent: to remind his listeners ("brethren") that Boris' and Gleb's spiritual feats are part of Kievan Christian history, rather than the history of a particular Kievan clan.

With the same homiletic goal in mind, Nestor replaces the genealogy of Vladimir with a portrait of the ruler as a Christian prince who, though initially a pagan, came to see the light:

> Бысть бо, рече, князь въ тыи годы, володый всею землею Рускою, именемь Владимеръ. Бѣ же мужь правдивъ и милостивъ к нищимъ и к сиротамъ и ко вдовичамъ, Елинъ же вѣрою [Abramovič, 1916: 4].[23]

Vladimir's conversion is equated with the precedent of St. Eustace, a noble pagan general who, legend has it, converted after having a vision of a stag with a cross between its antlers. The fact that Vladimir not only saw the light, but converted his nation to Christianity, inspires the description of the prince as a second Constantine. After the baptism of Kievan Rus' in 988, adds Nestor, Vladimir went on to build the Cathedral of the Holy Mother of God in Kiev.[24]

Having broadened the context of the cult to extend beyond Vladimir's dynasty, Nestor proceeds to narrow the focus of his tale. He explains that while Vladimir had many sons, there is no point in listing them (as the author of the "Narration" does), for this story is about Boris and Gleb, the two who "shone like bright stars in the darkness" [*ibid.*: 5].

The central narrative of the saints' lives is supplemented in places where the added information will contribute to the portraits of the princes as potential saints. This information is never mechanically appended, but is integrated with the flow of the story and provided with logical motivation. The section describing the princes' youth, which is based on no surviving sources, has been regarded as a concession to a generic model that Nestor felt he had to follow regardless of the facts.[25] Closer reading suggests that this is an oversimplification. Gleb is depicted as a mere child, while Boris is represented as old enough to have some understanding of the faith. Certain assumptions could be made about Boris' behavior, but they would be less credible in the case of his younger brother. This situation, rather than any metaphrastic model, shapes the account of the princes' youth. Boris comports himself like an exemplary Christian and a potential saint, while Gleb follows the model of his brother.

Boris is described as an eager reader of *vitae* and *martyria*. This is the sort of information that we find in many saints' lives, either because the subject actually did read holy books at an early age (a possibility usually overlooked) or because such behavior is deemed appropriate to a saintly childhood. It is not, however, universal or required of a saint. In addition, Nestor continues, Boris recited prayers around the clock. Gleb, who could not read or understand the material, listened to his brother and repeated the words after him [*ibid.*: 5]. In much the same way, Nestor shows us how each brother followed the example of his father, the righteous Prince Vladimir, in ruling his kingdom, and how each resembled his patron saint. Like Romanus the Melodist, whose name he bore, writes Nestor, Boris was imbued with the gift of the Holy Spirit. The parallel explication of Gleb's affinity to his patron saint, King David, has to be stretched to fit the case in point. Like David, Gleb is the youngest of his brothers and the favorite of his father [Psalm 151: 1-2]. Gleb's victory over the devil, which took away the reproach from the sons of Rus', is equated with David's victory over Goliath, which took away the reproach from the sons of Israel [Abramovič, 1916: 6; I Samuel: 17].

Evidence that the facts known to Nestor were not sacrificed in the interests of maintaining a strict parallelism between the behavior of the two brothers may be seen in the treatment of Boris' marriage. Nestor does not suppress this information, which could conflict with the prince's image as a saint, but does reconcile the potential conflict by explaining that Boris acceded because of his desire to obey the commandment dictating filial obedience rather than because he desired to live with a woman [Abramovič, 1916: 6]. He was then sent by Vladimir to rule his own principality, which Nestor does not name. Gleb, he continues, remained with his father because he was still very young.[26]

While the catalyst for the murders remains Vladimir's illness and sudden death, Svjatopolk's motivation becomes his irritation at the brothers' exemplary conduct rather than his desire to attain unlimited power. Boris is represented as so righteous that the devil, who could not bear this sort of behavior, incited Svjatopolk to contemplate how he could do away with his brother and rule alone. Svjatopolk's hatred for Boris is equated with the hatred of Jacob's sons for Joseph [Gen. 37: 4]. Svjatopolk's enmity toward Gleb, who was too young to exercise any power, is similarly attributed to the fact that he followed the examples of his father and brother, adhering to the commands of the Lord, giving alms to the poor and the widow, and scorning the things of this world [Abramovič, 1916: 7].

Nestor's account of the actual murders and their aftermath follows three editorial principles: ordering, formalizing, and, when possible, deleting superfluous details from the version in the "Narration" so that the exemplary behavior of the protagonists stands in clear relief. We can see the sort of changes that Nestor typically introduced by comparing the two descriptions of Vladimir's illness and death. In the "Narration," Vladimir is depicted as sorrowful because he cannot fight the Pechenegs himself. Boris joyfully agrees to do his father's bidding. Upon hearing from a messenger that Vladimir has passed away, Boris expresses his distress in a lengthy monologue. Nestor's report of the same incident reads as follows:

> По времени же нѣкоемь нача болѣти благовѣрный отець има болѣзнью, ею же умре. Болящю же ему, въ страну его придоша ратнии. Слышавъ же князь, не могы изити противу имъ, пославый сына своего Бориса, давый ему множество вои. Блаженый же падъ поклонися отцю своему и облобыза честнѣи нозѣ его, и пакы въставъ, обуимъ выю его, цѣловаше съ слезами. Ти тако изиде с вои на ратьныя. И отшедшю же ему блаженому, умре отець его [*ibid.*: 7].[27]

The "Lection" version relates the events in sequence, but avoids mentioning concrete names and places that would localize, and therefore limit, the story.[28] Vladimir is referred to as the "pious father" and Boris as "the blessed one." The Pechenegs are identified simply as "warriors" who came to the prince's land. By the same token the emotional outpourings of the "Narration" are curtailed and formalized into scenes illustrating idealized decorum. Boris expresses his fidelity to his father physically by bowing and kissing his feet; he expresses his love no less formally by embracing his father "with tears."[29] Although Nestor announces Vladimir's death and Svjatopolk's seizure of the throne, we do not immediately see Boris' reaction to those events, as we do in the "Narration," because Boris himself does not learn of it until later on. Gleb, on the other hand, has remained in Kiev, according to the "Lection," and Nestor is therefore obliged to report his reaction to his father's sudden death. He does so, again, with reference to ecclesiastical decorum. Gleb enters the Cathedral of the Mother of God, falls to the ground, utters a fairly standard prayer for deliverance, kisses the icon of the Virgin with tears, and then goes to the river where a ship has been prepared for his escape from Svjatopolk.

Nestor's version of Boris' murder sacrifices the detail of the "Narration" in order to more clearly portray the analogy between Boris' passing and the passion of Christ. When Matins are finished the prince kisses his retainers, lies down on his bed and calls upon the men to execute what they had been ordered to do:

> И они же, акы звѣрие дивии, нападоша на нь и внизоша во нь сулици свои. И се единъ отъ престоящихъ ему слугъ паде на немь, они же и того пронизоша, и мьнѣвъ же блаженаго мертва суща, изидоша вонъ [*ibid.*: 11].[30]

Boris pulls himself up, goes outside the tent and, lifting his arms to the sky (a commonplace of saints' lives), offers a standardized prayer of thanks to God for having sacrificed His only Son on the cross. He expresses his joy at making a similar sacrifice and asks for absolution of his sins. When he has finished his speech, one of the murderers pierces his heart:

> ... и тако блаженый Борисъ предасть душю в руцѣ Божии, мѣсяца июля въ 24 день. Честьное же тѣло его въземше, несоша въ градъ, наричаемый Вышегородъ, еже есть отъ Кыева, града столнаго, 15 стадий, и ту положиша тѣло блаженаго Бориса у церквы святого Василия [ibid.: 11].[31]

Gleb's murder, too, is presented as a ritualized scene of slaughter. Svjatopolk sends his men to hunt the prince down. There is no further warning (Jaroslav's name does not come up until later in the narrative). Gleb reiterates his intention to submit to his brother and, just as Boris did, forbids his troops to intervene. The murderers board boats and sail toward Gleb, who passively awaits them together with a small group of retainers [otroki]. As Svjatopolk's men draw up alongside Gleb's boat, the terrified retainers let their oars fall. The hired assassins order Gleb's cook, who is sitting behind the prince, to slit his master's throat, threatening the man's life if he refuses. The cook, "not emulating the [retainer] who fell on St. Boris [to shield his master's body], but following the example of the treacherous Judas," unsheathes his knife and grasps the prince's head in preparation for the slaughter. Gleb utters a prayer, comparing his impending martyrdom to the slaying of Zacharias at the Lord's altar [Matt. 23: 35] and asking that his sins be forgiven. The cook then slashes the prince's throat. Nestor closes the scene with the statement that "St. Gleb commended his soul into God's hands on the fifth day of the month of September" [Abramovič, 1916: 13].

The tale of how Svjatopolk was driven from his kingdom into foreign lands and endured an agonizing death in a deserted place is discarded, no doubt, because it seemed superfluous to the biographies of the saints. Nestor explains the circumstances of Svjatopolk's overthrow and death in terms of divine will and in reference to the model of an ideal Christian prince. Svjatopolk wanted to go on killing his other brothers, he writes, but God did not allow him to continue his carnage:

> Крамолѣ бывшеи отъ людий и изгнану ему сущю не токмо из града, нъ изъ области всея: избѣжавше же ему въ страны чюжи и тамо животъ свой сконца и разверже. Бываеть бо смерть грѣшнику люта [ibid.: 14].[32]

Jaroslav enters the narrative only at this point. His revenge and his role in ending the civil wars, so central to the "Narration," are outside the frame of the "Lection." Nestor introduces Jaroslav as the brother of the saints who took over the Kievan throne after Svjatopolk's death and characterizes him as "a righteous man who followed God's commandments" [ibid.: 14]. He is important, not as a figure in his own right, but because he gives the order that Gleb's body be located and oversees the canonization process along with Metropolitan John. The account of the posthumous miracles follows, ending with the cure of a blind man, a miracle that occured at some time before the translations of 1115 (recounted at the end of the earliest copy of the "Narration," but absent in the "Lection").[33]

Periodically the narrative is interrupted by rhetorical apostrophes directed to Nestor's "brethren." Initially, the apostrophes serve as commentary on the behavior of Svjatopolk. Nestor draws an analogy between the prince's plot to kill his brother and Cain's murder of Abel:

> Видите ли, братие, немилосердие оканьнаго? Видите ли втораго немилосердие Каина явльшася? Мышлящю убо Каину, рече, како и кымъ образомъ погубить брата своего Авеля: не бяше бо тогда вѣдѣти, кымъ образомъ смерть бываеть. И се яви ему злодѣи врагъ, в нощи спящю, убиство. Въставъ же, увидѣвъ во снѣ, и тако уби брата своего Авеля [*ibid.*: 9].[34]

Having drawn the analogy, he then addresses a rhetorical question to Svjatopolk himself:

> О оканьний, си ли слышалъ, что рече Богъ Каину о убийствѣ брата своего? И како не убояся суда Божия, рекшаго: «аще кто гнѣвается на брата своего, повиненъ есть суду и муцѣ огньнѣи? Ты же не токмо, оканьный, гнѣваешися на брата своего, нъ и посылаеши на нь, рекы: «аще ся вы то кто противить, то и того с нимь погубите» [*ibid.*: 9].[35]

The narrative of the princes' death and posthumous miracles is also followed by a homily which sums up the moral lessons to be drawn from the brothers' example. This parenetic admonition stresses the importance of a humble heart and the willingness to submit to one's superiors. Nestor reminds his audience that Boris and Gleb would not have attained their miraculous powers of intercession merely by virtue of the fact that they were killed by their older brother:

> Мнози бо суть нынѣ дѣтескы князи, не покоряющеся старѣйшимъ и супротивящеся имъ, и убиваеми суть: ти не суть такои благодѣти сподоблени, яко же святая сия [*ibid.*: 25].[36].

Among the many princes who were murdered by their brothers, he continues, only Boris and Gleb received the gift of working miracles, and they did so because they went to their deaths without resisting their murderers.

The example of the other murdered princes has been taken literally—perhaps too much so—as an admonition to junior members of the clan to obey their elders.[37] While we cannot rule out the possibility that Nestor was taking an opportunity to offer advice to particular princes, the context of his remarks suggests more straightforward connotations. One purpose of this homily is to clarify the princes' claims to sainthood, to explain why

Boris and Gleb were canonized when others who may have been murdered were not. We can also read it as a short sermon on the virtue of humility. Nestor reminds his brethren, the Kiev Cave monks among other possible audiences, that humility is a virtue prized by God; though it is no easy task for a man or a monk to achieve the humility of a saint, we could all benefit by trying.[38]

There follows a eulogy, which echoes the eulogy that we find in the "Narration" [Abramovič, 1916: 50], praising Boris and Gleb for the healing powers which they extend to all who come to visit their graves:

Сказание	Чтение
О, блаженая убо гроба, приимъши телеси ваю чьстьнѣи, акы съкровище мъногоцѣньно! Блаженая црькы, въ неи же положенѣ быста рацѣ ваю святѣи, имущи блаженѣи телеси ваю! О Христова угодьника! Блаженъ по истинѣ и высокъ паче всѣхъ градъ Русьскыихъ и вышии градъ, имый въ себе таковое скровище, ему же не тъчьнъ ни вьсь миръ! По истинѣ Вышегородъ наречеся: вышии и превышии городъ всѣхъ, въторыи Селунь явися въ Русьскѣ земли, имый въ себе врачьство безмьздьное [50].	О, блаженому гробу, идеже лежить богатьство некрадомо! О, честьному гробу, из него же текуть источници цѣльбамъ неоскудѣюще! О, святому гробу, събирающе людие вѣрнии на честь и славу блаженую, память! о преблаженому гробу, сущю в тебѣ честному тѣлу на славу Божию, иже его почьстьть блаженую страстотерпцю и врачю, до вѣка память имуще съ похвалами! О граде честный, истиньный бо наречен именемь прозванъ еси, се бо всѣхъ вышьши градъ славою възнесенъ еси, заступника бо имяше, исцѣлителя всѣмъ, притѣкающимъ в тя! [25-26][39].

Both eulogies, as I mentioned above, are based on the same liturgical archetype, one which differs from the eulogy that we find in the Laurentian Chronicle. The eulogy in the "Narration," however, is only a segment of an extended tribute and prayer to Boris and Gleb which praises them as saints who intercede for their city and the land of Rus' like St. Demetrius.[40] It localizes the graves of these unmercenary physicians in Vyšgorod, a second Thessalonica, and represents the city as a center of pilgrimage, providing a natural preface to the subsequent account of the saints' canonization and posthumous miracles.

Nestor's eulogy, like the "Lection" as a whole, presents the saints, less as local patrons of Vyšgorod or the land of Rus', than as intercessors for all Christians. As a monk of the Kiev Cave Monastery, Nestor is naturally less interested in promoting pilgrimages to the grave site in Vyšgorod, but speaks instead of "a blessed grave" where the faithful gather to be cured, leaving only the paranomastic clue that the city he has in mind is "higher" than all others [се бо всѣхъ вышьши градъ] because it holds the relics of the divine intercessors and healers. This eulogy brings the "Lection" to a close, preparing the reader for the concluding remarks, much as the final litany of a service prepares the worshipper for the dismissal.

The "Lection" ends with decorous apologies for Nestor's crudeness and a brief prayer:

> Се же се азъ, Нестеръ грѣшный, о житии и о погублении и о чюдесѣхъ святою и ближьную страстотерпцю сею, опаснѣ вѣдущихъ исписавъ я, другая самъ свѣды,--отъ многыхъ мала въписахъ, да почитающе славять Бога. Молю же вы и почитающа, да любве ради Божия въспоминаите мя и глаголите: «Боже, молитвами преблаженую страстотерпцю Бориса и Глѣба, очисти грѣхы списавшаго си». Некли вы оставление грѣховъ получить благодатию и щедротами, человѣколюбиемь Господа нашего Исуса Христа, с Ним же Отцю слава, купно съ Святымь Духомь, и нынѣ и присно вѣкы вѣкомъ. Аминъ [Abramovič, 1916: 26].[41]

Our analysis illustrates how two extended narratives, based on the same subject matter and composed in the same principality only a few decades apart, took on very different shapes. The structural and stylistic divergences of these two narratives cannot be accounted for by differing generic models or attributed to the tastes of a particular literary-ecclesiastical circle. They can, however, be traced back to a specific *Sitz im Leben* in communities whose institutions and needs dictate a particular treatment of special themes.[42]

At the time when the "Narration" was composed, the Christian cult of the saints and pagan ancestor worship overlapped. The two princes are portrayed as representatives of a righteous clan that prospers by the will of God and as Christian martyrs. They rely on the Lord's will, but they also rely on the help of their dead ancestors. Jaroslav is depicted as the divinely-blessed successor to his father's throne and the guardian of his brothers' memory: he avenges his brothers' death according to the traditions of pre-Christian Rus' and he supervises their canonization as Christian saints. Cultural models that we perceive as conflicting—pagan vs. Christian, sovereign vs. saint—are inseparably intertwined in the text. In order to portray the pagan bond between clan members and to prove that Jaroslav's rule is divinely sanctioned, as we have seen, the writer turns to Scripture. By the same token he explicates Boris' and Gleb's martyrdom in terms of kinship loyalties that predate any Kievan exposure to the Judeo-Christian concept of *philadelphia*. The resulting mixture of genuinely monastic piety with syncretism shapes a text that seems anomalous when compared with *vitae* produced by communities long assimilated to a Christian world view. For the author of the "Lection," on the other hand, Christianity is a given. I do not mean to imply that all traces of syncretism had actually been obliterated in the late eleventh or early twelfth century, but merely to emphasize that Nestor identifies with a monastic community. His residence in the Kiev Cave Monastery allows him the luxury of addressing an audience united by a common faith. For Nestor, as for his "brethren," the struggle between Jaroslav and Svjatopolk is not relevant to the martyrdom of Boris and Gleb. There is no conflict between the behavior of a good prince and the behavior of a saint.[43] Vladimir, Boris, Gleb, and Jaroslav all conform to the ideal of the righteous prince: they give alms to the poor, care for widows and orphans, and promote the interests of the Church. Boris and Gleb distinguish themselves by their voluntary sacrifice, for which they earn the crown of martyrdom and the power to intercede for the faithful. The desire to record as full a history as possible, while presenting the princes' behavior as a lesson that transcends a specific place or time, shapes a biography which shares commonplaces and certain general structural features (an introduction, middle and conclusion) with some biographies of Byzantine saints.

The preference accorded by the medieval community to one or the other version is no less dependent upon a particular *Sitz im Leben*. There is a certain irony in the fact that the anonymous "Narration," initially addressed to a specific community with highly localized interests and differing radically from other sacred biographies, has survived in so many copies, while the "Lection," which attempts to address universal Christian issues and corresponds to the Byzantine ideal of a proper saint's life, enjoyed a very limited circulation. This apparent anomaly has a logical explanation, however. Most of the extant manuscripts date to the Muscovite period, when the princes were venerated as patrons of imperial power. The portrait of Boris and Gleb conveyed by the "Narration," though lacking certain information, better corresponded to this final stage of their cult. The lyrical prayers, laments, and picaresque plot of the original, extended biography, which Nestor found distracting, appealed to the well-documented Muscovite taste for melodramatic ornamental prose.

Metropolitan Makarij's editors, who were concerned with encyclopedic fullness, included both versions side by side in the *Velikie Minei Četii*. Dmitrij Rostovskij administered the *coup de grâce* to Nestor's version by selecting the "Narration" for his Menaion, which remains definitive to the present day for all Orthodox communities where the lives of the saints are read in Church Slavic. His judgment was made primarily on religious grounds, but one cannot deny that his editorial treatment of Boris' and Gleb's *vita*, like his treatment of other East Slavic saints' biographies, was influenced by his personal taste [Deržavin, 1976]. Modern literary historians, most of whom have no interest in the religious commemoration of Boris and Gleb, share Dmitrij Rostovskij's preference for the "Narration" over the "Lection" on the basis of belletristic criteria. They praise the "Narration" as an original work of art that transcends the stereotypes of its age, and for that very reason retains its appeal. All of these judgments, however, derive from premises which postdate the period in which the *vitae* were conceptualized and composed.

5

CHRONICLES

> *Not to know what happened before you were born is to be forever a child, for what is the span of life of a man unless it is tied to that of his ancestors by the memory of earlier events?*[1]
> Cicero

> *I have written this work to keep alive the memory of those dead and gone, and to bring them to the notice of future generations. My style is not very polished, and I have had to devote much of my space to the quarrels between the wicked and the righteous. . . .*[2]
> Gregory, Bishop of Tours

The wish to leave a record of one's own time is as basic as the instinctual need to mark a certain area as one's own. In preliterate societies such marks involve claims to space designated by pictorial symbols or actual physical barriers. The ability to write permits an individual or group to carry this spatial function into a second dimension and to carve out a place in time. Such is the motivation of the most elementary form of history-writing, a series of chronologically ordered entries recounting the events of any given year that are deemed to be significant.

In the case of Old Russian chronicles it is difficult to be more specific about motivation because here, just as in the spheres of poetics and rhetoric, the medieval writer is chary of metatextual commentary. Where ancient and medieval European chroniclers preface their work with historical apologias, the writer of the Kievan Primary Chronicle simply announces: "These are the narratives of bygone years." This editorial indifference to the issue of what one might call "historiodicy" is particularly troublesome because it extends through whole generations of texts: the earliest extant version of the hypothetical "first" chronicle postdates its presumed inception by several centuries.

The fact that the "Tale of Bygone Years" [*Povest' vremennyx let*] begins with the flood and that most latter chronicles incorporate this digest of Kievan history, however, suggests a motivation beyond that of temporal marking: the desire to place the nation's past and present within the sequence of Christian history. This fact alone is of great importance in analyzing the Primary Chronicle, for it means that both secular and sacred cultural systems contribute to the generation of the annals. The systems were naturally more diffuse in their impact because the texts produced were not required for the operations or protocol of either Church or State. Chronicles would have been of secondary importance to the Church, and they had no concrete legal or administrative function that would necessitate their production by the Court. Yet the function of these documents was not a neutral one. The Christian historical perspective makes it imperative that the past be presented as a justification of the present, and also as an example or warning to the future. A chronicler had to take full advantage of the cultural models at his disposal in order to fulfil this goal. That is why the search for order in the annals, more than in any other type of Old Russian writing, reveals the importance of tracing the vertical bonds between the text and the extra-literary sources of which it is an analogue.

The flexible structure of the chronicles reflects the variety of these bonds. Their broad documentary function effectively precludes the sort of mandatory constraints on length and phrasing that apply to texts used in formal worship. The order in which they are put together is chronological, but only loosely so. Yearly entries need not be symmetrical in length and form, nor need they be comprehensive or aesthetically unified. Narrative per se is only one of several modes of discourse. Fragmentation and contradictions, sometimes in the space of a single sentence, are the norm. The multiple vantage points which chronicles reflect are not merely the consequence of their paratactic organization, but also derive from earlier chronicles which serve as a point of departure. A chronicler did not simply begin anew: he merged contemporary reports with annals reporting on the reigns of earlier princes. These sources themselves are almost invariably compilations [*svody*] of still earlier annals.

The extraordinary complexity of this network is illustrated in Lur'e's comprehensive stemma of Old Russian chronicles composed for the Academy's *Slovar' knižnikov i knižnosti drevnej Rusi* [Lur'e, 1985]. Boris' and Gleb's story, as conveyed in the chronicles, is a microcosm of the tangled morphology of the whole with its interconnected digests, recensions and redactions. A preliminary analysis of the latter will lay the textual ground for an examination of the cultural institutions and models that shape this account of the murdered princes.

Redactions

The narrative of Boris' and Gleb's murder is a part of the *Povest' vremennyx let*. There are three primary versions. The first is in the Codex Laurentianus, copied by the monk Lavrentij for Prince Dmitrij Konstantinovič of Suzdal' in 1377. The second is in the Codex Hypatianus, a mid-fifteenth century copy discovered at the Hypatian Monastery in Kostroma, but believed to have been written in Pskov around 1425. The third is in the *mladšij izvod* of the Novgorod I Chronicle.[3] Scholars disagree on the archetype of these versions, as well as on its sources. Šaxmatov believed that all of the versions stem from a single archetype, a tale recorded for the hypothetical *Drevnejšij svod* of 1039. This original version, he writes, was composed by a Kievan chronicler during the reign of Jaroslav [1908: 473-476]. Its heterogeneity reflects heterogeneous sources rather than multiple archetypes. In addition to information that was recorded in official documents of one sort or another, Šaxmatov speculates, the author probably incorporated Kievan oral legends which circulated locally following the official glorification of the princes. These legends focus on the particulars of the princes' death and the fate of their murderers. They identify Boris' and Gleb's assassins as men from Vyšgorod, recount how Svjatopolk fled into the wilderness and died of a terrible disease, and testify that his grave site can be located because it exudes a foul smell to the present day [*ibid.*: 485].

Other historians prefer to reserve judgment on the question of annalistic digests precedent to the hypothetical *Načal'nyj svod* of 1093 [see Lur'e, 1985, 196-197, for a review of the discussion to date]. Il'in's conviction that Jaroslav murdered his brothers and attempted to cover up his own guilt by encouraging a cult leads him to conclude that the first written narrative of Boris' and Gleb's death had to have been a *martyrion* like the "Narration," composed on the models of Wenceslas' and Ludmila's passions for the canonization. He accounts for the mixture of hagiography and historiography in the chronicle account by citing evidence that the chronicler shortened the passion, deleted or altered the lyrical digressions, and added concrete factual references [1957: 189-209].

Literary scholars, who have traditionally approached chronicles as important components in the alleged "literary-generic system" of Early Russian writing, have devised two strategies to cope with the problem of the Laurentian Chronicle account's heterogeneity, one synchronically, and the other diachronically, oriented. The former approach is best represented by the work of Lixačev. He regards the Laurentian Chronicle entries on Boris and Gleb as the first Kievan *vita*, a narrative forming part of the hypothetical "Tale of the Spread of Christianity" (i.e., the religious foundation of the Primary Chronicle as distinct from the pre-Christian, oral sources). It differs from more standard hagiographical texts, in his view, only because of its attention to Kievan politics [1950: 357]. The impression of heterogeneity is attributable to the fact that this *vita* is incorporated in the chronicle, which Lixačev conceptualizes as a "sovereign" genre. "Just as each political unit in a feudal system comprises part of a larger unit," he writes, "so in Early Russian writing. . . . genres are not equal or homogeneous, but comprise a distinct hierarchical system" of sovereign and vassal texts [1979: 59]. The chronicle's status as a genre is determined by the predominance of yearly entries, but it also contains complete works, of which the "tale" of Boris and Gleb is one.

The principal problem with Lixačev's "synchronic" solution is that, in all surviving chronicle versions, the story of Boris and Gleb is intimately bound up with preceding events in Kievan history and cannot be successfully isolated from its annalistic context. An entire complex of discrete and noncontiguous chronicle entries relating directly or indirectly to the murders (977, 980, 1015, 1016 and 1019), corresponds to the information incorporated in the anonymous "Narration" and in Nestor's "Lection" [cf. Šaxmatov, 1908: 474]. Sometimes the chronicle entries coincide word for word with passages or phrases in the extended lives, but often the texts that bear on the murdered princes are interspersed with yearly entries that deal with other events perceived by the chronicler as important for a given year.

A second problem with the solution proposed by Lixačev is that it has a hidden diachronic component. If the "vita" of Boris and Gleb is a vassal genre incorporated into the sovereign genre of the chronicle, it presumably existed prior to the compilation of the latter. Had this been the case, we would have difficulty accounting for the production of the "Narration" and the "Lection," which are identical in function. In any case, as we have seen in the preceding chapter, textual evidence suggests that both narratives borrow from the chronicle entries that have come down to us.

Müller discerns more ancient, generically pure textual strata in the chronicle entries. He regards the primary source of the Laurentian Chronicle account as a prose saga. This hypothetical saga, which Müller has attempted to reconstruct, ostensibly reflects the concerns of the Kievan royal guards [*družina*] and was probably written soon after the events described [1954: 210; 1956[a]]. In addition to its primary source, the "Saga," the Laurentian Chronicle entries on Boris and Gleb contain extracts from a *martyrion* (referred to as the *Urlegende*) based on the "Saga" and composed in connection with the canonization [*ZSPh* 30: 14-20].

We have already dealt at length with Müller's hypotheses concerning the existence of *Urtexts* as well as with Il'in's suggestion that the original chronicle account of Boris' and Gleb's life and death is based on a text such as the "Narration" (see Chapter Four). In both cases Occam's razor may appropriately be cited: there is no need to appeal to generically pure texts in one's search for the sources of the annalistic accounts. The existence of an annalistic archetype of the kind posited by Šaxmatov is more than sufficient. Moreover the remarkable stability of the textual tradition as traced through the evolution of the chronicle accounts provides a highly convincing literary-historical analogy for the correlation of the Laurentian redaction and its prototype.

The Laurentian codex, which by consensus is viewed as closest to the initial version of the annalistic text, scarcely differs from the "extended" redaction preserved in the Hypatian codex. Two types of editorial interpolation typical for the authority-conscious medieval period are at work here:

the addition of scriptural citations and the updating of "commemorative" citations—material reflecting the current state of the saints' cult and/or the current status of other figures for the community, most notably Vladimir and Jaroslav. None of these interpolations, as we shall see below, substantially alters the thematics or viewpoint of the narrative.

The text in the *mladšij svod* of the Novgorod I Chronicle constitutes a mixed redaction. Up to the episode depicting Gleb's death, this version essentially follows the expanded redaction in the Hypatian Chronicle. Beginning with the phrase "to i selika postiže mja" [NPL, 1950: 173, lines 6-7], the variants correspond to a fifteenth-century northern *svod* preserved in the Sophia I and Novgorod IV chronicles.[4] Two major editorial changes characterize the northern digest:

1) the deletion of the extended eulogy to the saints;

2) the addition of an account of how Gleb's remains were recovered and brought to Vyšgorod for burial next to the body of Boris. This account is close, though not identical, to the entry in the Sophia I Chronicle for the year 1019, and appears to summarize information based on later hagiographical narratives [cf. PSRL, 1851: 133-134; Šaxmatov, 1908: 31-32].

The greatest variation between the Novgorodian *svod* and the Kievan versions may be seen in entries which frame the narrative of Boris' and Gleb's death and place it in its historical context. Here the predominant consideration is clearly local interests as reflected in the contents of local archives. The chronicle versions that were originally composed in Kiev relate Boris' and Gleb's story to the question of the Kievan throne. We see this most clearly in the narration of events *subsequent* to the princes' murder. In the Laurentian and Hypatian chronicles, following the extended eulogy to the saints, without breaking up the entry, the chronicler recounts the following series of events:

1015

1. Svjatopolk's men pursue a third brother, Svjatoslav, and murder him in the mountains;

2. Svjatopolk usurps the Kievan throne, distributing gifts to the population in order to win their support;

3. Jaroslav, who allegedly does not know of his father's death, has executed a number of Novgorodians who attacked members of his Varangian guards. Upon learning of Svjatopolk's murders, he is obliged to appeal to the Novgorodians for support;

4. Having gathered an army, Jaroslav meets Svjatopolk at Ljubeč and prepares to do battle.

1016

5. Jaroslav's army drives Svjatopolk into Poland;

6. Jaroslav ascends the throne of his forefathers.

1017

7. Jaroslav takes up residence in Kiev.

1018

8. Polish King Bolesław, together with Svjatopolk, drives Jaroslav back to Novgorod.

9. Jaroslav again gathers an army and retakes the city of Kiev.

1019

10. Svjatopolk, who had fled to the Pechenegs, once again returns to face Jaroslav on the River Al'ta.

11. Svjatopolk is defeated and forced to flee.

12. He is possessed by a demon who weakens his bones so that he cannot sit upon his horse and has to be carried on a stretcher.

13. Svjatopolk dies in the wilderness.

14. Jaroslav ascends the Kievan throne.

The First Novgorod Chronicle follows the account of Gleb's burial with a new yearly entry which announces that Svjatopolk was defeated by Jaroslav at Ljubeč and had to flee to Poland. Jaroslav then has a number of his Novgorodian soldiers executed as punishment, learns of his father's death, and meets Svjatopolk at Ljubeč. Thus the order of events, as compared to the order in the Laurentian and Hypatian versions, is 4-5-3-4. Events nos. 1 and 2 are eliminated, as are events nos. 6 through 9. Perhaps the most striking variation comes in the depiction of the final battle on the River Al'ta. The Laurentian and Hypatian Chronicles portray this battle as an epic confrontation between the two brothers:

> Ярославъ ста на мѣстѣ идеже оубиша Бориса, въздѣвъ руцѣ на небо, рече: «Кровь брата моего вопьеть к тобѣ, Владыко! Мьсти от крове праведнаго сего, якоже мьстилъ еси крове Авелевы, положивъ на Каинѣ стенанье и трясенье;—тако положи и на семь». Помоливъся и рекъ: «Брата моя! Аще еста и тѣломь [отошла] отсюда, но молитвою помозѣта ми на противнаго сего убиицю и гордаго». И се ему рекшю поидоша противу собѣ, и покрыша по[ле] Летьское обои от множьства вои. Бѣ же пятокъ тогда, въсходящю солнцю, и сступишася обои, бысть сѣча зла, яка же не была в Руси, и за рукы емлюче сѣцяхуся, и сступашася трижды, яко по удольемь крови тещи. К вечеру же одолѣ Ярославъ, а Святополкъ бѣжа [PSRL 1926: 144].[5]

The Novgorodian version preserved in the *staršij izvod* treats the battle of Ljubeč as the victory that secured Jaroslav's right to the Kievan throne:

> И начя Дьнѣпрь мърознути. И бяше Ярославу мужь въ приязнь у Святопълка; и посла к нему Ярославъ нощью отрокъ свои, рекъ к нему. И рекъ к нему: «оньси, что ты тому велиши творити; меду мало варено, а дружины много». И рече ему мужь тъ: «рчи тако Ярославу: даче меду мало, а дружины много, да къ вечеру въдати». И разумѣ Ярославъ, яко въ нощи велить сѣцися. И томь вечере перевозися Ярославъ съ вои на

> другыи полъ Дънѣпра, и лодь отринуша от берега; и тои нощи поидоша на сѣцю. И рече Ярославъ дружинѣ: «знаменаитеся, повиваите собе убрусы голову». И бысть ссчи злѣ, и до свѣта побѣдиша Святопълка. И бѣжя Святопълкъ въ Печенѣгы, а Ярослав иде Кыеву, и сѣде на столѣ отця своего Володимира [NPL, 1950: 15].[6]

The *mladšij izvod* adds a few commonplaces describing the battle as well as an account of Svjatopolk's end:

> И бысть сѣча зла, оже за рукы емлющеся сѣчаху и по удолиемъ кровь течаше; мнозѣ вѣрнии видяху аггелы Божиа помагающа Ярославу; и до свѣта побѣдиша Святополка. И бѣжа Святополкъ в Печенѣгы, и бысть межи Чахы и Ляхы, никимъ же гонимъ пропаде оканныи, и тако злѣ живот свои сконча; яже дымъ и до сего дни есть; а Ярославъ иде къ Кыеву, сѣде на столѣ отца своего Володимира [*ibid.*: 175].[7]

This conclusion differs from the account in the Kievan chronicles in a number of particulars. Svjatopolk is first described as going to the Pechenegs (which happens after the second battle in the Laurentian and Hypatian redactions), and only then reported to have fled to a place between Poland and Bohemia. The details of Svjatopolk's illness and demonic possession are not provided here. Nor does the chronicler interpret the moral implications of the prince's death as a punishment for his sins. Finally, the site of the grave in the Novgorodian version is marked not by an evil odor, but by a cloud of smoke.

The fact that the two primary redactions correspond so closely in their sequence and details to the later mixed redaction, where insignificant variations are introduced, speaks for Šaxmatov's hypothesis of a single heterogeneous archetype which editors followed with remarkable consistency. Kievan editors enhanced the archetype with interpolations from Scripture and from liturgical texts reflecting later stages in the cult. The Novgorodian tradition, insofar as we can judge it, appears to have relied on local compilations which, though ultimately based on the same archetype, give a garbled version of some events (i.e., the final battle for the Kievan throne) and eliminate others altogether. Later Novgorodian editors "updated" the entries with information suggested, in part, by Kievan written sources (the *topoi* of battle, the account of the recovery of Gleb's remains) and in part by local oral tradition (the smoke over Svjatopolk's grave).

Point-of-View

The Laurentian Chronicle entries that deal directly or obliquely with Boris and Gleb do not concentrate exclusively on the story of their murder. Their heterogeneity becomes apparent when we arrange the events in two columns according to their mode and narrative focus:

Narrative: Jaroslav ceases paying tribute to Vladimir. Vladimir prepares to attack him.

THE MARTYRED PRINCES BORIS AND GLEB

Narrative: Vladimir falls ill.
Narrative: Vladimir sends Boris to repulse the attacking Pechenegs.
Narrative: Vladimir dies and is buried.

    Eulogy: praising Vladimir.
    Apostrophe: to Vladimir.

Narrative: Svjatopolk settles in Kiev and consolidates his power.
Narrative: Boris learns of his father's death and mourns him. The army asks him to take his father's throne. When Boris refuses, they leave him. Svjatopolk's men find Boris on the Al'ta and kill him.

    Eulogy: praising Boris as a martyr.

Narrative: Boris' body is secretly buried by the Church of St. Basil in Vyšgorod.

    Homily: on evildoers

Narrative: Gleb is summoned to Kiev under the pretext that his father is ill. He then learns from Jaroslav that Vladimir has died and that Boris has been murdered. Svjatopolk's men murder Gleb.

    Eulogy: describing how, for his sacrifice, Gleb joins his brother receiving a martyr's crown.

Narrative: Svjatoslav's men report their deed. Gleb's body is thrown in the wilderness, then later recovered and buried beside the body of Boris.

    Apostrophe: a long hymn addressed to Boris and Gleb, praising them and asking for their intercession.

Narrative: Svjatopolk murders a third brother.

    Homily: on righteous and evil princes.

Narrative: Svjatopolk begins his reign in Kiev.
Narrative: Jaroslav's Varangian mercenaries are murdered by the Novgorodians. He has the murderers killed. Upon learning of his father's and brother's death, Jaroslav gathers an army and marches against Svjatopolk. Initially Svjatopolk is driven to Poland. He then regains the throne of Kiev and is driven out a second time. The brothers meet on the banks of the Al'ta River.
Narrative: Svjatopolk flees and is struck by a disease. He dies in the wilderness.

Homily: on the lessons to be drawn from Svjatopolk's death.

Narrative: Jaroslav settles in Kiev.

The above scheme illustrates that the chronicle entries for the years 1014-1019 fall into blocks of text which are both narrative and non-narrative in mode. Part of the entry for the year 1015 is a "tale" of two saints which resembles other hagiographical narratives. Other parts resemble homilies, eulogies and prayers. Much of the text is about persons who are not saints, but play an important role in the history of the principality. This role, however, extends beyond the confines of any single year. If we want to understand why the chronicler follows the given sequence of events that he does, why he interpolates non-narrative material and how he selects such material, we must examine several cultural underlays. The first of these is essentially political, and the others are ethical or religious.

The Socio-Political Model

The documentation of "significant" events in the life of a Christian principality will be affected by a broad spectrum of subsystems which need have no other source of unity but the fact that they operate in a given land under a given ruler. In the year 1015, even this unifying principle can no longer be taken for granted because Vladimir has died suddenly without naming a successor. His failure to designate an heir to the throne had created a crisis because Kievan Rus' had no institutionalized protocols for the transfer of power. The story of Vladimir's sons owes what narrative suspense and unity it possesses, as well as its heterogeneity, to this situation. The chronicler perceives the struggle between Svjatopolk and his brothers as a struggle for the survival of a land threatened by *besknjaž'e*. His perception of events in terms of a political crisis and its resolution gives epic shape to a text that would otherwise constitute a mere chronological record.

Besknjaž'e inspired very real fears because a prince performed functions indispensable to the maintenance of community order. It was the prince who organized the defense of a kingdom's borders and initiated campaigns to acquire more territory. Other important functions included administrative responsibilities (apportionment of land and agricultural products, policing the community), codification and enforcement of the law, and certain religious duties connected with princely patronage of Christianity and its institutions. A period of interregnum could pose a profound threat to a community. Many annalists express their fears of being invaded by hostile forces. A vacant throne could also mean starvation due to the breakdown of channels for the distribution of food supplies [Frojanov, 1980: 8-63].

The idea of a communal order maintained by the ruling prince and the potential anarchy resulting from a prince's death represents the unmarked political background structuring the chronicle account. Its spatial loci are the lands occupied by Vladimir's sons, and its temporal loci the points between Vladimir's death and Jaroslav's ascent to the Kievan throne, a period of time in which no single prince has firm control over the land. The plot is arranged in such a way as to reflect the configuration of forces. Since no central ruler's actions are *ipso facto* in force throughout Rus', the narrator's focus drifts from prince to prince. The chronicler tends to concentrate on the person who seems to have the upper hand at any given moment in time, reporting not only his speech but frequently his thoughts.

Boris initially attracts the attention of the chronicler because he is the candidate of the prince's personal retainers, who played an important role in the distribution and maintenance of power. Vladimir's men formally request Boris to take the throne from Svjatopolk, who has occupied it without asking. Boris refuses to oppose his elder brother.

> Рѣша же ему дружина отня: «Се дружина оу тобе отьня и вои. Поиди, сяди Кыевѣ на столѣ отни». Онъ же рече: «Не буди мнѣ възняти рукы на брата своего старѣишаго: аще и отець ми оумре, то сь ми буди въ отца мѣсто». И се слышавше вои, разидошася от него [PSRL, 1926: 132].[8]

From the standpoint of the Church, this refusal is a fitting expression of Boris' willingness to give up his life for the sake of the common good. From the perspective of the guards, the community and the chronicler, however, Boris' refusal to fight is an abdication of his princely responsibilities. His ceding of the kingdom to Svjatopolk, acknowledged from the start as the devil's agent, is a tragic error that will cost many men their lives.

Following the account of Boris' "abdication," the chronicler focuses on

Svjatopolk, who hopes to consolidate power by eliminating all contenders. As the most likely successor to the throne and the people's choice, Boris is the logical first victim. For the same reasons, his death is described in the most detail. Less attention is devoted to Gleb's death by the chronicler, and it is portrayed in a different light than the death of Boris, because Gleb never was a candidate for Vladimir's throne. Young and naive, he goes "like a lamb to be slaughtered" by the agents of Svjatopolk. The murder of yet a third brother, Svjatoslav, is described in a single sentence. This distribution of narrative material is clearly correlated to the political viability of potential claimants to power. By the time we hear of Svjatoslav's fate, we have seen enough to realize that Svjatopolk's ambition is boundless. Any lingering doubts are dispelled when the chronicler reports Svjatopolk's thoughts on the subject, confirming that the prince intends to kill all his brothers if need be to secure the throne [PSRL, 1926: 139-140].

It becomes apparent that the chronicler regards Svjatopolk's rule as temporary when he shifts his narrative focus abruptly to Jaroslav. The shift is particularly noticeable because it begins with a marked departure from the annalistic norm. The chronicler violates chronological order by taking us back in time to the period *before* Gleb's death. The flashback is set in Novgorod, which was Jaroslav's patrimony. After having refused to pay tribute to Vladimir in 1014, Jaroslav anticipated an attack from his father and sent for Varangian reinforcements. These mercenaries, we now learn, abused the Novgorodians. Jaroslav's retainers attacked the Varangians and killed them in the marketplace. The angry prince arranged to have the instigators of the riot put to death.[9] That very night a messenger arrived from his sister Predslava in Kiev, reporting that Vladimir had passed away, that Boris had been murdered, and that Svjatopolk was plotting Gleb's death. Jaroslav was advised to be wary of his brother. The repetition of a warning which, earlier in the narrative, Jaroslav conveyed to Gleb,[10] appears to be motivated by the chronicler's desire to present a complete, unified account of Jaroslav's actions as they relate to the issue of succession for the throne.

A second flashback, accompanied by parallel shifts in time and place, occurs within the entry for 1018. Here the narrator initally focuses upon Polish king Bolesław Chrobry, who together with Svjatopolk drives Jaroslav from Kiev. Jaroslav flees to Novgorod where he makes plans to escape overseas, removing himself from the picture entirely. His plans are thwarted by his retainers who actually go so far as to destroy the prince's boat (in contrast to the retainers who passively accept Boris' refusal to enter the fray). The spatial dislocation is motivated by the chronicler's conviction that the thwarting of Jaroslav's escape and his decision to renew the struggle for the throne are critical links in the restoration of a fitting prince to power. This break then necessitates a return to the central location, Kiev, and a description of what happened *while* Jaroslav was in Novgorod. The closing focus of the chronicle on Svjatopolk [*PSRL*, 1926: 144-145], even though he has clearly lost the struggle, finds its motivation in another model (see below).

Limits imposed by the overriding issue of who will occupy the throne also affect the selection of material for the entries from 1015 to 1019. If we compare this account with information from Scandinavian and German sources, we realize how much has been left out of the Laurentian Chronicle entries for this period. Among seemingly significant events in Kiev that remain off the record is Jaroslav's marriage to Ingigerd, the daughter of King Olaf Skotkonung of Sweden, and several major confrontations between Jaroslav and Bolesław Chrobry of Poland[11] prior to the battle that forces Jaroslav to withdraw with his retainers to Novgorod.

Jaroslav's actions portray him as a prince who stands in clear opposition to the other contenders for the Kievan throne. In contrast to Boris, he is usually prepared to assert his right to power and to fulfill his dynastic responsibilities. Even when he appears to be ready to give up his claims and flee abroad, the members of his retinue come to his rescue and force him to resume the struggle against the "impious Svjatopolk." He hastily gathers together an army and prepares to wrest the kingdom from his brother. In contrast to Svjatopolk, Jaroslav is portrayed as behaving exactly as a prince should. It is especially marked in the account of the final battle (which occurs in the year 1019). We see him praying piously to his dead brothers for help and, when the morning sun rises, leading his men into combat, and then driving the enemy from the land.

The impact of the chronicler's concern with *besknjaž'e* and the issue of succession extends so far as to create the illusion of aesthetically motivated unity and closure. One can take as the opening of the tale the first instance of annalistic inconsistency and achronology, the point at which we are told that "Upon his father's death Svjatopolk settled [сѣде] in Kiev,"[12] and as the closure, the parallel remark that "Jaroslav settled in Kiev, together with his retainers." The "tale" concludes with a summation that relates to the entire preceding narrative, in which the chronicler depicts Jaroslav wiping the sweat from his brow and notes that the prince and his men have labored hard and won a great victory. What we might perceive as aesthetically dictated violations of annalistic chronology, however, are clearly dictated by the historical analogy of princely power and its negative reflection in the anti-institution of *besknjaž'e*. The maintenance of chronology and a measured attention to all critically important events in the life of the principality are contingent upon secure and just princely rule. Its disruption brings about a narrative structure that is historically and annalistically imbalanced, but aesthetically cohesive.

The Ethical Models

The chronicler's concern with the succession to the Kievan throne, accounts for the way narrative textual blocks function in the Laurentian redaction. For all his preoccupation with the person who is recognized as the reigning prince, however, the chronicler is no less concerned with moral questions. Ultimately the legitimation of any claim to be grand prince of Kiev rests on the claimant's moral stature. This ethical dimension accounts for much of the material that is not in a narrative mode: the apostrophes, the eulogies, the homilies and polemical scriptural citations through which the narrator expresses his judgment of the personae. There are essentially three operative moral codes here. Orthodox Christianity, representing a new dispensation, plays what may be characterized as a "sovereign" role. Two subordinate, but still active, ethical models are the East Slavic pagan tradition and Mosaic law. They function as "vassals" in the hierarchy of moral codes.

Each prince's narrative role and cultural significance conforms to the dictates of one or more of these ethical systems. Their combination plays a crucial role in the shaping of the chronicle narrative. When two or more sharply contrasting moral standards are applied to the same character, they generate a variety of non-narrative textual blocks that contribute to the structural heterogeneity of the text. When a relatively pure ethical model is applied to a character, the resulting textual block achieves a semblance of aesthetic unity comparable to the sort that we saw in what might be called "the tale of the succession." In order to fully appreciate the ways in which these codes interact we must extend the boundaries of the text to include chronicle entries which illustrate and comment upon the behavior of the grand princes who rule in the periods immediately preceding and immediately following Boris' and Gleb's death.

The moral standpoint most limited in its application is the Old Testament expectation that a prince is answerable to the law, and that a nation will share the grace or infamy of its head. It is operative exclusively for the personae of Svjatopolk and the men who execute his orders. In all of the narrative accounts we have examined, Svjatopolk is consistently portrayed as one who is on the side of the powers of darkness, but each source provides its own interpretation of the nature of Svjatopolk's crimes. For the author of the anonymous "Narration," as we have seen, Svjatopolk's transgression represents a betrayal of the code of his clan. He is punished for violating the bonds of kinship as much as for violating the norms of Christian behavior, and is contrasted to his martyred brothers and Jaroslav, who uphold the family honor. This syncretic viewpoint is minimized in the "Lection," where Svjatopolk, the devil's agent, serves as the counter-example to the ideal Christian princes (Vladimir, Boris, Gleb, Jaroslav) who serve God. The chronicle accounts foreground Svjatopolk's similarity to Old Testament incarnations of lawlessness and highlight the opposition between him and the other princes in terms of an essentially Judaic model of royal conduct.

A series of quotes and scriptural allusions reproach Svjatopolk as a renegade who defies God's commandments without a thought of repentance or a pang of conscience. When his agents report the outcome of the second murder, Svjatopolk's heart fills with pride and the chronicler reproaches him with the words of King David: "Why boasteth thou thyself in mischief [*bezakon'e*], O mighty man?. . . . Thy tongue deviseth mischiefs" [Psalm 51: 1-2]. In similar fashion, the men who serve Svjatopolk are identified through Old Testament scriptural allusions as servants of the devil whose "feet run to evil" and who "make haste to shed innocent blood" [cf. Isaiah 59: 7-8; Proverbs 1: 16-19] and later as sinners whose domicile is Hell [Psalm 9: 17]. The chronicler himself includes a long excursus on how evil men (and Svjatopolk is, of course, included by implication) are even worse than demons because they fear neither their fellow men nor the wrath of God [PSRL, 1926: 135].

The theme of lawlessness is directly related to the issue of Svjatopolk's right to the throne. The chronicler seeks to know why Svjatopolk has been permitted to rule Kiev and what the consequences may be for his subjects. These issues are addressed on two rhetorical levels: indirectly, through the equation of Svjatopolk to evil kings in the Old Testament who suffered terrible deaths for their crimes, followed in some versions by citations of scriptural passages prophesying the ruin of the lawless; and directly, in a homiletic discourse comparing the situation in Kiev to the situation in Israel in the time of the prophet Isaiah.

In searching for Old Testament parallels to Svjatopolk, the chronicler labels him a new Abimelech. The analogy is strikingly precise. Abimelech was of dubious parentage, the product of a liason between Gideon and a Shechemite concubine. After Gideon's death, the prince murdered his seventy brothers with the aid of his Shechemite clansmen. Only the youngest, Jotham, managed to save himself. The Shechemites then elected Abimelech as their king. After he had ruled for three years, however, God caused the Shechemites to rebel. Abimelech retook his kingdom at great cost, but suffered an ignominious death a short time thereafter. During an attack on the city of Thebez, a woman threw a millstone at him, breaking his skull. To save his honor, Abimelech asked his armorbearer to finish him with a spear so that people could not say that he was slain by a woman. This fate, writes the Old Testament narrator, was God's retribution upon Abimelech for the slaughter of his brothers [Judges 9].

A second parallel equating Svjatopolk with King Ahab of Israel is added in the Hypatian and Novgorodian redactions following the commentary on evil servants. The exact phrase that is added reads as follows in the Septuagint:

For [the Lord] said: who goes forth to deceive Ahab? and a demon said: I will go forth [III Kings 22: 20-22].

It refers to the following situation. Ahab, who has acted against God's will, is unable to conquer Ramoth in Gilead. He asks the prophets what has impeded him and whether he will prevail. All of the prophets except Micaiah predict victory. The messenger sent to Micaiah urges him to do the same, but Micaiah insists on speaking the truth. He has a vision of Israel scattered about the hills "as a flock without a shepherd" [III Kings 22: 17] and then sees the Lord sitting on his throne. The Lord predicts that Ahab will fall in this battle and seeks about for a lying spirit to persuade the king to go to his death. Ahab disguises himself so that the enemy archers will not recognize him, but he is slain despite this precaution. He is buried in Samaria:

> ... and the swine and the dogs licked up the blood, and the harlots washed themselves in the blood, according to the word of the Lord which he spoke [III Kings 22: 38].

The reference to Ahab is followed in the Hypatian Chronicle by verses 1-5 from Psalm 57 which enhance the accusation of evil intent:

> Do ye indeed speak righteousness, O congregation? Do ye judge uprightly, o ye sons of men? Yea, in heart ye work wickedness; ye weigh the violence of your hands in the earth. The wicked are estranged from the womb: they go astray as soon as they be born, speaking lies. Their poison is like the poison of a serpent: they are like the deaf adder that stoppeth her ear; which will not hearken to the voice of charmers, charming never so wisely [cf. PSRL, 1908: 121-122].

After the report that Gleb's murderers have returned to Svjatopolk, the Hypatian Chronicle adds a citation from Psalm 36 (verses 14, 15, 19, 20) that foretells the fate of those who, like Svjatopolk, have engaged in violence against the righteous:

> The wicked have drawn out the sword, and have bent their bow, to cast down the poor and needy, and to slay such as be of upright conversation. Their sword shall enter into their own heart, and their bows shall be broken. . . . [the righteous] shall not be ashamed in the evil time: and in the days of famine they shall be satisfied. But the wicked shall perish, and the enemies of the Lord shall be as the fat of lambs: they shall consume; into smoke shall they consume away [cf. PSRL, 1908: 123].

Precedent to the notice that Gleb's relics have been translated, the Hypatian Chronicle adds a series of scriptural citations in the same vein:

> Thou lovest evil more than good; and lying rather than to speak righteousness . . . . Thou lovest all devouring words, O thou deceitful tongue. God shall likewise destroy thee for ever, he shall take thee away, and pluck thee out of thy

dwelling place, and root thee out of the land of the living... [Psalm 51: 3-7].

I also will laugh at your calamity; I will mock when your fear cometh. . . . Therefore shall they eat the fruit of their own way, and be filled with their own devices [Proverbs 1: 26, 31; cf. PSRL, 1908: 124].

The issues that provoke the scriptural comparisons and allusions to the fate of lawless men are directly addressed in the homily on kingship and the law provoked by Svjatopolk's murder of a third brother:

Поставляетъ бо цесаря и князя Вышнии, емуже хощетъ дасть. Аще бо кая земля оуправится пред Богомь, поставляеть еи цесаря или князя праведна, любяща судъ и правду, и властеля оустраяеть, и судью, правящаго судъ. Аще бо князи правьдиви бывають в земли, то многа отдаются согрѣшенья [земли], аще ли зли и лукави бывають, то болше зло наводить Богъ на землю, понеже то глава есть земли. Тако бо Исаия рече: «Согрѣшиша от главы и до ногу, еже есть от цесаря и до простыхъ людии». «Лютѣ бо граду тому, в немь же князь оунъ, любяи вино пити съ гусльми и съ младыми свѣтникы». Сяковыя бо Богъ даеть за грѣхы, а старыя и мудрыя отъиметь, якоже Исаия глаголеть: «Отъиметь Господь от Иерусалима крѣпкаго исполина, и человѣка храбра, и судью, и пророка, и смѣрена старца, [и дивна свѣтника, и моудра хитреца, и] разумна, послушлива. Поставлю оуношю князя имъ, и ругателя обладающа ими» [PSRL, 1926: 139-40].[13]

The notion "that God appoints emperor and prince, and confers authority according to his desires" is, of course, central to the Greek and Roman tradition which the Russians inherited via Byzantium. "For his subjects the Emperor was Lord and God; and everything connected with his person was regarded as holy," writes William Ensslin. "And this remained so, even after Constantine, when the Emperors had become Christian, and when the conception of the God-Emperor had to give way before the belief in a special sanctification of the ruler conferred on him through God's grace [1961: 269]." In regarding the emperor as annointed by God, the Byzantines also viewed his actions as divinely sanctioned. Ultimately, the degree to which the emperor retained his favor in the eyes of the Lord was measured by his success. A successful revolt against the emperor was interpreted as a sign that the regent had fallen from God's grace. The question of an emperor violating the *law* and thereby inviting God's wrath upon his people, however, is outside of the Byzantine model, as is the premise that an evil ruler may be enthroned in a lawless nation as a punishment from God.[14]

The chronicler himself identifies his immediate source for these notions as the Book of Isaiah. Isaiah describes a people "laden with iniquity" who have sinned "from the sole of the foot even unto the head" [1: 4-6]. The princes are "rebellious and companions of thieves: every one loveth gifts and followeth after rewards: they judge not the fatherless, neither doth the cause of the widow come unto them" [1: 23]. If the nation continues its lawlessness, predicts Isaiah, it will be punished by the Lord. Among other punishments, the people will be deprived of "the judge and the prophet, the prudent and the ancient, the captain of fifty, and the honorable man, and the [able] counsellor, and the cunning artificer, and the eloquent orator . . . . and I [the Lord] will give children to be their princes, and babes shall rule over them" [3: 2-4].

The choice of Isaiah is no coincidence. Its political-historical context is, in many ways, closer to the situation in Kiev than the Hellenistic or Byzantine contexts. The kings of Israel, as Moses Hadas reminds us, were not regarded as deities or divine regents:

> Kingship [in Israel] had grown out of the institution of "judges," and had been inaugurated for the specific purposes of military defense; its only claim was that it had received divine approval, which, however, was given with reluctance (I Samuel 10.17 and elsewhere). Nor was the king an intermediary between God and his people; that function was reserved to the prophets, who were consistently antimonarchial and insisted on their priority in time and authority. King and people alike were responsible to the [Mosaic] law [1959: 267-268].

A similar state of affairs existed in Kievan Rus' under Vladimir and his immediate successors. The hegemony of the grand prince was continually contested, often by his own immediate family members. Converted princes regularly violated elementary notions of Christian conduct on an individual level (murder, broken oaths, fornication) and in the political sphere (challenging other princes). This *Sitz im Leben* inspires the choice of the Old Testament model for addressing the issue of a ruler's crimes and leads the chronicler to attribute Svjatopolk's rule of Kiev to the sins of the population (who are won over with costly gifts and bribes).

Svjatopolk's death inspires a final homily on the ultimate consequences when a ruler defies divine law. Svjatopolk's fatal wound, writes the chronicler, is a sign of God's wrath. The impious prince is driven from his land into the wilderness where he dies a miserable death. His tomb has no monument. It can be located only by an evil stench, which is the physical manifestation of the prince's moral decay. Even after death, continues the chronicler, this accursed prince must sit in Hell, bound and subjected to unending torments. Svjatopolk's fate is a divine admonition to the princes of Rus'. Those who follow his example will suffer the same punishment and perhaps even worse, just as Lamech was chastised more severely than Cain because he committed murder even though he knew it was a sin. The thesis that Lamech's sin is greater than the sin of Cain (with whom Svjatopolk is equated in every one of the cult texts) reveals a characteristically Old Testament perspective. Murder is viewed as a transgression against God's laws, regardless of the victim. The fact that Lamech killed a man *knowing* that murder was forbidden is more important than the fact that Cain killed his own brother. The violation of kinship bonds, which is primary in the anonymous "Narration," remains a secondary concern within this moral universe.

Vladimir and Jaroslav, in contrast to Svjatopolk, are subjected to a dual pagan-Christian moral standard. In the case of Vladimir, there is a clear distinction made between two periods of his life: a pagan period and a Christian period. Before his conversion to Christianity, Vladimir challenges his brother Jaropolk, then the reigning grand prince of Kiev. When he is unable to take the city by force, Vladimir contracts with his brother's general, Blud, to murder Jaropolk, exactly as Svjatopolk contracts for the murders of Boris, Gleb and Svjatoslav. Jaropolk's murder by two Varangian mercenaries enables Vladimir to occupy the Kievan throne. He then has intercourse with Jaropolk's Greek widow, a nun. The fruit of this union is Svjatopolk "the accursed" [PSRL, 1926: 75-78]. The attitude of the chronicler toward all of these events, which are preconditions of Boris' and Gleb's murder, is essentially pagan. He condemns Blud as a false retainer, and notes that the violated nun will bear defective fruit. Vladimir's behavior, on the other hand, occasions no comment. What he has done is clearly regarded as within the limits of his authority.

Only after Vladimir converts and suddenly passes away does the chronicler attempt to reconcile the prince's earlier behavior with Christian mores. He does so in a eulogy, generally regarded as part of the chronicle archetype:

Се есть новыи Костянтинъ великого Рима, иже крестивъся сам и люди своя: тако и сь створи подобно ему. Аще бо бѣ и преже на скверньную похоть желая, но послѣже прилежа к покаянью, якоже апостолъ вѣщаваеть: «Идеже оумножиться грѣхъ ту изобильствуеть благодать» [PSRL, 1926: 130-131].[15]

The chronicler first praises Vladimir as the baptizer of Rus', who brought the Kievans from darkness to light. He then admits that the prince had committed certain sins, but stresses the importance of repentance. The Laurentian redaction explains that "where sin abounded, grace did much more abound" [Romans 5: 20]. The Hypatian Chronicle contains a long excursus citing further scriptural evidence that a man will be judged by his spiritual state at the time of his death:

Аще бо прѣже в невѣжьствѣ, етера быша сгрѣшения, послѣди же расыпашася покаяньемь и милостынями, яко же глаголеть: «В нем тя застану в том ти и сужю». Яко же пророкъ глаголеть: «Живъ азъ Адана Господь, яко же не хощю смерти грѣшника, яко же обратитися ему от пути своего и живу быти; обращениемь обратися от пути своего злаго». Мнози бо

> праведнии творяще и по правдѣ живуще и къ смерти совращаються, праваго пути и погыбают, а друзии развращено пребывають и къ смерти вьспомянуться и покаяньемь добрымь очистить грѣхы, яко же пророкъ глаголеть: «Праведныи не возможе спастися въ день грѣха его. Егда рекуть правѣдному, живъ будеши: сьи же оуповаеть правдою: своею, ти сотворить безаконье, вся правда его не въспомянеться, в неправдѣ его, юже створи, и в неи оумреть. И егда рекуть нечестивому, смертию оумреши, ти обратиться от пути своего, и створить судъ и правду и заимъ судъ лъжю отдаеть, и вьсхищение възвратить, вси грѣси его, яже сгрѣшилъ есть, не помянеться, яко судии вь правду створилъ есть, и живъ будеть в них. Комужь то васъ сужю по пути его, доме Израилевъ». Съи же оумеръ во исповѣдании, добрьмь покааньемь расыпа грѣхы своя милостынями, иже есть паче всего добрѣи. «Милости бо хощю, а не жерьтвѣ». Милостьни бо есть всего луче и вышьше възводящи до самого небеси пред Ббъ [sic.]; яко же ангелъ Корнильеви рече: «Молитвы твоя и милостыня твоя взиидоша в память предъ Богомь.» [PSRL, 1908: 116-117].[16]

Šaxmatov regards the passage as part of the original text on the grounds that the eulogy in the Laurentian Chronicle seems inappropriately short [1908: 30]. One could, of course, argue the reverse, that the Hypatian chronicler extended the eulogy. However one explains the editorial process, the appropriateness or inappropriateness of the text is clearly linked to the issue of whether the prince's repentance has been sufficiently emphasized. Both accounts then resume with praises of Vladimir's apostolic act, followed by an apostrophe to the deceased prince and a prayer for the newly baptized Russian Christians:

> Дивно же есть се, колико добра створилъ Русьстѣи земли, крестив ю. . . . намъ бо достоить за нь Бога молити, понеже тѣмь Бога познахом. Но дажь ти Господь по сердцю твоему, и вся прошенья твоя исполни, егоже желаше царства небеснаго. Дажь ти Господь вѣнець с праведными, в пищи раистѣи веселье и ликъствованье съ Аврамомь и с прочими патриархы, якоже Соломонъ рече: «Оумершю мужю праведну, не погыбаеть оупованье». Сего бо в память держать Русьстии людье, поминающе святое крещенье, и прославляють Бога въ молитвахъ и в пѣснехъ и въ псалмѣхъ, поюще Господеви, новии людье, просвѣщени Святымь Духомь, чающе надежи великаго [Бога] и Спаса нашего Иисуса Христа въздати комуждо противу трудомъ неизреченьную радость, юже буди оулучити всѣмъ хрестьяномъ [PSRL, 1926: 131].[17]

Interestingly enough, Vladimir is still not reproached for having killed his brother, although the Old Testament analogies with Cain and Abimelech would fit his case nearly as well as they fit the case of Svjatopolk. So, too, while the sin that is explicitly mentioned as the object of the ruler's contrition is the sin of lust and Vladimir's ultimate responsibility for Svjatopolk's bad character is acknowledged, a very basic contradiction is passed over in silence. Vladimir's case shows how an impious prince can become a righteous prince by following the straight and narrow path. Had Svjatopolk changed his ways, the chronicler implies, he too might have been a worthy successor to his father. Svjatopolk's inability to repent is caused by the circumstances of his conception which mark him as "accursed" in the eyes of God. To address this issue, however, would require addressing Vladimir's pagan life according to the Old Testament code whereby the sins of the father are visited upon the son, as well as upon the nation as a whole. Such an approach is clearly incompatible with the sovereign moral standpoint of the chronicler.

Jaroslav's revolt against his father (1014) and his draconian measures in Novgorod are likewise treated as princely prerogatives rather than condemned as violations of moral law. The chronicler does not pass judgment on his apparent cowardice in seeking to flee abroad. His role as the avenger of his brothers' blood (an act which occasions a conflict with another brother) is not subjected to censure from the standpoint of the Old or New Testament, but is accepted as a matter of familial obligation. While the Christian Jaroslav has no real excuse for continuing what is essentially unchristian behavior, he is exempted from the sovereign moral code so long as he plays a subordinate role in the narrative. It is only when Jaroslav finally consolidates his power in Kiev that the chronicler provides a moral characterization of the grand prince, and then only as an ideal Christian ruler. He is praised, for example, in the year 1037 as one who is distinguished by his services to the faith and his enlightened cultural policies: he is the builder of the Golden Gate and the Church of St. Sophia, the patron of learning, the comfort of the poor and unfortunate, and so on.

This portrait of Jaroslav is based on essentially the same material as the portraits in the anonymous "Narration" and in Nestor's "Lection." It differs primarily in its polyphonic character. The "Narration," while stressing Jaroslav's status as head of the clan and protector of its honor, carefully reconciles "pagan" functions with the Christian ideal, leaving examples of behavior which would conflict with Christian mores outside of the narrative frame. The "Lection" reduces Jaroslav's role to that of one who promotes the veneration of the martyred princes. All of these facets of Jaroslav's character may be found in the chronicle narrative, but the multiplicity of contradictory features results in an image that lacks the sharp focus of the hagiographical accounts. In the final scenes of battle he acquires a kind of epic stature, emerging as the personification of the king who triumphs because he enjoys the favor of divine forces. Ironically, this epic function which spans the pagan, Old Testament and Christian traditions, is also the catalyst that activates the sovereign moral code implicit in Jaroslav's new status as grand prince of Kiev.

The only characters whose behavior is portrayed consistently as that of model Christians are Boris and Gleb. Their response to their father's death and to their brother's perfidy is beyond reproach. They mourn Vladimir, but express their readiness to submit to their brother's authority. Warned beforehand of Svjatopolk's murderous intentions, Boris does not raise a hand in his own defense. Gleb's reaction here lacks the pagan undertones of his laments in the anonymous "Narration." He does not pray to his dead relatives, but weeps at their fate and expresses his distress at having been left "alone" in the evil world. Gleb's servants are terrified as his assassins approach, but the prince himself accepts his death as a fitting sacrifice to God without protest. Upon his murder, writes the chronicler, he takes up his martyr's crown and enters the heavenly mansion where he rejoices because he has been reunited with his dead brother.

The eulogy that follows takes up the theme that the two martyred princes act as intermediaries between Rus' and God, bestowing their gifts of healing and good fortune on their countrymen.

> Радуитася, страстотерпца Христова [застоупника] Русьскыя земля, яже ицѣленье подаета приходящим к вамъ вѣрою и любовью. Радуитася, небесная жителя, въ плоти ангела быста, единомысленая служителя, верста единообразна, святымъ единодушьна; тѣмь стражющимъ всѣм ицѣленье подаета. Радуитася, Борисе и Глѣбе богомудрая, яко потока точита от кладязя воды живоносныя ицѣленья, истѣкають вѣрным людемъ на ицѣленье [PSRL, 1926: 137-8].[18]

That the account of Boris' and Gleb's martyrdom should be so consistently Christian in its viewpoint suggests that the original records underlying the account were subjected to unusually intensive editing. There is scarcely a sign of the syncretism that emerges so clearly in contiguous chronicle entries and in the anonymous "Narration." The exceptional features which distinguish the circumstances of Boris' and Gleb's death from typical martyrdoms, together with the consistency of all chronicle versions and their organic connection to contiguous entries, support Šaxmatov's scenario that the tale of the princes' murder is probably very close to the hypothetical archetype.

Viewed in terms of the syncretic political and moral codes that were operative in Rus' at the time, the tale's unified Christian perspective emerges quite naturally from the fact that neither Boris nor Gleb ever achieves the status of grand prince. In life, their role for the chronicler is the role of the righteous victim rather than the role of an earthly prince. Jaroslav's victory is an earthly victory and he acts as Christ's regent in the world. Boris' and Gleb's authority begins in the world to come. There they act as charismatic intermediaries who deliver their land from strife, disease and civil war. In life and in death, the realm of Boris and Gleb is the heavenly kingdom, which knows only a single moral code: the code of Grace.

CONCLUSION

My analysis of the literary responses to Boris' and Gleb's cult is based on a theory that the earliest Russian writings are protogeneric. Hymns, sermons, saints' lives and chronicles, as well as the many other medieval texts which are less readily categorized, sometimes resemble modern belletristic genres. Ultimately, however, most such texts are produced with the needs of specific institutions, customs or modes of behavior in mind. Sociocultural categories, rather than literary-generic models or empirically verifiable verbal features, dictate the shape of the text, its classification, and its concrete function. The tradition is conservative, but also far less stable than a modern literary tradition: a single text can be reclassified without undergoing any structural alterations; a text may be radically altered and yet remain in the same category; works which modern typology would distinguish as separate genres may be identified by the medieval community as two-of-a-kind when they fulfill the same cultural function.

I have argued that the nature of this writing process cannot be conceptualized within the theoretical boundaries of genre, however radically we attempt to expand that concept. The notion of genre is inseparable from the belletristic literary tradition in which texts are laterally related, i.e., produced and defined with reference to each other. Medieval texts, in contrast, are formed primarily by vertical bonds to extra-textual cultural systems and subsystems. The notion of protogenres reflects the socio-cultural realities that account for certain sets of texts. While answering the need of modern critics to seek some analogy with the other literary traditions—a need that the medieval community did not experience—it provides a theoretical apparatus that accounts systematically for the production of texts which have no clear belletristic analogy.

In seeking to apply this unified theoretical approach to Kievan, Muscovite and other writings produced in the medieval period, I do not wish to imply that we are dealing with a static, immutable tradition. Most of the texts produced in newly christened Kievan Rus' are shaped by extra-literary considerations, with the partial exception of liturgical texts. Beginning with the orthographic reforms introduced as a result of the so-called Second South Slavic influence and the coming of professional hagiographers and refugee scribes, one observes a piecemeal lateralization of East Slavic writing. *Vitae* and services reworked by Paxomij Logofet, for example, were perceived as models of style and structure. Russian writers who attempted to imitate Paxomij, however, had only a weak grasp of such concepts as style or form. Thus, while they sensed that a proper *vita* should follow certain verbal norms, they viewed those norms in terms of edifying rhetoric rather than as guidelines for an artistically composed structure. Too often they produced awkward, asymmetrical texts consisting of materials copied word for word from all manner of sources and mechanically joined together without any attempt to compose transitions or to unify the different styles.

In the second half of the sixteenth century texts appear that are consciously composed or edited with reference to other verbal structures. They cannot be regarded as genuine belletristic works, but they do foreshadow the belletristic literary process. The editors of the *Stepennaja kniga*, for instance, appear to have been guided by literary considerations of plot, style and format. Nonetheless the relatively sophisticated level of some *vitae* rewritten for *Stepennaja kniga*, which must be viewed as a turning point in the written tradition, is ultimately occasioned by vertical considerations. The book's function as a tool for the legitimation and glorification of the Muscovite imperial dynasty dictates both the entertaining, often fantastic, plots and the pompous, carefully unified official style of the individual entries. Not until the mid-seventeenth century do the Eastern Slavs make regular, albeit unsystematic, efforts to adjust their literary house to the order of their European neighbors. Protogeneric literary production remains the dominant framework for writing in the medieval period, so much so that a number of fictional works and literary treatises translated from Greek, Latin or Polish are perceived as moralistic tracts.

The customs and needs of the Kievan community at the time of Boris' and Gleb's murder created fertile soil for their cult. From its very inception the saints were venerated by people from a variety of social strata. The middle and lower strata of the population, whose Christian convictions cannot be taken for granted, appear to have responded to phenomena which were regarded as portentous in pre-Christian Slavic beliefs. The response of Jaroslav and his sons to the murder and the miracle likewise display evidence of a syncretistic world view. Metropolitan John's decision to sanction, first limited, and then national, veneration of the saints is justified by the miraculous preservation of the relics and by miraculous healings. These miracles and their formal verification find parallels in the great majority of subsequent canonizations of East Slavic saints, as do the periodic translations of the princes' relics. As the cult evolved and spread it inspired an increasing variety of texts, some composed according to highly restrictive parameters to meet specific functions and others responding to a broader spectrum of institutional and local needs.

For the initial official veneration of the saints, a minimal number of hymns was composed and integrated into the office of St. Christine, whose feast fell on the same day. These hymns show traces of the dual nature of the veneration, but do so from an essentially Christian perspective. The miraculous healings reported at the grave site play a primary role and are viewed, in conjunction with the princes' untimely death, as signs of the power given by God to innocent victims whose passion is in some way analogous to the passion of Christ. The first office (attributed to Metropolitan John) was composed in Kiev by Greek monks who drew heavily on hymns praising pairs of saints with healing powers. A later, fuller Kievan office was adapted for Novgorodian use. Here, many local references to Vyšgorod, the place where the saints' relics were kept, have been eliminated in favor of other, penitential motifs. Later services adjusted to the changing role of the princes as patrons, first of Jaroslav's dynasty, then of individual princes in North and Northeast Rus', and eventually to the patrons of the imperial Muscovite State. The intermediate services also reflect the elevation of the saints' feast to a middle status and new liturgical rules which called for more hymns. In conjunction with strictly liturgical commemoration, a number of readings and homiletic texts singled out aspects of particular importance to a given community.

Some years after the canonization, two extended biographies were composed. While it is impossible to date either narrative with any certainty, they reflect the interests of successive stages of the cult, which suggests the most plausible period of their composition. The anonymous "Narration," which in all probability was written between 1036 and 1054, represents a reworking of earlier annalistic entries and documents in local church archives in order to portray Boris and Gleb's death as what might be called a "dynastic" martyrdom. Two models—that of saints who died for the faith and that of the avenger and defender of a dynasty—shape this hybrid, uneven, but nonetheless appealing work. The "Lection" attributed to Nestor reflects a mature, monastic mode of veneration. It was, in all likelihood, produced at some time after 1072 and aimed primarily at a cenobitic community. In keeping with its audience, the "Lection" replaces many references to Jaroslav and his dynasty with ascetically oriented literary motifs and analogies which resemble the commonplaces that we find in services and biographies of Byzantine saints. In this way, two narratives composed only a few decades apart treat the same subject matter in very different ways because they are, themselves, shaped by different cultural institutions.

The annalistic entries were based upon records made immediately following Boris' and Gleb's murder. In tracing the earliest surviving versions of the entries, one is struck by their remarkable stability: apart from certain moralistic interpolations, updatings, and deletion of information which was superfluous for a given locality, the later texts essentially follow the account preserved in the Laurentian Chronicle. The narratives of the murder, the Kievan civil wars, and other "tales" are arranged, for the most part, in chronological order and supplemented with non-narrative material. The heterogeneity of the material has traditionally been attributed to its status as a repository of vassal genres. Its shifting point of view has been taken as a marker of one or another such genres. All of these "characteristic" features are more simply and compellingly accounted for, not by literary models, but by Kievan political realities and moral imperatives. The narrator naturally shifts his viewpoint in accordance with the shifting occupancy of the Kievan throne—his primary concern due to the central role played by the grand prince for the community. The nature of Kievan politics and its relationship with the institution of the Church dictate non-narrative interpolations. These moralistic commentaries are shaped by the competing ethical systems by which one or another of the primary characters are judged. Orthodox Christianity plays the dominant role, but it is replaced and/or supplemented by ethical models derived from the pagan tradition and from Mosaic law, both of which contribute to the hybrid, fragmentary quality of the exposition.

Taken as a set, the texts associated with the cult of Boris and Gleb can provide us with an excellent idea of the range of forms that we may expect in the East Slavic protogeneric literary corpus. They illustrate the typical constraints placed on the medieval writer by institutional protocol and doctrine, and also point to broad areas of latitude which permitted the medieval writer to respond to specific, localizable cases and needs. This local factor, which plays a role even in the most strictly controlled liturgical hymns, must be viewed as the counterbalance to what Lixačev called literary etiquette: the verbal expression of socio-cultural decorum. Kievan, North and Northeast Russian writings are far more likely than Muscovite texts to permit regional interests to outweigh decorum. As the rich manuscript tradition is gradually collated and studied, we will be better able to assess the range and patterns of deviations from what was formerly assumed to have been a norm and to discern a new order in the legacy of medieval Rus'.

NOTES

1 INTRODUCTION

1 Dibelius [1933: 8].

2 "Lo I have recounted the life of our saintly and blessed father Feodosij, from his youth to [his old age] selecting a small part of many [events and deeds] for my tale. But who could describe the wise guidance of that blessed man in good order! Who could praise him as he deserves!" From Nestor's *vita* of Feodosij of the Caves (d. 1074) in Uspenskij Sbornik [1971: 125, f. 61^a, lines 14-29].

3 Picchio concurs with Lixačev that a literary system of sorts is operative in medieval Russian letters, but not one based on genres. The system that Picchio perceives in the corpus of early Russian texts is an ecclesiastical poetics where artistic principles are directly linked to the propagation of the Word [1984^a]. A complex of stylistic patterns and ideological themes combine in fluid compositional structures marked by the isocolic principle and other types of rhythmic, syntactic, grammatical and phonetic parallelism [1973; 1982].

2 THE KIEVAN CULT

1 "In the year 1044 the bodies of two princes, Jaropolk and Oleg, sons of Svjatoslav, were dug from their graves; their bones were baptized and then buried in the Church of the Holy Virgin" [PSRL, 1926: 155].

2 "Come, oh Lord, and bless this water with Thy Holy Spirit and with fire," from the account of what Dionisij, archimandrite of the Trinity-Sergius Laura, found in 1616 when he was ordered by Tsar' Mixail Fedorovič to correct the service books [Dionisij's *vita* (GIM, Sinodal'noe sobranie, no. 850) as cited by Solov'ev, 1851-79: vol. 9, 317].

3 Svjatopolk, Boris and Gleb are actually half-brothers to Jaroslav, but are referred to in the hagiographical texts simply as brothers. I have chosen to maintain this form of reference, which reflects the broad connotations of the term in the pre-Mongol period.

4 See Cook [1986] on editions and the research tradition. Rydzevskaja [1978: 89-104] provides a modern Russian translation in a very useful posthumously edited collection of other translated Scandinavian documents with information on Rus'.

5 Only Členov [1971] wholly accepts Il'in's theory that the behavior of the princes as depicted in the saga reflects historical fact. Aleškovskij accepts the identification of Burislafr with Boris, while acknowledging the contradictory nature of the saga as a source [1972: 121].

6 Cf. Šaxmatov [1908: 78-79] and Müller [1954: 198-199], as well as my discussion of their theories in note 10 of Chapter Five.

7 "'It was not I who began to kill our brethren, but Svjatopolk himself. May God be the avenger of the blood of my brothers inasmuch as Svjatopolk, despite their innocence, has shed the just blood of Boris and Gleb. Perhaps he will even visit the same fate on me. But judge me, oh Lord, according to the right, that the malice of the sinful may end'" [Cross and Sherbowitz-Wetzor, 1953: 131].

8 "Jaroslav halted at the site where Boris had been slain and, lifting up his hands to heaven, exclaimed, 'The blood of my brother cries aloud to thee, oh Lord. Avenge the blood of this just man. Visit upon this criminal the sorrow and terror that thou didst inflict upon Cain to avenge the blood of Abel.' Then he prayed and said: 'My brethren, although you be absent in body, yet help me with your prayer against this presumptuous assassin'" [*ibid.*: 133].

9 "When judgment thus rightly fell upon him as a sinner, torments seized this impious prince after his departure from this world. That is clearly proved by the fatal wound which was dealt him and which mercilessly drove him to his end; and since his death, he abides in bonds and in torment everlasting. His tomb is in the wilderness even to this day, and an evil

odor issues forth from it. "This retribution was exhibited by God as an admonition to the princes of Rus' so that, if they do likewise after hearing of this dread example, they shall incur the same punishment, yet even more severe because they, though familiar with this story, shall commit the same evil crime. For Cain received seven punishments for killing Abel, and Lamech seventy, because Cain did not know the penalty to be exacted by God, while Lamech knew of the chastisement visited upon his ancestor, yet still committed murder notwithstanding" [*ibid.*: 133].

10 "ARTICLE 1. If a man kills a man [the following relatives of the murdered man may avenge him]; the brother is to avenge his brother; the son, his father; or the father, his son; and the son of brother [of the murdered man] or the son of his sister, [their respective uncle]. If there is no avenger, [the murderer pays] 40 *grivna* wergeld . . ." [Vernadsky, 1969: 26].

11 The importance of ancestor worship in the formation of Boris' and Gleb's cult is emphasized by Maczko [1975: 73] and Sciacca [1985] (the latter also identifies Jaroslav's invocation of Boris and Gleb as a relic of the ancestral cult), and noted in passing by Poppe [1973: 14], Cherniavsky [1961: 9], and Pritsak [1981: 32]. Scandinavian pagan customs and practices attested in the sources show striking parallels to those of the Slavs and, as Vries indicates, are characteristic of a society organized around institutions of kinship:

> The clan united the dead and the living into a single community whose members were bound together by their very being. . . . [They] had no choice but to stand by one another with unswerving loyalty. . . . Blood revenge is neither the unbridled expression of pain or rage at the death of a relative nor a personal vendetta: it is intended to redress the wounded honor of the clan. One could go so far as to say that the clan must demand [blood revenge] in order to restore its world image, which has been shattered by the death [1956: 145-146].

12 "Slovo svjatago Grigor'ja izobrěteno v tol"cěx o tom", kako pervoe pogani sušče jazyci, klanalisa idolom", i treby im klali, to i nyne tvorat" [Paisiev Sbornik cited from Tixonravov 1862: 97; cf. GPB, Nov. Sof. Bib. 1285 *loc. cit.: 99;* GPB, Kir. Bel. 43/1120, 17th c. *loc. cit.: 105*]; "Slovo svjatogo otca našego Ioana Zlatooustago arxiepiskopa Kostantina grada o tom' kako p'rvoe poganii věrovali v" idoly i treby im" klali, i imena im" narekali jaže i nyne mnozi tako tvorat' i v" krest'jan'stve soušče, a ne vědajut' čto est' krest'jan'stvo" [GPB, Nov. Sof. sobor, no. 1262, 14th c., ff. 93-94, *loc. cit.: 108*]; "Slovo Kirila nedostoinago mnixa po pascě, poxvalenie v"skresenija, i o ar"tusě, i o Fomině ispytan"i rebr gospodnix" [Eremin, 1957[a]: 415].

13 "And though the saintly one lay there a long time, he remained entirely unharmed, for He [the Lord] left him not in oblivion and neglect, but gave signs: now a pillar of fire was seen, now burning candles. Moreover, merchants passing by on the way would hear the singing of angels; and others, hunters and shepherds, also saw and heard these things" [Kantor, 1983: 193].

14 "The Christ-loving prince ordered that the body of the holy Gleb be sought. Though they searched long and hard, no one could find it. Then one year later hunters came upon the saint's body lying unharmed, for neither beasts nor birds had touched it. They went to the town and informed the town's senior official. Together with servants, he went [to the place] and saw how the saint's [body] glowed like lightning, and the official was awestruck. He ordered his servants to guard the holy body in that place, while notification was sent to the Christ-loving Jaroslav . . .".

15 "People flocked to the sight and, as the church was burning from the top down, they carried out all the icons and chalices, and nothing was consumed save the church itself. Jaroslav was told of this. And he summoned the Metropolitan John and told him everything concerning the holy martyrs, his brothers. And he [the Metropolitan] was very awed and in doubt, and then filled with courage and joy in God" [Kantor, 1983: 209].

16 "And all this, I think, was allowed by God to happen—for the [Church of St. Basil] was a poor decrepit wooden one—so that another church would be erected on the site in the name

of the holy and blessed passion-sufferers Boris and Gleb. . . . For they are the luminaries in the shrine, God's servants, and it was not fitting for such luminaries to be buried in the earth: they should be laid in a pure place that they might shine forth to all inside the church."

17 St. Wenceslas' body, for example, is described in the "Nikol'skij legend" merely as being "illuminated by divine power" [Rogov, 1970: 83].

18 The association of Boris and Gleb with pagan agrarian festivals is discussed by Rybakov [1965] and Sciacca [1977]. While I cannot agree with Sciacca's thesis that early worshipers integrated veneration of Boris and Gleb into the ancient harvest cycle [*ibid.*: 8], his article is well worth examining for its ethnographic evidence on the mature (nineteenth-century) cult. Reisman also discusses the pagan aspects of the cult, theorizing that Boris and Gleb were venerated as priest-kings according to the Scandinavian cult practice [1978: 141-157].

19 The service was a *panixida* [παννυχίς] rather than a *moleben* because the brothers had not yet been canonized [Golubinskij, 1903: 271-2; Müller, 1962: 43].

20 "When day broke Archbishop John came with crosses to the place where the venerable bodies of the saints lay. Upon offering a prayer, he ordered that the earth over the grave of the saints be removed. Then those digging noticed a fragrant aroma issuing from the grave of the holy ones. After removing the earth, they took them out of the ground. And then Metropolitan John came forward with presbyters, and with fear and love he opened the coffins of the saints. They saw a most glorious miracle: the bodies of the saints were not corrupted but were entirely whole; and their faces were as radiant as those of angels. So the archbishop was greatly amazed, and an abundant fragrance filled all the people. And they carried [the coffins] into the shelter which had been placed on the site of the burned-out church, and placed them above the ground, on the right side of the place" [Kantor, 1983: 210-11].

21 "The senior official of the town had a lame servant: [this boy's] leg was bent and withered like a reed, and he had no feeling in it, it was like a dead [limb]. Being unable to walk on it, he had a wooden limb made for himself. This [boy] came to pray at the grave of the saints, where he stayed, praying, day and night. One night he had a vision of the holy passion-sufferers in Christ Boris and Gleb, who said to him: "Why do you cry out to us?" He showed them his leg and petitioned them to heal it. The swift physicians and healers took the withered leg [in their hands] and, making the sign of the cross three times, healed it. [The boy also] saw the retainer [Georgij], who had fallen on the blessed Boris [in order to shield him from Svjatopolk's men], holding a candle in front of the saints. When [the boy] awoke, he no longer needed a wooden leg, but jumped up and hastened to the place where the caskets of the saints stood. Falling down before them, he prayed and wept and told everyone how the saints had been merciful to him."

22 ". . .the archbishop was awed. Inspired by this blessed light, he said to the Christ-lover [Jaroslav]: 'It would be fitting, oh pious Tsar' [sic], for us to erect a church in their name and set a day for their commemoration.'"

23 "When relics make themselves manifest in the earth [they must be associated with] three miracles—that a deaf person hear, a mute person speak, and a blind person see; if miracles occur these are from God and the Holy Apostles. If these miracles do not occur, then [the relics] should not be accepted."

24 Historians of East Slavic canonization stress the special significance accorded by the Russians to uncorrupted relics. A large percentage of medieval Russian saints proved to be "netlennye." In certain cases (Prince Fedor Rostislavovič of Jaroslavl', for instance) the fact of uncorrupted relics appears to have been a primary impetus for canonization despite the behavior of the person in life. The attitude of the monks to the elder Zosima's body, in Dostoevsky's *Brothers Karamazov*, is very close to the medieval attitude

25 Aleškovskij accords significance to the fact that, even after the alleged canonization in Jaroslav's reign, several Russian princes gave their sons the name "Svjatopolk," among them Izjaslav Jaroslavovič. He claims that no prince could have named a child after a person who had killed two sovereign-saints, taking this as yet another piece of negative evidence for a

1072 canonization [1972: 122-131]. Poppe wisely questions the value of this evidence. He points out that several princes were named Svjatopolk after 1072: Svjatopolk Mstislavovič of Novgorod (born 1113) and Svjatopolk of Turov, the son of Jurij Jaroslavovič (born after 1144) [PSRL, 1908: 286-295 and 665]. Specific references in the Hypatian Chronicle, writes Poppe, suggest that at least the second Svjatopolk received his name in honor of Svjatopolk Izjaslavovič [1969: 369-371; 1973: 10, notes 15-17]. At the same time he insists that Izjaslav could only have named his son Svjatopolk *before* the canonization, since the referent is clearly Svjatopolk "the accursed." To reconcile these contradictory facts we would have to accept the premise that, when a person was condemned by official hagiographical sources, one could not name one's son after him *unless the name was meant to refer to a specific ancestor of honorable character*. This hypothesis is superfluous. A Kievan prince was given a Christian name and a royal name. The Christian name had to conform with Church dogma, the royal name evidently had certain associations for the *clan*. The gradual disappearance of the name Svjatopolk would seem to be linked, neither to any official condemnation of Svjatopolk Vladimirovič nor to the canonization of Boris and Gleb, but to the diminishing influence of pre-Christian customs in princely circles.

26 From Jaroslav's death through the reign of Vladimir Monomax, each Kievan prince attempts to provide physical evidence that the relics of the saints are not only in his domain, but have been "marked" (i.e., adorned or translated) by him personally. This behavior marks what I consider to be an elementary stage in the princes' veneration and has a strong syncretic element that may reflect beliefs held in common by the Slavs and the Scandinavians. Nordic sagas use the epithet *ársael* with respect to certain kings whose personal *virtus* brought fertility to the fields, healthy livestock, abundant fishing and military success [Schmidt, 1941: 80-81]. Upon the death of the pagan Norwegian king Hálfdan "Whiteleg" in 860 "men of influence . . . came and prayed, all of them, to take the body with them to be buried in their lands; for it was thought that he who got possession of it could expect good seasons. They reached an agreement in this wise, that the body was assigned to four places: the head was laid in a mound at Stein in Hringaríki, but each of the others carried away his share and interred them in burial mounds in his homeland, and all are called the Mounds of Hálfdan" [*Heimskringla*: Chapter 44, p. 45].

27 Izjaslav's political motives for the ceremony are generally stressed by modern historians. Those who believe that the canonization took place in 1072 ascribe it to an attempt by Izjaslav to consolidate his precarious rule over Kiev [cf. Il'in, 1957: 182-183; Poppe, 1969: 381; Aleškovskij, 1972: 125; Xorošev, 1986: 220-21].

28 "On the Translation of the Holy Martyrs. This came to pass at the time of the translation of the holy martyrs, Roman and David. And when all the brothers had gathered, Izjaslav, Svjatoslav, and Vsevolod, the metropolitan George of Kiev and another, Neofit of Černigov, and the bishops Peter of Perejaslavl', Nikita of Belgorod, and Michael of Gurgev, and the hegumens Feodosij of the Cave Monastery, Sofronij of Saint Michael's, and German of the Holy Savior, and all of the other hegumens arranged a solemn holiday. And having first raised Saint Boris in his wooden coffin, the princes raised the coffin to their shoulders, and preceded by venerable monks with candles, and after them deacons, and then presbyters, and after them the metropolitans and bishops, they followed after them with the coffin. They carried it into the church and set it down. Upon opening the coffin, the church was filled with a fragrance and an aroma most wonderful, and all who saw this praised God. But terror overcame the Metropolitan, for he did not firmly believe in the saints, and he prostrated himself to beg forgiveness. Kissing the relics, they put them in a stone coffin" [Kantor, 1983: 215].

29 A number of these descriptions have been published. They may be found in chronicle entries (especially in the protocol-conscious Sophia II and Nikon Chronicles) and in later redactions of saints' lives. For an overview see W.-H. Schmidt,"Slavische Translationsberichte: Zum Profil einer Gattung" to appear in the proceedings of the Third Berlin Conference on Early Slavic Literatures sponsored by the Freie Universität's Forschungsgruppe "Ältere Sla-

vische Literaturen" (June 13-16, 1988). On the alleged translation of Boris' and Gleb's relics to Smolensk in 1191 see S. P. Pisarev [1897], N. K. Nikol'skij [1907], I. I. Orlovskij [1909], and Voronin and Žukovskaja [1969].

30 "[H]olding the hand of the saint, he pressed it to his injury, for he had pain in his neck, and [then pressed it] to his eyes, and to his forehead, and then placed the hand back into the coffin" [Kantor, 1983: 215].

31 Lesjučevskij attempts to argue that this incident reflects "some specific connection between the erection by Izjaslav of a church with a single cupola and Gleb" [1946: 238], supporting this conjecture by citing images of Gleb holding a church with a single cupola on *enkolpia* [see Poppe's critique, 1966: 41-42].

32 Ajnalov interprets the focus on Izjaslav in the "Lection" as one indication that the writer of this version worked during Izjaslav's reign, while the writer of the version of the miracles appended to the "Narration" worked during the time of Vladimir Monomax [1910: 124-125]. Lesjučevskij attempts to reconcile this reasoning with his own conviction that Gleb was venerated before Boris by arguing that the compiler of the "Narration" had other sources which "in all probability" led him to replace Boris' name in the account (if it was in the account at all) with the name of Gleb [1946: 238]. The latter hypothesis is both superfluous and unsupportable.

33 The hypothesis that three writers composed the "Narrative," and that the third writer worked between 1115 and 1118, was first proposed by Bugoslavskij [1914: 135; cf. the discussion in Chapter Four on the textual history of the "Narration"].

34 ". . . [H]e came at night and measured the graves. He then removed the silver slabs and gilded them. And again he came at night, and having covered them, he adorned the miracle-working and praiseworthy holy graves of Christ's sufferers and martyrs Boris and Gleb, and then left that same night" [Kantor, 1983: 229].

35 "And all the boyars walked, pulling the sledge with great ropes, crowding and pressing. A fence had been built on both sides where they were pulling the holy coffins, but it was possible neither to move nor to pull because of the multitude of people. Then Volodimir ordered marten furs and skins, and brocades thrown to the people. Upon seeing this, the people turned back, but others remained and hastened to the holy coffins that they might be worthy to touch them" [*ibid.*: 235].

36 "As they pulled with force, the ropes, which were so large that a man could scarcely put both hands around them, snapped; and they snapped at once, while the people were crying *kyrie eleison*. And throughout the entire town, and along the walls, and along the parapets of the city, there was a great multitude, just like bees. The voice of the people rose from everyone: 'Lord, have mercy!' It was like thunder. And thus they were barely able to transport the relics to the church in the time between Matins and the liturgy" [*ibid.*: 235-236].

An interesting footnote on this idealized depiction of the translation is given in the Hypatian Chronicle which describes how Vladimir Monomax and the princes of Černigov bickered over where to place the sarcophagi in the new church. Vladimir wanted to place the coffins in the center of the church and to place a silver canopy over them, but David and Oleg wished to place them in a *komara* [literally a vaulted space; most probably a side chapel] which Svjatoslav, their father, had built especially for the sarcophagi. The princes agreed to cast lots, and in accordance with the will of God and the martyrs, David and Oleg were permitted to "place the [sarcophagi] in that vaulted area on the right [side of the church] where they remain to this day" [PSRL, 1908: 281].

37 Boris' and Gleb's names are mentioned by Vladimir Monomax in his Testament (describing a battle against the *Polovci* [Kipchaks] in 1094). In 1174 Mstislav Rostislavovič calls upon the saints to defend him from Andrej Bogoljubskij [PSRL, 1908: 576-577]. Andrej also invokes their help in 1175; so, too, when he is attacked by his retainers, he calls for the "sword of Boris" and invokes the names of the two saints [*ibid.*: 587; cf. Hurwitz, 1980: 51-52]. Their names are also invoked by Svjatoslav Vsevolodovič in 1185 [PSRL, 1908: 636]. The Novgoro-

dian cult of the mid-thirteenth century built upon this tradition, praises the saints as Christian warriors [Janin, 1974]. They are invoked by Aleksandr Nevskij and credited with divine intervention in his *vita* [Mansikka, 1913: 3-4].

38 The evolution I describe is reflected in the hymns and sermons to the saints (see Chapter Three), in the textual history of the "Lection" and the "Narration" (see Chapter Four), and in the various chronicle traditions (see Chapter Five). For a discussion of the cult artifacts and their sources, see Lesjučevskij [1946] and Aleškovskij [1972]. The rich iconographic tradition is discussed by Gusev [1898], Lixačev [1907], Ajnalov [1910], Smirnova [1959], Černogubov [1963], Alpatov [1966], and Poppe [1966]. On the churches, see Orlovskij [1909], Karger [1952; 1958-1961; 1964], Xolostenko [1967], Janin [1974] and Vorob'eva and Tic [1974].

3 RITUAL COMMEMORATION

1 "While eating after hunting in the forest, some men noticed the light that shone from your face. 'What is this vision?' they asked each other. 'Come, and we shall see a most glorious vision' [was the answer]. Those who witnessed this miracle told everyone of it" [Ode 8 of the kanon attributed to Metropolitan John, cited from Abramovič (1916: 142)].

2 "Righteous martyrs and true followers of Christ's word, chaste Roman and meek David, you did not oppose your enemy, who was also your brother and slayer, who killed your flesh but could not kill your spirits: while the evil lover of power weeps, you rejoice in the choir of angels and stand at the throne of the Holy Trinity. Pray for the government of your kinsmen, that it may be more worthy in the eyes of the Lord, and that the Russian people may be saved" [the modern troparion to the saints, cited from Bulgakov (1900: 254)].

3 See *Svodnyj katalog* [1984: mss. no. 42, 50, 54, 64, 76, 93, 98, 99, 100, 103, 107, 131, 139, 153, 173, 204, 205, 219].

4 Three stichera from ms. CGADA f. 381, no. 121 are published in Mur'janov [1981: 274-275].

5 Liturgical terminology, definitions of hymns and descriptions of modern service protocol follow Gardner [1976; 1980]. Ch. Hannick offered detailed criticisms of this chapter in manuscript and commented on the Greek hymnographic tradition. Remarks on the form and composition of East Slavic saints' offices in the fifteenth century are primarily based on my own reading of mss. in CGADA, GBL, GPB and BAN and published offices. The Menaia currently being published by the Moscow Patriarchate (1976-) still retain services going back to the medieval period: some of them have not been standardized.

6 Hannick points out that these hymns may not have always been sung after the sixth ode of the kanon since their position varies in Greek and Slavic mss. prior to the thirteenth century.

7 In our correspondence Hannick called my attention to the thirteenth-century notational reform in Greece which led to the abandonment of "generically" ordered liturgical codices. Even before the thirteenth century, however, Old Russian scribes do not consistently follow the Greek precedent (two interesting examples discussed below are the Tipografskij Typikon which contains kontakia and the Novgorod Sticherarion which contains a kanon). I take these codices as further proof that the Old Russians approached hymns as protogenres.

8 Mur'janov regards the misplaced kanon as a sign that the text is very ancient, noting that the tenth c. Putjatina Menaion [*Svodnyj katalog* (1984: 63-4) lists the ms. as eleventh century] also places kanons before the service proper [1981: 270]. St. Christine's service (undoubtedly more ancient than the service for the princes) in the same codex has the kanon in its usual place, however, which suggests that the unusual order is attributable to something other than the early provenance of the office. Many eleventh-thirteenth century mss. contain services or hymns arranged in a way that would strike a modern observer as erratic.

9 Noting that the Greeks tended to record troparia in special codices called Tropologia, Hannick concludes that the "missing" troparia in the earliest Old Russian Service Menaia may in fact have been recorded separately as well. Further study is required to determine whether this applies to the Old Russian liturgical tradition.

10 "**Sedalen, tone 1, prosomoion: 'The Choir of Angels...**' Having both come to love Christ at an early age, oh honorable brothers, and having espoused a life free from passions, glorious [ones], you chose chastity and abstinence from passions that imperil the soul: for this reason, having been granted Divine grace through good works, you heal the sick."

11 "**Kontakion, tone 3, prosomoion: 'Today a Virgin...**' Today your most glorious memory, martyrs in Christ, Romanus and David shone forth, summoning us to praise Christ our God. Therefore hastening to your coffins, we receive the gifts of healing—you are divine physicians!"

12 "**Oikos, prosomoion: 'Bethlehem hath opened Eden...**' Completing an enlightened life, oh most blessed one, you were adorned from youth with an imperial crown, most wealthy Romanus: you had great power over your native land and all creation. Seeing your success, Christ God in his judgment summoned you to martyrdom and gave you the strength from heaven to vanquish the enemy courageously together with David, your brother, who suffered and lived with you."

13 For a detailed discussion of the kanon's provenance and evolution see Wellesz [1961: 206-228].

14 The fullest study of the diachronic concept of the saint is to be found in Delehaye [1927]. See, in particular, pp. 95-6 and 105-8. Schmemann discusses the changing cultic functions of the saint, noting that by the end of the third century the intercessory function had gained increasing prominence over the original eschatological and sacramentary functions of the saint and his or her relics [1961: 209-217].

15 On the pre-Christian context of saints who appear in "pairs" and its reflection in the language and iconography of works dealing with Boris and Gleb, see Toporov [1985].

16 "Come, newly christened congregations of Rus', and we shall see how the innocent Boris submits to judgment by his brother's envy. His body was pierced with a spear, and his blood was shed at the devil's instigation; Gleb was cut down with a knife [at the command of] that same brother, Svjatopolk, and [his body] hidden between two tree trunks, but [the brothers] received a martyr's crown and he [Svjatopolk] died in obscurity. [Now the saints] pray to the Lord Christ for the salvation of our souls."

17 "Grant me forgiveness, Christ, for my evil sins, for I have defiled myself with evil deeds that I might glorify your martyrs as befits them, without reproach."

18 "Most-holy Vyšegrad teems with your miracles, you pour forth healing from your grave like rivers, you heal the infirm and comfort the despondent: you are blessed."

19 "When you camped on the field by the L'to [Al'ta River], Prince Boris, armed men sent by your brother Svjatopolk approached you without warning; when your retainer saw that you were to be stabbed with lances, he fell upon your breast, crying: 'Until you pierce me, you shall not pierce my master.' And this the lawless ones did, having pierced him [the retainer], they then pierced your [body], oh Prince.

20 "Come, all you faithful congregations of Rus', that we may praise the good princes Boris and Gleb; having received the gift of their father's love, and holding sway over many warriors of the Russian Land, they did not oppose their brother, contemplating that other glory: in this way they were adorned with the crown by Christ, God and Savior of our souls."

21 "Blessed is your fatherland and the city in which you were raised, and the holy shrine which received your bodies as though putting on the Crown of the Kingdom: gracious guardians and warriors who fight the enemy and drive him far from your fatherland, glorious Romanus and most wondrous David, pray for the salvation of our souls."

22 "Today, we, the congregations of those who honor the holiday, coming together with joyful countenances and pure in heart, forming a chorus praising, not with cymbals in the Jewish manner, but with contrite hearts, Christ, our true God, Who has glorified His saints, the noble Romanus and David: we stand around their healing and miraculous sarco-

phagi, and lovingly kiss [them], saying: 'Rejoice, you who follow Christ's teachings according to His example; rejoice, you who have received Christ's humility [by] not opposing your enemy and brother [who] mercilessly slaughtered your [mortal] bodies; rejoice, you who guided your people to the true faith and who now preserve them. Most wondrous Romanus and gentle David, you most bright luminaries of your fatherland and confident intercessors for our souls."

23 Delehaye lists the *topoi*, based on Menander's late third-century treatise Περὶ ἐπιδεικτικῶν and provides examples from early Christian panegyrics [1966: 141-65]. On analogous *topoi* in Slavic eulogistic prose of the fourteenth and fifteenth centuries see Alissandratos [1982].

24 "Oh, honorable brothers, sending the shining rays of miracles throughout the land ... you intercede for your kinsmen, our pious princes, and keep them in peace and in health, praying [on their behalf] to God, for now you repose [with Him], holy and glorious passion-sufferers in Christ, intercessors for all Christians. Oh, honorable and resplendent brothers, blessed Princes Boris and Gleb, most brilliant luminaries, holy crowned ones, beautiful pearls who speak out boldly to the Lord!"

25 There is no consensus on the date when the original was composed. Golubovskij views it as a response to the internecine strife of 1174 and dates it to the year 1175 [1899: 491-510]. Golubinskij attributes it to the second half of the twelfth century [1901-1910: I, 1, p. 824]. Pogodin, who discovered the first copy, suggests that it might have been written as late as the first half of the thirteenth century [1856: VII, 406-408].

26 "Hear, brothers, how, spurred on by the devil, the accursed Svjatopolk conceived a hatred for his elder [*sic*] brothers and opposed them, leading an army of pagans against his brothers; these saints [in contrast] bore no hatred [for their brother], but endured all [his abuses] in this transient life and received a [martyr's] crown from Christ."

27 "Hear [me], princes who oppose elder brothers and provoke war and led an army of pagans against your brothers, [for] God has not yet denounced [you] at the Last Judgment."

28 "Once, when the Israelites feared that Chaldean armies would fall on Jerusalem, they sent to Pharaoh in Egypt, requesting help to prevent the Chaldeans from taking Jerusalem. God sent a prophet to the Israelites, saying: 'Because you did not rely on the God who created you but set all your hopes on the Egyptians, I shall drive the Chaldeans away from you, but you shall be captured by the Egyptians, for you have set your hopes on them and you shall perish [through them]' and so it came to pass." The muddled reference may allude to Isaiah 31: 1-3 or possibly to II Kings: 18-20. No exact biblical parallel has been found.

29 "And suddenly the roof of the church where the prince lay opened up, terrifying the people [who were inside], and a white dove flew in: it alighted on the prince's worthy chest, and parted his lips with its beak. The prince gave up his soul, and the dove vanished, and the church was filled with a sweet fragrance."

30 "'Holy is the Father, holy the Son, holy the Spirit in one God and unto the ages,' Amen." This may be a catechetical restatement of the Trisagion.

31 Loparev notes many historical errors, which he explains by claiming that the author, though from Černigov, wrote about events that had occurred in the distant past [1894: 10]. Abramovič suggests that the text was authored in Vyšgorod [1916: XIX-XX], which would explain the errors but not the inclusion of the references.

32 See Aleškovskij on the archaeological evidence [1972: 117-118 and *passim*] that Boris and Gleb were first revered as thaumaturgic saints and only later became the patrons of princes. Lesjučevskij's comments, while often insightful, are based on misinterpretations of archaeological evidence [1946; cf. Poppe's criticisms (1966: 41-42; 1981: 34)].

33 "Just as Abraham took vengeance against the enemy for Lot's sake [cf. Gen. 14: 13-16], so Jaroslav marched against Svjatopolk for the sake of his brothers, invoking the Lord and saying: "It was not I who began to kill our brethren, but he [Svjatopolk] shed the blood of these righteous ones, who were not guilty. May vengeance be taken upon him; let God return

blood for the blood of my brother. For they lived out their lives in the fear of God, knowing that, like immortal gold, they were tested in this mortal life, and were slaughtered by their brother; like innocent and most pure lambs they came to Christ."

34. Soboleva's line by line comparison of the two texts points out how general references are replaced with references to brothers, fratricide and civil war [1975: 108-110].

4 TESTIMONIALS

1 ". . . and seeing the third miracle, they were awed and then rejoiced. The life of the saint had not yet been recorded. I, the humble and miserable servant, feared to be condemned like the slothful servant who hid his master's talent [Matt. 25: 25-30] . . . [and] wrote a little [about the] life of our holy father Ignatij, Bishop of Rostov. Glory be to our God" cited from GBL, f. 304 (TSL), ms. 745, f. 210^v. R. Bosley, who is currently preparing a scholarly edition of Ignatij's life for publication, generously permitted me to use his copy of the ms. which was dated by B. M. Kloss to the 1420's.

2 "In the year 1436 . . . the aforementioned Savatij, who was named before, was at St. Kirill's monastery, one of those in Belozersk. We were not able to find out what city or village he was born in or where his parents lived, for many years had passed before the writing of this [life]; nor do we know how old he was when he was clad in the robes of a monk. But, from godloving men, and spiritual conversations with those who came from [the Solovki] island, we have learned a few things [which I shall now relate], inspired by these talks, for the spiritual benefit of those who wish to save their souls and to imitate these virtuous lives in God. . . ." Cited from the *vita* of Savvatij and Zosima Soloveckie, CGADA, f. 187, no. 61 (second half of the sixteenth century): ff. 81^v-82^r.

3 For texts and descriptions see Bugoslavskij [1928^a]. Cf. M. P. Bulgakov who proposed initial groupings of the "Narration" mss. [1857-1883: vol. 2, 137-138], and N. K. Nikol'skij [1906: 258-271]. Thirteen additional copies of the "Narration" are described in Revelli [1977-1979: 11-21].

4 See, among other studies arguing for the primacy of the chronicle to the "Narration," Butkov [1852: 85-106], Sobolevskij [1890: 801-804], Šaxmatov [1908: 34-36], Ajnalov [1910: 4], Serebrjanskij [1915: 105-106], Bugoslavskij [1928^a: XIX-XXIII] and Müller [ZSPh 25: 335-343]. Among the scholars who believe that the Primary Chronicle entry used the "Narration" as a source are M. P. Bulgakov, Golubinskij, N. K. Nikol'skij, Il'in and Poppe.

5 The most recent printing of the Slavonic legends (with notes and modern Russian translations) is in Rogov's edition of 1970. The Latin texts may be found in Fontes [1873], Pekař [1906] and Chaloupecký [1939].

6 Among the scholars who have remarked upon the "Narration's" unorthodox form and dynastic connection are Golubinskij [1901-1910: I,1, 746-9], Bugoslavskij [1914: 132-48, 156-176], Eremin [1968: 17-21], Maczko [1975: 72-74] and Ingham [1983: 230-1]. Müller, noting that the biblical citations glorify the princely house, believes that they are more appropriate to a eulogy or a chronicle account than to his hypothetical *Urlegende* [ZSPh 27: 277-278].

7 "His mother, a Greek, was formerly a nun, and Jaropolk, Volodimir's brother, took her, and because of the beauty of her face he unfrocked her, and begot of her this accursed Svjatopolk. But Volodimir, who was still a pagan, killed Jaropolk and took his wife, who was pregnant; and of her was born this accursed Svjatopolk. And he was of two fathers who were brothers, and for this reason Volodimir loved him not, for he was not of him" [Kantor, 1983: 167].

8 "For of such did the author of Proverbs say: 'I was my father's son, obedient and beloved in the sight of my mother'" [*ibid.*: 169].

9 The Russian term *bratoljubie* has political and theological connotations. D. S. Lixačev regards the *political* principle of *bratoljubie* (i.e., that junior princes submit to senior princes) as the ideological motivation for the promotion of Boris' and Gleb's cult [1954: 87-89; cf. my discussion in Chapters Two and Three on Jaroslav's guilt and the eulogies to the princes]. The

theological concept of *philadelphia* [cf. 1 John 3: 7-15 and 4:18] is discussed by Freydank [1983: 80-81] and Ingham [1984: 39-42, 47-49]. This notion of *philadelphia* is developed in a more orthodox manner in the Primary Chronicle entry, the paremia readings and the *Poxvala and mučenie*. In the "Narration" it has a special context, as we shall see below, and the emphasis is on Svjatopolk's affinity with Cain rather than Boris' or Gleb's affinity with Abel.

10 Lilienfeld emphasizes the resemblance between Boris' lament and oral folk laments [1957: 261-2]. Müller cites parallel laments from the *vita* of Alexis, "the Man of God," which was extremely popular in Rus' [ZSPh 27: 292-299].

11 "If he sheds my blood and attempts to slay me, then a martyr shall I be unto my Lord. For I shall not resist, because it is written: 'God resisteth the proud, but giveth grace unto the humble' [James 4:6]. And the Apostle says: 'He who says, I love God, and hateth his brother, is a liar' [I John 4: 20]. And again: 'There is no fear in love; perfect love casteth out fear' [I John 4: 18]. Therefore, what shall I say or what shall I do? Lo, I must go to my brother and say, 'Be a father to me. You are my brother and elder. What is your command, my lord?'"

12 The narrator appears to refer, not to the Gothic martyr, but to a St. Nicetas (286-305), identified in his legend as the son of the Emperor Maximian and reported to have been killed by his father because he converted to Christianity. This version was widely circulated among the Eastern Slavs [Müller, *ZSPh* 27: 310].

13 "And his sleep was troubled by many thoughts and a great, heavy, and terrible grief: How to give himself up to the martyr's passion; how to suffer and end the course and keep the faith so as to receive the predestined crown from the hands of the Almighty" [Kantor, 1983: 177]. On the traditional *topoi* of martyrdom (the image of the martyr as a lamb whose sacrifice imitates the sacrifice of Christ, the metaphor of the crown and the course), see Delehaye [1927: 95-108], Müller [ZSPh 27: 315-316] and Ingham [1984: 44].

14 "O dear and precious lord of ours, how filled with goodness you are that for the sake of the love of Christ you desired not to resist, though many were the troops you held in your hands" [Kantor, 1983: 179].

15 "Look down from Thy holy heights and see the sickness of my heart, which I caught from my kinsman, that for Thy sake I am killed this day. I am counted as a sheep for the slaughter. For Thou knowest, my Lord, that I shall neither resist nor speak contrarily. Though I had all my father's troops in my hands and all whom my father loved, yet I plotted nought against my brother. But he has found it possible to rise up against me so greatly. If an enemy reproached me, I could have borne it; if he that hated me did magnify himself against me, I would have hid myself [cf. Psalm 54: 12]. But, Thou, O Lord, behold and judge between me and between my brother; and, Lord, lay not this sin to their charge, but receive my spirit in peace [cf. Acts 7: 60]. Amen" [Kantor, 1983: 181].

16 Müller's commentary on the selection of this citation for the "Narration" [ZSPh 30: note 49, p.32] must be qualified. He writes: "The carefully selected biblical references are intended to show that Gleb's death fulfils a prophesy of Christ, and that the acceptance of suffering is a theological virtue. Only in this way can the political murder be construed as the sacrifice of a Christian saint." I would argue that the citation is not a shortened summary of Luke 21: 12-19 and Mark 13: 12, but a deliberate selection of Luke 21: 16 precisely because it prophesies that martyrs will be killed by family members. For that reason it draws an analogy logically precarious enough to have inspired much critical debate as to whether the princes were really Christian martyrs.

17 "Whoever acquits himself so after hearing of such things will receive the same, and even more than this, just as Cain, who knew not the retribution he would receive, received one wound, but Lamech, because he knew of the punishment visited upon Cain, was punished seventyfold [cf. Gen. 4: 24]. Such are the retributions for evildoers. For just as the Emperor Julian, who spilled much blood from the holy martyrs, received a bitter and inhuman death, stabbed in the heart with a lance, not knowing by whom he was run through, so too did this

one, fleeing, not knowing from whom, receive a vile death. And from then on discord ceased in the land of Rus', and Jaroslav assumed all power over it" [Kantor, 1983: 197].

18 An overview of various scholarly positions on the issue is given by Müller [ZSPh 25: 332-333]. Čiževskij [1948: 127], Il'in [1957: 180-188], Poppe [1969: 381-2], Maczko [1975: 71] and Ingham [1984: 229], though differing on the precise dating, all agree that the "Narration" was written before the "Lection." Voronin remains the exception to this rule, insisting that the "Lection" came first [1957: 47].

19 Šaxmatov himself eventually accepted 1109 as the most probable date of the "Lection's" composition [1940: 84].

20 In his study of the earliest stages of Kievan annalistic writing, Kuz'min reviews the arguments for the dating of Feodosij's life. He regards Nestor's failure to mention the invention of Feodosij's relics in 1091 as the only compelling negative evidence for dating the *vita* prior to that year, but suggests that Nestor's silence could be attributed to the fact that he was writing two or three decades after the invention, or could indicate that Nestor had left the Kiev Caves Monastery by 1091 [1977: 154].

21 Müller believes that the version in the "Narration" was based on local sources and legends [ZSPh 23: 68-74]. Ingham traces the theme to the literary tradition of Wenceslas, pointing out a series of parallel motifs. At the same time, he reminds us that "prisoner miracles of [this] kind . . . were current in hagiography" [1965: 181] and had numerous scriptural parallels [Acts 5: 17-26; 12: 1-11; 16: 23-24]. Poppe finds the most likely precedent to be the prisoner miracle in the life of St. Nicholas, which was circulated far more widely than the legends of Wenceslas among all classes of Kievan Rus' [Poppe, 1965: 303]. The details on Svjatopolk and the saints' church, in conjunction with the documentary nature of hagiographical writing, suggests to me that Müller's theory is the most probable: namely, that the local legend was recorded in the Vyšgorod archives by witnesses whose account may have been influenced by their familiarity with the biblical and hagiographical precedents. That the miracle is atypical of Boris and Gleb [cf. Ingham, 1965: 167], and would not be conducive to enriching the monastery (since prisoners are not the typical kind of pilgrims) would also speak against the likelihood of a deliberate borrowing and falsification. There is no perceptible economic or literary motive for introducing such a account: the only plausible reason is that such a legend had been handed down and seemed credible (here an analogy would be applicable).

22 "I, the humble hieromonk Paxomij, went to the saint's cloister and witnessed frequent miracles at the sarcophagus of the godbearing father. I learned more from one of the blessed man's disciples who had spent his life from early childhood with the saint. This Epifanij, who was the confessor for all the great laura's brothers, and who had known the blessed man personally, told me everything in order about [Sergij's] birth and youth and miracles, and of his life and death."

23 "In those years, it is said, there was a prince named Vladimir who ruled the entire land of Rus.' He was a righteous man and generous to the poor and to orphans and to widows, [but] he was a pagan."

24 Nasonov believed that this gratuitous reference to the Church of the Tithe, as well as other references (Gleb's prayer in that church before fleeing to northern lands) may indicate that Nestor sympathized with this political milieu, which he characterizes as favorable to Izjaslav Jaroslavovič and his sons [1969: 48-50]. For a review of this issue see Kuz'min, 1977: 183-220], who regards Izjaslav as "the most pro-Western of all eleventh-century Russian princes" [185].

25 See, among others, Eremin [1968: 21-22], Adrianova-Peretc [1970: 92] and Ingham [1983: 232]. Bugoslavskij, while not specifically ascribing the presence of such information to the *vita* as a genre, regards it as part of Nestor's effort to portray typical saints (Čiževskij agrees [1954: 110]). Such a motive could explain certain new facts: Boris' fervent prayers and edifying reading, for example. But it cannot really explain the references to Boris' marriage or to the number of troops that he led [Abramovič, 1916: 10]. Šaxmatov, therefore, concluded that

Nestor must have had additional source material [1908: 66].

26 This statement contradicts the Laurentian Chronicle and the "Narration," where we read that Vladimir sends Gleb to rule Murom. Bugoslavskij attributes this and other factual discrepancies to the fact that political considerations were secondary to Nestor [1914: 172, 188]. Ingham attributes it to hagiographical stylization which, for him, implies a willingness to alter historical facts [1983: 232]. I know of no hagiographical precedent that would dictate such an alteration. The principle of eliminating superfluous details (the name of the kingdom) does not generally involve denying or contradicting facts unless there is a concrete political motivation. Šaxmatov's hypothesis that Nestor was working on the basis of other sources [1908: 66] provides a more plausible motivation for the contradiction. It may be that Nestor was unable to verify Gleb's rule of Murom and deduced that this state of affairs was implausible in view of the prince's youth; he therefore concluded that Gleb must have remained at home with his father. This assumption, as we shall see, involved further amendations of the "Narration."

27 "After some time [had passed] their pious father fell ill of the disease that would kill him. During his illness, [enemy] soldiers invaded his land. The prince heard this, but could not march against them, and so he sent his son Boris, having supplied him with many troops. The blessed one fell [to the ground] and bowed to his father, kissing his venerable feet, and then rose and embraced him, and kissed him with tears. Then [Boris] went out to do battle with the [enemy] troops. And after the blessed one had departed, his father died. . .".

28 Nestor's preference for generalities has been noticed by many scholars who comment on the "Lection," among them Šaxmatov [1908: 64], Ajnalov [1910: 40] and Bugoslavskij [1914: 172].

29 Lilienfeld characterizes the scene in the "Narration" as monastic in its orientation: in her interpretation Boris is depicted as possessing the gift of shedding many tears and his protestations show his scorn for the things of this world. She contrasts this to Nestor's treatment of the encounter, which strikes her as far more emotional and worldly. Here, she writes, the tears underscore Boris' obedience which earns him sainthood in the "Lection" [1957: 268]. My own impression is that the "Narration" consistently stresses feelings but oscillates between pious and chivalric emotions (Boris' meditations on the beauty of his body, for example, or Georgij's fealty to his lord) while the "Lection" either eliminates expressions of feeling altogether or molds them into expressions of decorum. Eremin calls it severe and schematic with a solemn, liturgical pathos [1968: 23].

30 "And like wild beasts they fell upon him and pierced him with their lances. And then one of his retainers fell on him, but they pierced him [the retainer] too, and, thinking that the blessed one was dead, departed."

31 "And thus the blessed Boris commended his soul into the hand of God on the twenty-fourth day of the month of July. His holy body was taken and carried to the town called Vyšgorod, which is located 15 furlongs from the capital city of Kiev, and there they laid the body of the blessed Boris by the Church of St. Basil."

32 "His subjects rebelled and he was driven, not only from the city [of Kiev], but from his principality; he fled to foreign lands and there ended and lost his life. For a sinner dies a difficult death."

33 See Bugoslavskij's extensive comparison of the posthumous miracles in the "Narration" and "Lection" [1914: 165-172].

34 "Brethren, do you see the mercilessness of the accursed one? Do you see the mercilessness of the second Cain who has appeared? For Cain, it is said, pondered how and by what means he
might kill his brother Abel: he could not know the way in which death came about. And, lo, at night as he slept the villain [and] enemy revealed murder to him [i.e., the devil caused Cain to have a vision of how one man could kill another]. After having this vision in his sleep, he arose and killed his brother Abel."

35 "Oh, accursed one, have you heard what God said to Cain about the murder of his

with his brother shall be liable to judgment and hell fire [cf. Matt. 5: 22]?' Not only are you angry with your brother, oh accursed one, but you send men to [kill] him, saying: 'if anyone opposes you, kill him as well.'"

36 "For there are many young princes today who do not submit to their elders and oppose them and are killed; but they are not granted the grace that these saints [were vouchsafed]."

37 See, for example, Fedotov [1931: 22-23], Lixačev [1954: 88], Maczko [1975: 72] and Ingham [1984: 41-42]. There is some discussion as to whether Nestor is referring to concrete junior princes, since this reference would affect the dating of the "Lection." Bugoslavskij, who believed that the work was written after 1108, identifies these princes as Izjaslav Vladimirovič, who was killed in a battle with Oleg Svjatoslavovič, his cousin once-removed, in the year 1096, and Mstislav Svjatopolkovič, who died around 1099-1100 in a battle with his uncle David Igorevič [1941: 328]. Poppe believes that Nestor is most probably referring to princes (and namesakes of Boris and Gleb) involved in the internecine conflicts that reached a peak during the years 1078-1079. At this time senior princes Vsevolod and Izjaslav Jaroslavovič agreed upon an alliance and marched against younger princes who challenged their authority. Among the junior princes who died during this period were Gleb Svjatoslavovič, Boris Vjačeslavovič, and Roman Svjatoslavovič [Poppe, 1965: 305].

38 Nestor's homily anticipates Bishop Simon's (d. 1226) rebuke to the ambitious monk Polikarp contained in the patericon of the Kiev Cave Monastery [Abramovič, 1930: 99-103]. The legends of the monastery indicate that disobedience and arrogance had long been a problem, suggesting that Nestor's rebuke may have been oriented toward his own brethren who constituted his immediate audience.

39 **The Narration**

"O blessed are the graves that received your venerable bodies like a treasure most valuable! Blessed is the church in which the holy coffins containing your blessed bodies were placed! O righteous men of Christ! Blessed in truth and exalted more than all the cities of Rus', the most exalted city is the one that holds such a treasure; the whole world is not its equal. Verily, it is called Vyšgorod: an exalted, the most exalted city of all; a second Thessalonica has appeared in the land of Rus' possessing the power of unmercenary healing" [Kantor, 1983: 201].

The Lection

"O [let us commemorate the] blessed grave where the treasure that cannot be stolen reposes! O [let us commemorate the] venerable grave from which inexhaustible sources of healing flow! O [let us praise the] memory of the holy grave where the faithful gather to the honor and glory of the blessed ones! O may the most blessed grave where the venerable bodies rest to the glory of God who has glorified the [relics] of the blessed passion-sufferers and physicians be commemorated and praised unto the ages! O venerable city, you have been truly named: for you are glorified above all other cities because you hold the [relics of] the intercessors and healers of all who come to you."

40 St. Demetrius was born in Thessalonica. According to his legend he became proconsul of the city and began to preach Christianity openly. He was imprisoned and stabbed to death with a lance in the reign of Maximian (d. 305). Other details that entered into Church Slavonic versions of his life and miracles parallel the cases of Boris and Gleb: Demetrius' servant Lupus is said to have been killed shortly after the death of his master because he, too, was a Christian; Demetrius' grave became a center of healing; Demetrius is a patron of his city, of soldiers, and of kings just as Boris and Gleb came to be [Bulgakov, 1900: 390]. Nestor leaves out this comparison, as well as the comparisons of the princes to Wenceslas, Barbara and Nicetas, perhaps because the motifs of murder by one's clansmen and the patronage of a specific city figure less prominently in the "Lection" than in the "Narration."

41 "I, the sinful Nestor, have written of the life and death and miracles of these holy and blessed passion-sufferers diligently [recording the words of] those who knew [of them] and [adding] other [things] I learned myself. I have written only a few of many things that could be written so that whoever reads this may do so to the glory of God. I also entreat you who read this for the love of God to remember me and ask that you say [this prayer on my behalf]: 'Lord, by the prayers of the most blessed passion-sufferers Boris and Gleb, expunge the sins of the man who wrote this.' May you, too, be forgiven for your sins by the grace and mercies and love for mankind of our Lord, Jesus Christ. Glory be to Him, and the Father and the Holy Spirit, today and forever and unto the ages. Amen."

42 Ingham's position is that subject (also special themes) and function (the intended application of a work) direct a writer to choose an appropriate literary *genre* [cf. 1983: 227; 1987^a: 239 and the discussion in Chapter One].

43 The behavior of Vladimir and Jaroslav as described in the Laurentian Chronicle entry is, on occasion, incompatible with that of a saint; the "Narration" conveys information that might compromise Vladimir, but deletes any facts that would detract from Jaroslav's image (his rebellion against his father, his draconian measures in Novgorod against certain retainers, his attempt to flee abroad [see Chapter Five]). Nestor takes this editorial process one step further by depicting all princes, with the exception of Svjatopolk, as ideal Christian rulers who might potentially be counted among the saints. In the "Lection" only Boris and Gleb reach this goal, although Vladimir would later be canonized in his capacity as the baptizer of Rus'.

5 CHRONICLES

1 *Orator* 120 [cited from Hadas, 1959: 115].

2 Preface to the *Historiae Francorum* [Gregory, Bishop of Tours, 590-594: 63].

3 In his 1950 edition of the Novgorod I Chronicle, Nasonov distinguishes between the older recension [*staršij izvod*] represented by the Sinodal'nyj ms. [GIM, Sin. sob., no. 786] and the younger recension [*mladšij izvod*] represented by the Komissionnyj ms. [LOII, sob. b. Arxeografičeskoj komissii, no. 240]. The initial 128 folia of the Sinodal'nyj ms. have been lost. It begins in the middle of the entry for the year 1016, and therefore most entries concerned with Boris' and Gleb's fate must be cited from the Komissionnyj ms.

4 Lur'e believes that Šaxmatov has no grounds for identifying this digest as the "*svod* of 1448" or the "Novgorod-Sophia *svod* of the 1430's," which Šaxmatov traces back to the *Sofijskij vremennik* and, ultimately, to Fotij's *Vladimirskij polixron* of 1421. He suggests that it seems to reflect the interests of the Muscovite metropolitan and the grand prince in their disputes with Novgorod, and estimates the most probable dates of its compilation to be in the 1440's [1985: 199].

5 "Jaroslav halted at the site where Boris had been slain and, lifting up his hands to heaven, exclaimed, 'The blood of my brother cries aloud to thee, O Lord. Avenge the blood of this just man. Visit upon this criminal the blood of Abel.' Then he prayed and said, 'My brethren, although ye be absent in the body, yet help me with your prayer against this presumptuous assassin.' When he had thus spoken, the two armies attacked, and the plain of the Al'ta was covered with the multitudinous soldiery of both forces. It was then Friday. As the sun rose, they met in battle, and the carnage was terrible, such as had never before occurred in Rus'. The soldiers fought hand to hand and slaughtered each other. Three times they clashed, so that blood flowed in the valley. Toward evening Jaroslav conquered, and Svjatopolk fled" [Cross and Sherbowitz-Wetzor, 1953: 133].

6 "And the Dnepr' [began] to freeze. And one of Jaroslav's men was in Svjatopolk's [camp]. And that night Jaroslav sent his retainer to this man [in Svjatopolk's camp] and [told the retainer to ask the following question]. [The retainer] said to [Jaroslav's agent]: 'What do you advise us to do? Only a small amount of mead has been brewed, but we have many retainers?' [Jaroslav's] man answered: 'Tell Jaroslav that if there is only a small amount of mead for a large group of retainers, then he should distribute it in the evening.' And Jaroslav understood

that he had been advised to attack at night. And that evening Jaroslav and his troops crossed over to the other side of the Dnepr', and they pushed their boat from the shore, and prepared their attack that night. And Jaroslav said to his retainers: 'Wind scarves around your heads as an identifying mark.' And there was a terrible battle. And before dawn, they had conquered Svjatopolk's [army]. And Svjatopolk fled to the Pechenegs. Jaroslav, however, went to Kiev and ascended the throne of his father, Vladimir" [cited, with some changes, from the translation of Michell and Forbes, 1970: 2].

7 "There was a terrible battle. The [soldiers] fought hand to hand, and blood flowed in the valley. Many of the faithful saw angels of the Lord helping Jaroslav. And before dawn [Jaroslav] conquered Svjatopolk. And Svjatopolk fled to the Pechenegs. And he remained [in the wilderness] between Poland and Bohemia, driven by no man. [There] the accursed one perished and thus he ended his evil life. To this day there is smoke [on the site]. And Jaroslav went to Kiev [and] ascended the throne of his father, Vladimir."

8 "His father's retainers then urged him to take his place in Kiev on his father's throne, since he had at his disposal the latter's retainers and troops. But Boris protested, 'Be it not for me to raise my hand against my elder brother. Now that my father has passed away, let him take the place of my father in my heart.' When the soldiery heard these words, they departed from him" [Cross and Sherbowitz-Wetzor, 1953: 126].

9 Šaxmatov notes that this episode is dislocated [1908: 501-503]. In his reconstruction of the Novgorodian *svod* of 1050 he places it in the entries for the years 1015-1016, i.e., in its proper chronological order [*ibid*.: 617-618]. Kuza has published a reconstruction of what he regards as an aesthetically closed tale [1978].

10 Šaxmatov, who was the first to remark upon this "seam" in the text, believes that the message was originally conveyed to Gleb at the time when it was allegedly delivered. He argues that the Kievan chronicler probably repeated and expanded it in order to clarify the account of Jaroslav's difficulties with his retainers, which was borrowed from an eleventh-century Novgorodian episcopal *svod* [1908: 78-79]. Müller takes the opposite position. The warning is conveyed in greater detail in the latter entry and seems to be central to the narrative about Jaroslav's retainers, he writes, whereas it is clearly secondary in the narrative of Gleb's death. He suggests that it was interpolated in abbreviated form as a means of establishing Gleb's status as a martyr (i.e., one who knows of his impending death but offers no resistance) [1954: 198-199]. I an inclined to accept Šaxmatov's theory, first, because it is based on the documentable premise that chronological ordering is the annalistic norm, and, second, because it can account for the repetition more simply and plausibly than the explanation provided by Müller. Jaroslav's warning to Gleb fits naturally into the sequence of events. The hypothesis of a hagiographical editor is rendered superfluous by the fact that the Kievan chronicler himself had a vested interest in copying this information from an archival record. The original purpose would be to document Jaroslav's role as his brothers' protector and champion. That he would later repeat it in greater detail in a second context should not surprise us, for there are any number of parallels in the annals illustrating that such repetition was entirely acceptable and, indeed, to be expected in a text where redundancy and contradiction are the rule.

11 On Jaroslav's marriage to Ingigerd (later baptized Irene) see *Heimskringla* [Chapter 93, pp. 342-343]. Bolesław's conflict with Jaroslav is most thoroughly reported in the eighth and ninth books of Thietmar's *Chronicon* [1012-1018]. For bibliography and a discussion of the sources, see Cross [1929], Stender-Petersen [1953] and Birnbaum [1978].

12 Svjatopolk's location before and immediately following Vladimir's death is problematic. The Laurentian Chronicle states: "потаиша и, бѣ бо Святополкъ Кыевѣ" [PSRL, 1926: 130, lines 20-21], which is generally translated as "they kept [his death] secret, for Svjatopolk was in Kiev" [Cross and Sherbowitz-Wetzor, 1953: 124]. This would seem to contradict the statement that "Святополк же сѣде Кыевѣ" [PSRL, 1926: 132, line 2]. Lixačev explains the situa-

tion as follows: "Vladimir's death was hidden in the interests of Svjatopolk. The people who were concealing the death did so because Svjatopolk was in Kiev and, accordingly, had the power to command them" [PVL, 1950: 356-357]. This would certainly seem to be the case, but even when the verb *сѣдѣти* is translated in its narrowest sense as "to rule" and we assume that the chronicler is referring to the actual usurpation of the throne, the chronology of events is far from clear. When did Svjatopolk leave his own patrimony? Why did he come to Kiev? What was his precise authority? Who were his supporters? All of these questions, themselves, create an obscure, contradictory situation which fuels the fears of the chronicler for the state of the land.

13 "For the Most High God appoints emperor and prince, and confers authority according to his desires. Wherever a nation is justified before God, he there appoints a just emperor or prince who loves law and righteousness, and sets up a governor and a judge to render judgment. For if the princes are righteous in the land, many sins are remitted. But if they are evil and deceitful, then God visits yet greater evil upon that country, for the prince is its head. Thus Isaiah said, 'They have sinned from head to foot,' [Isaiah 1: 6] meaning from the king down to the common people. 'Woe unto that city in which the prince is young, loving to drink wine amid music and in the company of young councillors. God bestoweth such princes in requital for sin, and taketh away from Jerusalem the strong, the giant, the valiant man, the judge, the moderate elder, the able councillor, the cunning artificer, the learned, the wise, and the obedient. I shall appoint a youth to be their prince, and a brawler to be their ruler' [Isaiah 3: 1-4]" [Cross and Sherbowitz-Wetzor, 1953: 130].

14 Manfred Hellmann identifies these two premises with the Western European traditions of the king's charisma [*Königsheil*] [1967: 234]. In its strictest sense, charisma refers to the belief that a divinely-sanctioned king has powers confirming his status as *vicarus Christi*, chief among them the power to heal illness by touching the victim with his hands [Hauck, 1950; *Lexikon*, 1983: 1719-1723]. Some analogy can be drawn between the chronicle passage and the widespread belief that a king brings good or evil fortune to a land [see Chapter Two, note 26]. Given the absence of any specific markers that would point to a particular European antecedent, however, and the concrete references to a biblical source (see below), the analogy seems pointless.

15 "He is the new Constantine of mighty Rome, who baptized himself and his subjects; for the [prince of Rus'] imitated the acts of [Constantine] himself. Even if he was formerly given to evil lusts, he afterward consecrated himself to repentance, according to the teaching of the Apostle that 'when sin increases, there grace abounds the more'" [Cross and Sherbowitz-Wetzor, 1953: 124].

16 "Even if he had previously committed other crimes in his ignorance, he subsequently distinguished himself in repentance and almsgiving. As it is written, 'As I shall find you, so shall I judge you' [Wisdom 11: 17]. Thus the Prophet says, 'as I the Lord Adonai live, I desire not the death of a sinner, but rather that he shall turn from his way and live; turn in repentance from your wicked way' [Ezekiel 33: 11]. For many of those who act justly and live in righteousness turn from the virtuous road to death and are destroyed; while others live unrighteously, yet are admonished before their deaths, and atone for their sins through laudable repentance. Thus the Prophet says, 'The righteousness of the righteous shall not save him in the day of his transgression. When I say to the righteous man, 'Thou shalt live,' if he trust to his righteousness and commit iniquity, all his righteousness shall not be remembered, and he shall die in the iniquity that he hath committed. And when I say to the wicked, 'Thou shalt die the death,' if he turn from his sin and perform equity and justice, restore his pledge, and give back what he hath stolen, then all his sins that he hath committed shall not be remembered, because he performed equity and justice, and in them shall he live. I shall judge each of you according to his way, o house of Israel' [Ezekiel 33: 12-16, 20]. [Vladimir] died in the orthodox

faith. He effaced his sins by repentance and by almsgiving, which is better than all things else. For the Lord says, 'I desire alms, and not a sacrifice' [Matt. 9: 13]. Alms are better and more exalted than all other things, since they lead us into the presence of God, even to heaven itself; as the angel said to Cornelius, 'Thy prayers and thy almsgiving are remembered before God' [Acts 10: 4]" [Cross and Sherbowitz-Wetzor, 1953: 124-125].

17 "It is indeed marvelous what benefits Vladimir conferred upon the land of Rus' by its conversion. . . . It is fitting for us to pray God for his sake, inasmuch as through him we have come to know God. But may God grant thee according to thy heart's desire and fulfill all thy requests, giving thee the kingdom of heaven which thou didst desire! May God confer upon thee the crown among the righteous, happiness in paradisiacal sustenance, and association with Abraham and the other patriarchs! As Solomon said, 'When a righteous man dieth, his hope is not lost' [Proverbs 11: 7]. The people of Rus', mindful of their holy baptism, hold this prince in pious memory, and glorify God in prayers and hymns and psalms, singing to God as his new people, enlightened by his Holy Spirit, maintaining the hope of our great God and of our Savior Jesus Christ, that He will give each one of us joy ineffable according to his labors. And may such be the lot of all Christians" [*ibid.*: 125-126].

18 "Rejoice, martyrs in Christ from the land of Rus', who give healing in them who draw near to you in faith and love. Rejoice, dwellers in heaven. In the body were ye angels, servants in the same thought, comrades in the same image, of one heart with the saints. To all that suffer ye give relief. Rejoice, Boris and Gleb, wise in God. Like streams ye spring out from the founts of life-giving water which flow for the healing of the faithful" [*ibid.*: 129]. This doxology is dense with reminiscences from the saints' offices. Allusions to a wide range of miracles worked through the saints' intercession —including the healing of the lame, blind, and sick, and the liberation of prisoners—suggest that it was composed after the translation of 1072 and most probably after the records of posthumous miracles contained in the appendices to the extended lives [Golubovskij, 1900: 148-149; Bugoslavskij, 1900: 63; Müller, 1954: 215]. Golubovskij's theory that the doxology represents a late corruption of the Ivaniči Menaion service is not borne out by textual analysis.

BIBLIOGRAPHY

Abrahamse, D.
1984 "Rituals of Death in the Middle Byzantine Period," *Greek Orthodox Theological Review* 29, no. 2, 125-134.
Abramovič, D. I.
1916 *Žitija svjatyx mučenikov Borisa i Gleba i služby im.* Pamjatniki drevne-russkoj literatury 2. Petrograd.
1930 *Kyjevo-Pečers'kyj Paterik*, Pam'jatky movy ta pys'menstva davnjoji Ukrajiny, 4. Kiev; reprinted under the editorship of D. Čiževskij (Munich, 1964).
Adrian
1873 "Žitie i stradanie svjatogo prepodobnogo mučenika Adriana igumena, Pošexonskogo čudotvorca," *JEV*, nos 4 (Jan. 24), 25-31; 5 (Jan. 31), 33-42; 7 (Feb. 14), 55-61; 9 (Feb. 28), 71-78.
Adrianova-Peretc, V. P.
1970 "Sjužetnoe povestvovanie v žitijnyx pamjatnikax XI—XIII vv." in *Istoki russkoj belletristiki*. Ed. Ja. S. Lur'e. Leningrad, 67-107.
Afanas'ev, A. N.
1865-69 *Poetičeskie vozzrenija slavjan na prirodu*. 3 vols. Moscow.
Ajnalov, D. V.
1910 "Očerki i zametki po istorii drevne-russkogo iskusstva," *IORJaS* XV, 3, 1-128.
Aleškovskij, M. X.
1971 *Povest' vremennyx let: sud'ba literaturnogo proizvedenija v drevnej Rusi*. Moscow.
1972 "Russkie glebo-borisovskie enkolpiony 1072-1150 godov" in *Drevnerusskoe iskusstvo: xudožestvennaja kul'tura domongol'skoj Rusi*. Moscow, 104-25.
Alissandratos, J.
1982 *Medieval Slavic and Patristic Eulogies*. Studia Historica et Philologica XIV, Sectio Slavica 6. Florence.
Alpatov, M. V.
1966 "Gibel' Svjatopolka v legende i v ikonopisi," *TODRL* XXII, 18-23.
Ammann, A. M.
1955 *Untersuchungen zur Geschichte der kirchlichen Kultur und des religiösen Lebens bei den Ostslawen. Heft 1: Die ostslawische Kirche im jurisdiktionellen Verband der byzantinischen Grosskirche (988-1459)*. Das östliche Christentum, N.F. 13. Würzburg.
Angelov, B. St.
1956 "Materialy za pronikvane na ruskata kniga v B"lgarija do XIV v.," *Godišnik na B"lgarskija bibliografski institut za 1954 godina*, kn. 4, Sofia, 113-26.
Aničkov, E. V.
1913 *Jazyčestvo i drevnjaja Rus'*. St. Petersburg.
A. P.
1971 "Izobraženie svjatyx knjazej Borisa i Gleba v lit'e XV veka," *Žurnal moskovskoj patriarxii* 5, 76-78.
Atadžanjan, I. A.
1977 "Ob istočnike, motivax i xaraktere armjanskogo perevoda 'Skazanija o Borise i Glebe'" in *Literaturnye svjazi, tom 2: Russko-armjanskie literaturnye svjazi. Issledovanija i materialy*. Erevan, 47-62.
Baetke, W.
1942 *Das Heilige im Germanischen*. Tübingen.

Bamborschke, U., Kośny, W., Meyer-Harder, H., Schmidt, W.-H. and Seeman, K.-D.
1979 *Die Erzählung über Petr Ordynskij. Ein Beitrag zur soziologischen Erforschung altrussischer Texte.* Berlin.
Baumgarten, N. de
1927 "Généalogies et mariages occidentaux des rurikides russes du xe au xiiie siècle," *Orientalia Christiana*, IX, 1, no. 35, 5-95.
1930 "Le dernier mariage de saint Vladimir," *Orientalia Christiana* XVIII, 2, no. 61, 165-168.
Beck, H.-G.
1959 *Kirche und theologische Literatur im Byzantinischen Reich.* Byzantinisches Handbuch 2, 1. Munich.
Belobrova, O. A.
1985 "Miniatjury 'Skazanija o Borise i Glebe,'" in *Skazanie o Borise i Glebe.* Vol. 1: *Naučno-spravočnyj apparat izdanija.* Moscow, 90-101.
Beneševič, V. N.
1909 "Armjanskij prolog o svjatyx Borise i Glebe," *IORJaS* XIV, 1, 201-236.
Beumann, H.
1948 "Widukind von Korvei als Geschichtsschreiber und seine politische Gedankenwelt," *Westfalen* 27, 161-176. Cited from the reprint [Lammers, 1961: 135-164].
Biljarskij, P. S.
1861 "Sostav i mesjaceslov Mstislavova spiska evangelija. Izvlečenija iz sočinenija prof. N. K. Nevostrueva," *Izvestija Imperatorskoj Akademii nauk po russkomu jazyku i slovesnosti* X, 110-137.
1862 "Zamečanija o jazyke Skazanija o sv. Borise i Glebe, pripisyvaemogo Nestoru, sravnitel'no s jazykom letopisi," *Zapiski Imperatorskoj Akademii nauk* II, kn. 1-2, 109-120.
Birkfellner, G.
1975 *Glagolitische und kyrillische Handschriften in Österreich*, Schriften der Balkankommission, Linguistische Abteilung XXIII, Vienna.
Birnbaum, H.
1960 "Linguistische Beobachtungen an einem altrussischen Text. Einige syntaktische Erscheinungen des Skazanie von Boris und Gleb nach der Handschrift des sog. Uspenskij Sbornik," *International Journal of Slavic Linguistics and Poetics* 3, 45-68.
1962 "On Old Russian and Scandinavian Legal Language: Some Comparative Notes on Style and Syntax," *Scando-slavica* 8, 115-140.
1978 "Yaroslav's Varangian Connection," *Scando-slavica* 24, 5-25.
1985 "Orality, Literacy and Literature in Old Rus'," *Die Welt der Slaven*, 30, 161-96.
Bloch, M.
1961 *Feudal Society: Volume 2. Social Classes and Political Organization.* Trans. L. A. Manyon. Chicago.
Bodjanskij, O. M.
1859 "Čtenie o žitii i o pogublenii i o čudesex svjatuju i blaženuju strastoterp'cu Borisa i Gleba, spisanie Nestora, po xaratejnomu spisku Moskovskoj Sinodal'noj Biblioteki," *ČOIDR* I, otd. III., pp. 1-19; a-kg [text]; I-XXVIII.
1870 "Žitie Svjatyx mučenikov Borisa i Gleba: 1. Po xaratejnomu spisku XII-go veka. II. Po xaratejnomu že spisku XIV veka," *ČOIDR* I.2, otd. III, pp. 1-31; 1-17.
Börtnes, J.
1988 *Visions of Glory: Studies in Early Russian Hagiography.* Tr. J. Börtnes and P. Nielsen. Slavica Norvegica V. Oslo-New Jersey.
Bosley, R. D.
1984 "The Saints of Novgorod: à propos of A. S. Chorošev's Book on the Church in Mediaeval Novgorod," *Jahrbücher für Geschichte Osteuropas* 32, 1-15.

Bražnikov, P. V.
1955 *Blagoveščenskij Kondakar'*. Leningrad.
Bugoslavskij, G. K.
1900 "Ivaničskie mesjačnye minei 1547-79 gg. i soderžaščajasja v nix služba sv. mučenikam-knjaz'jam Borisu i Glebu," *Čtenija v Istoričeskom Obščestve Nestora letopisca*, kn. 14, vyp. 2, otd. III, 29-70.
Bugoslavskij, S. A.
1914 "K voprosu o xaraktere i ob"eme literaturnoj dejatel'nosti prep. Nestora," *IORJaS*, XIX, 1, 31-186; 3, 153-91.
1924 "K literaturnoj istorii 'Pamjati i poxvaly' knjazju Vladimiru," *IORJaS* XXIX, 105-59.
1928[a] *Ukrajino-rus'ki pam'jatky XI-XVIII v.v. pro knjaziv Borysa ta Hliba. Rozvidka i teksty*. Kiev.
1928[b] "Literaturnaja tradicija v severnovostočnoj russkoj agiografii," in *Sbornik statej v čest' A. I. Sobolevskogo*. Leningrad, 332-36.
1939 "Drevnerusskie literaturnye proizvedenija o Borise i Glebe," Diss. (Institut mirovoj literatury im. Gorkogo, Moscow), 10 + xvi + 355 pp. [inaccessible to me].
1941 "Žitie" in *Istorija russkoj literatury* I. Moscow-Leningrad, 315-46.
Bulgakov, M. P. [Metropolitan Makarij]
1849 "Skazanie i strast' i poxvala svjatuju mučeniku Borisa i Gleba." *Xristianskoe čtenie* 2, 377-407.
1857-83 *Istorija russkoj cerkvi*. 12 vols. St. Petersburg.
1858 "Čtenie o žitii i o pogublenii blažennuju strastoterpca Borisa i Gleba," *Pravoslavnyj sobesednik* 1, 583-604.
Bulgakov, S. V.
1900 *Nastol'naja kniga dlja svjaščenno-cerkovno-služitelej*. 2nd ed. Khar'kov.
Bultmann, R.
1921 *Die Geschichte der synoptischen Tradition*. Marburg.
Butkov, P. G.
1852 "Razbor trex drevnix pamjatnikov russkoj duxovnoj literatury," *Sovremennik* 32, otd. 2, 85-106.
Černogubov, N. N.
1963 "Ikona 'Boris i Gleb' v Kievskom muzee russkogo iskusstva" in *Drevnerusskoe iskusstvo XV-XVI vv*. Moscow, 285-290.
Chaloupecký, V.
1939 *Prameny X. století legendy Kristiánovy o svatém Václavu a svaté Ludmile (Svatováclavský Sborník, II, 2)*. Prague.
Chase, F. H.
1891 *The Lord's Prayer in the Early Church*. Cambridge.
Cherniavsky, M.
1961 *Tsar and People. Studies in Russian Myths*. New Haven.
Čiževskij [Čyževskyj], D.]
1948 *Geschichte der altrussischen Literatur des 11., 12. und 13.Jahrhunderts*. Frankfurt.
1954 "On the Question of Genres in Old Russian Literature," *Harvard Slavic Studies* II, 105-15.
1956 "Zur Stilistik der altrussischen Literatur. Topik" in *Festschrift für Max Vasmer zum 70. Geburtstag am 26. Februar 1956*. Ed. Margarete Woltner and Herbert Bräuer. Berlin-Wiesbaden, 105-112.
Členov, A. M.
1971 "Zur Frage der Schuld an der Ermordung des Fürsten Boris," *Jahrbücher für Geschichte Osteuropas*, N. F. 19, 322-46.

Cook, R.
1986 "Russian History, Icelandic Story, and Byzantine Strategy in Eymundar þáttr Hringssonar," *Viator* 17, 65-89.
Cross, S. H.
1929 "Yaroslav the Wise in Norse Tradition," *Speculum* IV, 2, 177-197.
Cross, S. H. and Sherbowitz-Wetzor, O. (trans.)
1953 *The Russian Primary Chronicle. Laurentian Text.* Cambridge, Mass.
Cullman, O.
1925 "Les récentes études sur la formation de la tradition évangelique," *Revue d'histoire et de philosophie religieuse* 5, 459-77, 564-79.
Dachkévytch, Ya.
1975-76 "Les Arméniens à Kiev (jusqu'à 1240): 13. La Vie de Boris et Hlib en arménien," *Revue des études arméniennes*, n.s. 11, 346-75.
Dal', V. I.
1862 *Poslovicy russkogo naroda.* 2 vols. Rpt. Moscow, 1984.
1912 *Tolkovyj slovar' živogo velikorusskogo jazyka.* Ed. J. Baudouin de Courtenay. 4th ed. 4 vols. St. Petersburg-Moscow.
Delehaye, H.
1907 *Les légendes hagiographiques.* Brussels. Cited from *The Legends of the Saints.* Trans. V. M. Crawford. Notre Dame, Indiana, 1961.
1927 *Sanctus. Essai sur le cult des saints dans l'antiquité.* Subsidia hagiographica 17. Brussels.
1966 *Les passions des martyrs et les genres littéraires.* 2nd ed. Subsidia hagiographica 13. Brussels.
Demin, A. S.
1983 "Edinicy xudožestvennosti. Na materiale drevnerusskix i južnoslavjanskix pamjatnikov X-načala XII v." in *Slavjanskie literatury. IX Meždunarodnyj s"ezd slavistov, Kiev..* Moscow, 25-37.
Deržavin, A.
1976 "Četii-Minei svjatitelja Dmitrija, mitropolita Rostovskogo, kak cerkovnoistoričeskij i literaturnyj pamjatnik," *Bogoslovskie trudy* 15, 61-145.
Dibelius, M.
1929 "Zur Formgeschichte der Evangelien," *Theologische Rundschau* 1, 185-216.
1933 *Die Formgeschichte des Evangeliums.* Cited from the translation of the author and B. Wolf, *From Tradition to Gospel.* Greenwood, South Carolina, 1971.
1936 *A Fresh Approach to the New Testament and Early Christian Literature.* Hertford.
Dimnik, M.
1988 "Oleg Svyatoslavich and His Patronage of the Cult of SS. Boris and Gleb," *Mediaeval Studies* 50, 349-370.
Djačenko, G.
1900 *Polnyj cerkovno-slavjanskij slovar'.* Moscow.
Dmitriev, L. A.
1958 Ed. *Povesti o žitii Mixaila Klopskogo.* Moscow-Leningrad.
1972 "Žanr severnorusskix žitij," *TODRL* XXVII, 181-202.
1973 *Žitijnye povesti russkogo severa kak pamjatniki literatury XIII-XVII vv.* Leningrad.
1978 Trans. "Skazanie o Borise i Glebe" in *Pamjatniki literatury drevnej Rusi. Načalo russkoj literatury XI-XII veka.* Moscow, 279-304, 451-6.
1985 "'Skazanie o Borise i Glebe'—literaturnyj pamjatnik Drevnej Rusi" in *Skazanie o Borise i Glebe.* Vol. 1: *Naučno-spravočnyj apparat izdanija.* Moscow, 5-24.
Dostál, A. and Rothe, H.
1976– *Der altrussische Kondakar'.* 9 vols. Giessen.
Ebbinghaus, A.
1986 "Die altrussischen Marienikonen-Legenden." Ph.D. diss., Freie Universität Berlin [forthcoming in Veröffentlichungen der Abteilung für slavische Sprachen und Literaturen des Osteuropa-Instituts (Slavisches Seminar) an der Freien Universität Berlin].
1987 "Quellen und Typen der altrussischen Ikonenlegenden," in *Gattung und Narration in den älteren slavischen Literaturen.* Ed. K.-D. Seemann. Berlin-Wiesbaden, 71-84.

Èmin, N. O.
1877 "Skazanija o svjatyx Romane i Davide (Borise i Glebe) i o končine russkogo episkopa svjatogo Fomy. Po Armjanskim Četii-Minejam," *Russkij arxiv* XV, kn. 1, 273-288.

Ènciklopedičeskij slovar'
1890-1907 *Ènciklopedičeskij slovar'*. Ed. F. A. Brokgauz and I. A. Efron. 43 vols. St. Petersburg.

Ensslin, W.
1961 "The Emperor and the Imperial Administration" in *Byzantium: An Introduction to East Roman Civilization*. Ed. N. H. Baynes and H. Moss. Oxford, 268-307.

Eremin, I. P.
1947 "'Povest' vremennyx let' kak pamjatnik literatury," cited from the reprint in his *Literatura Drevnej Rusi*. Moscow, 1966, 42-97.
1957[a] "Literaturnoe nasledie Kirilla Turovskogo," *TODRL* XIII, 409-26.
1957[b] Trans. "Slovo o knjaz'jax" in *Xudožestvennaja proza Kievskoj Rusi XI-XIII vekov*, Moscow, 237-242 and 330-333. Reprinted in *Pamjatniki literatury Drevnej Rusi. XII Vek*, Moscow, 1980 (with the text from Loparev, 1894), 338-343 and 673-4.
1963 "'Skazanie' o Borise i Glebe," cited from the reprint in his *Literatura Drevnej Rusi*. Moscow, 1966, 18-27.
1968 *Lekcii po drevnej russkoj literature*. Leningrad.

Eymundar þáttr
1860-1868 *Eymundar þáttr Hringssonar*. In *Flateyjarbók*. Ed. G. Vigfusson and C. R. Unger. 3 Vols. Oslo, 2: 118-134.

Fedotov, G.
1931 *Svjatye drevnej Rusi (X-XVII st.)*. New York.
1946 *The Russian Religious Mind*, vol. I. Cambridge, Mass.

Fennell, J. and Stokes, A.
1974 *Early Russian Literature*. London.

Filippovskij, G. Ju. (ed.)
1982 "Skazanie o Leontii Rostovskom" in *Drevne-russkie predanija (XI-XVI vv.)* Sost. V. V. Kuskov. Moscow, 125-26.

Florja, B. A.
1978 "Václavská legenda a borisovsko-glebovský kult (shody a rozdíly)," *Československý časopis historický* XXVI, 1, 82-95.

Florovskij, A.
1929 "Počitanie sv. Vjačeslava, knjazja češskogo, na Rusi," *Naučnye Trudy Russkogo Narodnogo Universiteta v Prage*, 2, 305-25.
1958 "Češskie strui v istorii russkogo literaturnogo razvitija," *Slavjanskaja filologija* III, 211-51.

Fontes
1873 *Fontes Rerum Bohemicarum I*. Prague.

Fowler, A.
1982 *Kinds of Literature: An Introduction to the Theory of Genres and Modes*. Cambridge, Mass.

Fraehn, C. M. (ed.)
1823 *Ibn Foszlans und anderer Araber Berichte über die Russen älterer Zeit*. St. Petersburg; rpt. Hamburg, 1926.

Freydank, D.
1981 "Die Ermordung Glebs: Variationen eines hagiographischen Themas" in *Eikon und Logos. Beiträge zur Erforschung byzantinischer Kulturtraditionen*. Band 1. Wissenschaftliche Beiträge der Martin-Luther Universität, 35. Halle, 75-86.
1983 "Die altrussische Hagiographie in ihren europäischen Zusammenhängen: Die Berichte über Boris und Gleb als hagiographische Texte," *Zeitschrift für Slawistik* 28, 1, 78-85.
1985 "Povtory i ix funkcii v Čtenii o Borise i Glebe" in *Problemy izučenija kul'turnogo nasledija*. Ed. G. B. Stepanov. Moscow, 57-67.

Frojanov, I. Ja.
1974   *Kievskaja Rus'. Očerki social'no-èkonomičeskoj istorii.* Leningrad.
1980   *Kievskaja Rus'. Očerki social'no-političeskoj istorii.* Leningrad.
Gal'kovskij, N. M.
1913   *Bor'ba xristianstva s ostatkami jazyčestva v drevnej Rusi*, t. II. In *Zapiski Moskovskogo arxeologičeskogo instituta* XVIII.
Gardner, J. von
1976   *System und Wesen des russischen Kirchengesangs.* Wiesbaden.
1978   *Bogoslužebnoe penie russkoj pravoslavnoj cerkvi. Suščnost', sistema i istorija.* Tom 1. Jordanville, New York: Holy Trinity Russian Orthodox Monastery.
1980   *Russian Church Singing: Volume 1. Orthodox Worship and Hymnography.* Trans. V. Morosan. Crestwood, New York: St. Vladimir's Seminary Press.
Gimbutas, M.
1967   "Ancient Slavic Religion: A Synopsis" in *To Honor Roman Jakobson*, vol. 1. Paris-The Hague, 738-759.
Goldblatt, H. and Picchio, R.
1985   "The Formalist Approach and the Study of Medieval Orthodox Slavic Literature" in *Russian Formalism A Retrospective Glance. A Festschrift in Honor of Victor Erlich).* Ed. R. L. Jackson and S. Rudy. New Haven, 272-88.
Golubinskij, E. E.
1901-1910   *Istorija russkoj cerkvi.* 2 vols. Moscow.
1903   *Istorija kanonizacii svjatyx v russkoj cerkvi.* Moscow.
Golubovskij, P. V.
1899   "Opyt priuročenija drevnerusskoj propovedi 'Slovo o knjaz'jax' k opredelennoj xronologičeskoj date" in *Drevnosti. Trudy Arxeografičeskoj komissii imp. Moskovskogo Arxeologičeskogo obščestva* I, 3, Moscow, 491-510.
1900   "Služba svjatym mučenikam Borisu i Glebu v Ivaničskoj minee 1547-79 g.," *Čtenija v Istoričeskom Obščestve Nestora-letopisca*, kn. XIV, vyp. 3, otdel II, 125-166.
Gorskij, A. and Nevostruev, K.
1855-1917   *Opisanie slavjanskix ruskopisej Moskovskoj Sinodal'noj biblioteki.* 6 vols.
Gregory, Bishop of Tours
590-594   *Historiae Francorum* in *Monumenta Germaniae Historica, Scriptores rerum Merovingicarum, I.* Ed. W. Arndt and B. Krusch. Hannover, 1885; rpt. 1961. Cited from *The History of the Franks.* Trans. L. Thorpe. New York, 1974.
Grekov, B. D.
1940-1963   *Pravda Russkaja.* 3 vols. Moscow-Leningrad.
Grigor'jan, K. N.
1953   "Iz istorii russko-armjanskix kul'turnyx svjazej X-XVII vv.," *TODRL* IX, 323-36.
Gudzij, N. K.
1960   "Literatura Kievskoj Rusi i drevnejšie inoslavjanskie literatury" in *Issledovanija po slavjanskomu literaturovedeniju i fol'kloristike.* Ed. A. N. Robinson. Moscow, 1-60.
Gunkel, H.
1906   "Die Grundprobleme der israelitischen Literaturgeschichte," *Deutsche Literaturzeitung* XXVII, Nr. 29, cols. 1797-1800, 1861-1866.
Gusev, P. L.
1898   "Novgorodskaja ikona svjatyx Borisa i Gleba v dejanijax," *Vestnik arxeologii i istorii* X, 86-115.
Hackel, S.
1967   "The Creative Scribe: A Neglected Editor of the 'Tale, Passion and Eulogy of the Holy Martyrs Boris and Gleb,'" *Modern Language Review* 62, 3, 498-502.
1972   "The Tale of Boris and Gleb: A Creative Scribe and his Neglected Text," *Eastern Churches Review* IV, 1, 23-35.

Hadas, M.
1959 *Hellenistic Culture: Fusion and Diffusion.* New York.
Hannick, Ch.
1973 "Die Akrostichis in der kirchenslavischen liturgischen Dichtung," *Wiener Slavistisches Jahrbuch* 18, 151-162.
Hauck, K.
1950 "Geblütsheiligkeit" in *Liber Floridus. Mittellateinische Studien. Paul Lehmann zum 65. Geburtstag am 13. Juli 1949 gewidmet.* Ed. B. Bischoff and S. Brechter. Erzabtei St. Ottilien, 187-240.
Heimskringla
c.1223-1235 Ed. B. Adalbjarnarson. 3 vols. (Reykjavik: 1941-1951. Cited from *Heimskringla: History of the Kings of Norway by Snorri Sturluson.* Trans. L. Hollander. Austin, Texas, 1967.
Hellmann, M.
1967 "Das Herrscherbild in der sogenannten Nestorchronik" in *Speculum historiale. Festschrift für J. Spoerl.* Munich, 224-236.
Hollingsworth, P. A.
1987 "Rulership and Suffering in Kievan Rus' the Cult of Boris and Gleb." Unpublished Ph.D. diss., University of California, Berkeley.
Hruševʹskyj, M. S.
1895 "Ejmundova saga" in *Vyimky z žerel do istoryi Ukrainy-Rusy do polovyny XI veka*, Lʹviv, 109-22.
1913 *Istorija Ukrajini-Rusi.* 3rd ed. Lʹviv.
Hurwitz, E.
1980 *Prince Andrej Bogoljubskij: The Man and the Myth.* Studia Historica et Philologica XII, Sectio Slavica 4. Florence.
Ilʹin, N. N.
1957 *Letopisnaja statʹja 6523 goda i ee istočnik (opyt analiza).* Moscow.
Ingham, N. W.
1965 "Czech Hagiography in Kiev: The Prisoner Miracles of Boris and Gleb," *Die Welt der Slaven* 10, 166-82.
1968 "The Litany of Saints in 'Molitva sv. Troicě'" in *Studies Presented to Professor Roman Jakobson by his Students.* Ed. C. Gribble. Cambridge, Mass, 121-136.
1973 "The Sovereign as Martyr, East and West," *Slavic and East European Journal* 17, 1-17.
1983 "Genre Characteristics of the Kievan Lives of Princes in Slavic and East European Perspective" in *American Contributions to the Ninth International Congress of Slavists, Kiev. September 7-13, 1983. Volume II: Literature, Folklore and History.* Ed. P. Debreczeny Columbus, Ohio, 223-37.
1983[a] "Jedna opomenutá textová filiace a její význam pro studium církevněslovanské literatury," *Slavia* 52, 2, 161-163.
1984 "The Martyred Prince and the Question of Slavic Cultural Continuity" in *Medieval Russian Culture.* Ed. H. Birnbaum and M. S. Flier. California Slavic Studies 12. Berkeley-Los Angeles, 31-53.
1987[a] "Genre-Theory and Old Russian Literature," *Slavic and East European Journal* 31, 234-245.
1987[b] "Narrative Mode and Literary Kind in Old Russian: Some Theses" in *Gattung und Narration in den älteren slavischen Literaturen.* Ed. K.-D. Seemann. Berlin-Wiesbaden, 173-184.
Ivanov, V. V. and Toporov, V. N.
1965 *Slavjanskie jazykovye modelirujuščie semiotičeskie sistemy (drevnij period).* Moscow.
1974 *Issledovanija v oblasti slavjanskix drevnostej. Leksičeskie i frazeologičeskie voprosy rekonstrukcii tekstov.* Moscow.

Jacimirskij, A. I.
   1916   "Melkie zametki," *IORJaS* XXI, otd. 1, 192-201.
Jagić, I. V.
   1886   *Službenye Minei za sentjabr', oktjabr' i nojabr', v cerkovnoslavjanskom perevode po russkim rukopisjam 1093-1097 g.* St. Petersburg.
Jagoditsch, R.
   1957/58   "Zum Begriff der 'Gattungen' in der altrussischen Literatur," *Wiener Slavistisches Jahrbuch* 6, 113-37.
Jakobson, R. O.
   1940   [Olaf Jansen] "Český podíl na církevněslovanské kultuře" in *Co daly naše země Evropě a lidstvu.* Prague, 9-20.
   1944   "Some Russian Echoes of Czech Hagiography," *Annuaire de l'Institut de philologie et d'histoire orientales et slaves* VII, 155-80.
   1976   "Russkie otgoloski drevnečešskix pamjatnikov o Ljudmile" in *Kul'turnoe nasledie Drevnej Rusi. Istoki, stanovlenie, tradicii* [Festschrift for D. S. Lixačev]. Ed. M. V. Xrapčenko. Moscow, 46-50.
Janin, V. L.
   1970   *Aktovye pečati drevnej Rusi X-XV vv. I. Pečati X-načala XIII v.* Moscow.
   1974   "Cerkov' Borisa i Gleba v Novgorodskom detince (O novgorodskom istočnike 'Žitija Aleksandra Nevskogo)" in *Kul'tura srednevekovoj Rusi.* Leningrad, 88-93.
Kaiser, D. H.
   1980   *The Growth of the Law in Medieval Russia.* Princeton.
Kantor, M.
   1983   *Medieval Slavic Lives of Saints and Princes.* Michigan Slavic Translations 5. Ann Arbor.
Karger, M. K.
   1952   "K istorii kievskogo zodčestva XI v. Xram-mavzolej Borisa i Gleba v Vyšgorode," *Sovetskaja arxeologija* XVI, 77-99.
   1958-1961   *Drevnij Kiev.* 2 vols. Moscow-Leningrad.
   1964   *Zodčestvo drevnego Smolenska (XII-XIII vv.)* Leningrad.
Keller, F.
   1973   "Das Kontakion aus der ersten Služba für Boris und Gleb" in *Schweizerische Beiträge zum VII.Internationalen Slavistenkongress in Warschau. August 1973.* Ed. P. Brang, H. Jaksche and H. Schroeder. Slavica Helvetica. Lucerne, 65–74.
Kemp, E. W.
   1948   *Canonization and Authority in the Western Church.* London.
Ključevskij, V. O.
   1871   *Drevnerusskie žitija svjatyx kak istoričeskij istočnik.* Moscow.
Komarovič, V. L.
   1960   "Kul't roda i zemli v knjažeskoj srede XI-XIII vv.," *TODRL* XVI, 84-104.
Kondakov, N. P.
   1896   *Russkie klady. Issledovanie drevnostej velikoknjažeskogo perioda.* St. Petersburg.
Korzuxina, G. F.
   1954   *Russkie klady IX-XIII vv.* Moscow-Leningrad.
Kotljarevskij, A. A.
   1868   *O pogrebal'nyx obyčajax jazyčeskix slavjan.* Moscow.
Králík, O.
   1961   "Nové prace o Povesti vremenných let," *Československá rusistika* 3, 173-179.
   1963   "Povest' vremennyx let i legenda Kristiana o sv. Vjačeslave i Ljudmile," *TODRL* XIX, 177-207.
   1967   "Vztah Povesti vremenných let k legendě o Borisu a Glebovi," *Československá rusistika* 12, 99-102.

Krugovoj, G.
1973 "A Motif from the Old Russian *Vita Sanctorum* in Arthurian Romance," *Canadian Slavonic Papers* 15, 351-74.

Krumbacher, K.
1897 *Geschichte der byzantinischen Litteratur von Justinian bis zum Ende des oströmischen Reiches (527-1453)*. 2nd ed. Munich.

Kuza, A. V.
1978 "'Povest' o knjaze Jaroslave i o mužax novgorodskix'" in *Drevnjaja Rus' i slavjane*. Ed. T. V. Nikolaeva. Moscow, 233-239.

Kuz'min, A. G.
1977 *Načal'nye ètapy drevnerusskogo letopisanija*. Moscow.

Labyncev, Ju. A.
1985 "Ob odnoj belorussko-pol'skoj dramatičeskoj i grafičeskoj interpretacii XVII vv. sjužeta o Borise i Glebe," *TODRL* XXXVIII, 267-80.

Lammers, W.
1961 *Geschichtsdenken und Geschichtsbild im Mittelalter. Ausgewählte Aufsätze und Arbeiten aus den Jahren 1933 bis 1959*. Darmstadt.

Leclercq, J.
1962 *The Love of Learning and the Desire for God*. Trans. Catharine Misrahi. New York.

Lenhoff, G.
1982 "The Aesthetic Function and Medieval Russian Culture" in *The Structure of the Literary Process: Studies Dedicated to the Memory of Felix Vodička*. Ed. M. Červenka, P. Steiner, R. Vroon, 321-40.
1983 "Liturgical Poetry in Medieval Rus'," *Scando-Slavica* 29, 21-43.
1984 "Toward a Theory of Protogenres in Medieval Russian Letters," *The Russian Review* 43, 31-54.
1986 "The Ordering of Old Russian Narrative: *Po Rjadu* Versus *Nekako i Smutno*," in *Studia Slavica Mediaevalia et Humanistica. Riccardo Picchio dicata*. Ed. M. Collucci, G. Dell'Agata and H. Goldblatt. Florence, 442-452.
1987[a] "Categories of Medieval Russian Writing," *Slavic and East European Journal* 31, 259-271.
1987[b] "Problems of Medieval Narrative Typology. The Exemplum" in *Gattung und Narration in den älteren slavischen Literaturen*. Ed. K.-D. Seemann. Berlin-Wiesbaden, 109-118.

Lesjučevskij, V. I.
1946 "Vyšgorodskij kul't Borisa i Gleba v pamjatnikax iskusstva," *Sovetskaja arxeologija* VIII, 225-47.

Levickij, N.
1890 "Neskol'ko slov po povodu zametki prof. Sobolevskogo," *Xristianskoe čtenie* 2, 677-688.

Lexikon *Lexikon des Mittelalters*. Ed. Robert-Henri Bautier.
1981- Munich.

Lilienfeld, F. von
1957 "Die ältesten russischen Heiligenlegenden. Studien zu den Anfängen der russischen Hagiographie und ihr Verhältnis zum byzantinischen Beispiel" in *Aus der byzantinistischen Arbeit der Deutschen Demokratischen Republik I*. Ed. J. Irmscher. Berliner byzantinistische Arbeiten, 5. Berlin, 237-71.

Lixačev, D. S,
1950 "'Povest' vremennyx let' (Istoriko-literaturnyj očerk)," *Povest' vremennyx let. Čast' vtoraja. Priloženija*. Ed. V. P. Adrianova-Peretc. Moscow-Leningrad.
1954 "Nekotorye voprosy ideologii feodalov v literature XI-XIII vekov," *TODRL* X, 76-91.
1963 "Sistema literaturnyx žanrov drevnej Rusi" in *Slavjanskie literatury. V Meždunarodnyj s"ezd slavistov. Doklady sovetskoj delegacii*. Moscow, 47-70.

1968 "Drevneslavjanskie literatury kak sistema" in *VI Meždunarodnyj s"ezd slavistov. Doklady sovetskoj delegacii.* Moscow, 5-48.
1970 *Čelovek v literature drevnej Rusi.* Moscow.
1979 *Poètika drevnerusskoj literatury.* 3rd ed. M.
1983 *Tekstologija. Na materiale russkoj literatury X–XVII vekov.* 2nd ed. Leningrad.

Lixačev, N. P.
1907 *Licevoe žitie svjatyx blagovernyx knjazej russkix Borisa i Gleba po rukopisi konca XV stoletija.* Pamjatniki drevnej pis'mennosti i iskusstva, CXXIV. St. Petersburg.

Ljaščenko, V. G.
1926 "'Eymundar Saga' i russkie letopisi," *Izvestija Akademii nauk SSSR* XX, ser. 6, 1061-1086.

Ljaskoronskij, V. G.
1913 "Kievskij Vyšgorod v udel'no-večevoe vremja," *Žurnal Ministerstva narodnogo prosvěščenija*, n.s. Čast' XLV, April, 199-235; May, 64-100; June, 335-385; August, 223-277; September, 67-127; November, 45-91; December, 217-295.

Loparev, X. M.
1894 *Slovo poxval'noe na perenesenie moščej svv. Borisa i Gleba.* Pamjatniki drevnej pis'mennosti i iskusstva, XCVIII. St. Petersburg.
1910 "Vizantijskie žitija svjatyx VIII-IX vekov," *Vizantijskij vremennik*, 17, 1-224; 18 (1911), 1-47 and 19 (1912), 1-151.

Lotman, Ju. M. and Uspenskij, B. A.
1984 *The Semiotics of Russian Culture.* Ed. Ann Shukman. Michigan Slavic Contributions, 12. Ann Arbor.

Lunt, H.
1984 "On Editing Early Slavic Manuscripts: the Case of the Codex Suprasliensis, the Mstislav Gospel, and the Banica Gospel," *International Journal of Slavic Linguistics and Poetics* 30, 7-76.

Lur'e, Ja. S.
1985 "Genealogičeskaja sxema letopisej XI-XVI vv., vključennyx v 'Slovar' knižnikov i knižnosti Drevnej Rusi'," *TODRL* XL, 190-205.

Maczko, S.
1975 "Boris and Gleb: Saintly Princes or Princely Saints?" *Russian History* II, 1, 68-80.

Makarij
1869 *Velikie Minei Četii. Sentjabr'. Dni 14-24.* Pamjatniki slavjanorusskoj pis'mennosti. Izd. Arxeografičeskoju komissieju. St. Petersburg.

Manikovskij, F.
1890 *Vyšgorod i ego svjatynja.* 2nd ed. Kiev.

Mansikka, V.
1913 *Žitie Aleksandra Nevskogo. Razbor redakcij i tekst.* Pamjatniki drevnej pis'mennosti i iskusstva, CLXXX. St. Petersburg. Cited from the reprint (Leipzig, 1984).

Michell, R. and Forbes, N. (trans.)
1970 *The Chronicle of Novgorod: 1016-1471.* New York.

Miloradovič, G. A.
1889 *Opisanie černigovskix soborov Spaso-preobraženskogo i Borisoglebskogo.* Černigov.

Moszyński, K.
1934-39 *Kultura ludowa Słowian.* 2 vols. Cracow.

Müller, L.
1954-62 "Studien zur altrussischen Legende der Heiligen Boris und Gleb," *ZSPh* 23 (1954), 60-77; 25 (1956), 329-63; 27 (1959), 274-322; 30 (1962), 14-44.
1954 "Die nicht-hagiographische Quelle der Chronik-Erzählung von der Ermordung der Brüder Boris und Gleb und von der Bestrafung ihres Mörders durch Jaroslav" in *Festschrift für Dmytro Čyževskyj zum 60. Geburtstag am 23. März 1954.* Berlin-Wiesbaden, 196-217.

1956ᵃ "Die Urform der altrussischen Erzählung über Boris und Gleb" in *Vorträge auf der Berliner Slavistentagung (11.-13. November 1954)*. Berlin, 190-94.

1956ᵇ "Zur Rekonstruktion des 'Načal'nyj svod' der altrussischen Chronik aufgrund des 'Skazanie über die Ermordung der Heiligen Boris und Gleb" in *Festschrift für Max Vasmer zum 70.Geburtstag am 26. Februar 1956*. Ed. M. Woltner and H. Bräuer. Berlin-Wiesbaden, 341-48.

1963 "Neuere Forschungen über das Leben und die kultische Verehrung der Heiligen Boris und Gleb" in *Opera Slavica IV, Slawistische Studien zum V. Internationalen Slawistenkongress in Sofia 1963*. Göttingen, 295-317.

1967 *Die altrussischen hagiographischen Erzählungen und liturgischen Dichtungen über die Heiligen Boris und Gleb* [from Abramovič, 1916, with a new introduction, VII-XXIV].

Mur'janov, M. F.
   1981 "Iz nabljudenija nad strukturoj služebnyx minej" in *Problemy strukturnoj lingvistiki 1979*, Moscow, 263-278.

Nasonov, A. N.
   1969 *Istorija russkogo letopisanija XI-načala XVIII vekov*. Moscow.

Niederle, (Niderle), L.
   1924 *Byt i kul'tura drevnix slavjan*. Prague.

Nikolaeva, T. V.
   1968 *Russkaja melkaja plastika*. Moscow.

Nikol'skij, K.
   1900 *Posobie k izučeniju Ustava bogoslǔženija Pravoslavnoj cerkvi*. 6th ed. St. Petersburg.

Nikol'skij, N. K.
   1896 *Materialy dlja istorii ispravlenija boguslužebnyx knig*. Pamjatniki drevnej pis'mennosti i iskusstva, CXV. St. Petersburg.
   1906 *Materialy dlja povremennogo spiska russkix pisatelej i ix sočinenij (XI-XII v.)*. St. Petersburg.
   1907 "Proložnoe skazanie ob osvjaščenii cerkvi sv. Borisa i Gleba i perenesenii ix grobov iz Vyšgoroda na Smjadinu v 1191 godu," *Materialy dlja istorii drevne-russkoj duxovnoj pis'mennosti*. in *IORJaS* LXXXII, no. 6, 114-15.
   1909 *Legenda mantuanskogo episkopa Gumpol'da o sv. Vjačeslave češskom v slavjanorusskom preloženii*. Pamjatniki drevnerusskoj pis'mennosti i iskusstva, CLXXIV.

NPL
   1950 *Novgorodskaja pervaja letopis'*. Ed. A. S. Nasonov. Moscow.

Obolensky, D.
   1974 "The Cult of St. Demetrius of Thessaloniki in the History of Byzantine-Slav Relations," *Balkan Studies* 15, 3-20.

Odincov, N.
   1881 *Porjadok obščestvennogo i častnogo bogosluženija v drevnej Rossii do XVI veka*. St. Petersburg.

Orlov, A. S.
   1896 *Biblioteka Moskovskoj sinodal'noj tipografii. Čast' pervaja. Rukopisi. Vypusk pervyj: Sborniki*. Moscow.

Orlovskij, I.
   1909 "Borisoglebskij monastyr'" v Smolenske na Smjadyni i raskopki ego razvalin," *Smolenskaja starina*, vyp. 1, č. 1, 195-312.

Ostrowski, D.
   1981 "Textual Criticism and the *Povest' vremennyx let*: Some Theoretical Considerations," *Harvard Ukrainian Studies* V, 1, 11-31.

Pekař, J.
   1906 *Die Wenzels- und Ludmila-Legenden und die Echtheit Christians*. Prague.

Philipp, W.
   1940 *Ansätze zum geschichtlichen und politischen Denken im Kiewer Russland*. Breslau.

Picchio, R.
1963 "A proposito della Slavia ortodossa e della comunità linguistica slava ecclesiastica," *Ricerche Slavistiche* 11, 105-27.
1973 "Models and Patterns in the Literary Tradition of Medieval Orthodox Slavdom," *American Contributions to the Seventh International Congress of Slavists. Warsaw. August 21-27, 1973. Volume II Literature and Folklore*. Ed. V. Terras. The Hague-Paris, 439-67.
1977 "The Function of Biblical Thematic Clues in the Literary Code of 'Slavia Orthodoxa'," *Slavica Hierosolymitana* 1, 1-31.
1984[a] "The Impact of Ecclesiastic Culture on Old Russian Literary Techniques," *Medieval Russian Culture*. Ed. H. Birnbaum and M. S. Flier. California Slavic Studies 12. Berkeley-Los Angeles, 247-279.
1984[b] "Guidelines for a Comparative Study of the Language Question among the Slavs," *Aspects of the Slavic Language Question*, I. Ed. R. Picchio and Harvey Goldblatt. Yale Russian and East European Publications, 4-a. New Haven, 1-42.
Pisarev. S. P.
1897 "Bylo li perenesenie moščej sv. mučenikov Borisa i Gleba iz Vyšgoroda v Smolensk na Smjadyn'," *Smolenskie eparxial'nie vedomosti*, no. 8, 452-68; no. 9, 523-31; no. 10, 584-91; no. 11, 632-41; no. 12, 681-87.
Podskalsky, G.
1982 *Christentum und theologische Literatur in der Kiever Rus' (988-1237)*. Munich.
Pogodin, M. P.
1856 *Issledovanija, zamečanija i lekcii*. Moscow.
Poppe, A.
1965 "Chronologia utworów Nestora hagiografa," *Slavia Orientalis* 14, 3, 287-305.
1966 "O roli ikonografičeskix izobraženij v izučenii literaturnyx proizvedenij o Borise i Glebe," *TODRL* XXII, 24-45.
1966[a] "Predanie o Borise i Glebe v drevnerusskoj pis'mennosti XI-načala XII vv.," *Slavjanskaja filologija* 8, 55-57.
1968 *Państwo i kościół na Rusi w XI w.* Warsaw.
1969 "Opowieść o męczeństwie i cudach Borysa i Gleba," *Slavia Orientalis* 18, 267-292; 359-382.
1973 "O vremeni zaroždenija kul'ta Borisa i Gleba," *Russia Mediaevalis* 1, 6-29.
1981 "La naissance du culte de Boris et Gleb," *Cahiers de civilisation médiévale* XXIV, 29-53.
Presnjakov, A.
1909 *Knjažoe pravo v Drevnej Rusi. Očerki po istorii X-XII stoletij*. in *Zapiski Istoriko-Filologičeskogo Fakul'teta Sanktpeterburgskogo universiteta*, XC.
Priselkov, M. D.
1913 *Očerki po cerkovno-političeskoj istorii Kievskoi Rusi X-XIII vv*. St. Petersburg.
1923 "Bor'ba dvux mirovozrenij" in *Rossija i zapad. Istoričeskij sbornik*. Ed. A. Ja. Zaozerskij. Vol.I. St. Petersburg, 36-56.
Pritsak O.
1981 *The Origin of Rus'. Volume One: Old Scandinavian Sources Other than the Sagas*. Cambridge, Mass.
1985 "Die Anfänge der altnordischen Saga: Die Perspektive eines Historikers" in *The Sixth International Saga Conference Workshop Papers*, II. Copenhagen, 170-211.
Prochazka, H. Y.
1987 "Warrior Idols or Idle Warriors? On the Cult of Saints Boris and Gleb as Reflected in the Old Russian Military Accounts," *The Slavonic and East European Review* 65, 4, 505-516.

PSRL
1851 *PSRL. Tom. V. Pskovskie i Sofijskie letopisi.* St. Petersburg.
1908 *PSRL. Tom II: Ipat'evskaja letopis'.* St. Petersburg.
1926 *PSRL. Tom 1: Lavrent'evskaja letopis', vyp. 1: Povest' vremennyx let.* 2nd. ed. Leningrad.
PVL
1950 *Povest' vremennyx let. Čast' pervaja.* Ed. V. P. Adrianova-Peretc. Moscow-Leningrad.
Rančin, A. M.
1987 "K voprosu o tekstologii Borisoglebskogo cikla," *Vestnik Moskovskogo universiteta, Serija 9. Filologija*, 1, 73-80.
Reisman, E.
1978 "The Cult of Boris and Gleb: Remnant of a Varangian Tradition?" *The Russian Review* 27, 2, 141-57.
Revelli, G.
1977-1979 "Arxeografičeskie svedenija o neizvestnyx rukopisjax 'Skazanija o Borise i Glebe,'" *Ricerche slavistiche* XXIV-XXVI, 11-21.
1987 *Boris e Gleb. Due protagonisti del Medioevo russo.* Pubblicazioni dell' Istituto di Lingue e Letterature Straniere Moderne. Sezione di Slavistica. Facoltà di Lettere e Filosofia. Università di Genova. Abano Terme.
Rogov, A. I.
1970 *Skazanija o načale češskogo gosudarstva v drevnerusskoj pis'mennosti.* Moscow.
Rothe, H.
1981 "Kontakien auf russische Heilige[n] im altrussischen Kondakar," *Byzantine Studies/ Études byzantines* vols. 8, 11, 12 (1981, 1984, 1985), 333-341.
Rybakov, B. A.
1964 *Russkie datirovannye nadpisi XI-XIV vv.* Moscow.
1965 "Jazyčeskaja simvolika russkix ukrašenij XII v." in *Tezisy dokladov sovetskoj delegacii na Meždunarodnom kongresse slavjanskoj arxeologii (Sentjabr' 1965 g.).* Moscow, 64-73.
1981 *Jazyčestvo drevnix slavjan.* Moscow.
1982 *Kievskaja Rus' i russkie knjažestva XII-XIII vv.* Moscow.
1987 *Jazyčestvo Drevnej Rusi.* Moscow.
Rydzevskaja, E. A.
1978 *Drevnjaja Rus' i Skandinavija v IX-XIV vv. Drevnejšie gosudarstva na territorii SSSR.* Materialy i issledovanija, no. 2. Moscow.
Šajkin, A. A.
1986 "Svjatopolk, Boris i Gleb," in *Literatura Drevnej Rusi*, ed. N. I. Prokof'ev. Moscow, 41-47.
Šaxmatov, A. A.
1908 *Razyskanija o drevnejšix russkix letopisnyx svodax.* St. Petersburg.
1916 *Povest' vremennyx let.* St. Petersburg.
1940 "'Povest' vremennyx let' i ee istočniki," *TODRL* IV, 9-150.
Ščapov, Ja. N.
1976 *Drevnerusskie knjažeskie ustavy XI-XV vv.* Moscow.
Schmemann, A.
1961 *Vvedenie v liturgičeskoe bogoslovie.* Paris.
Schmidt, K.-D.
1948 *Germanische und germanisch-christliche Geschichtstheologie.* Göttingen. [Cited from Lammers, 1961: 76-90].
Schmidt, W.-H.
1975 *Gattungstheoretische Untersuchungen zur altrussischen Kriegserzählung (Zur Soziologie mittelalterlicher Gattungen).* Berlin-Wiesbaden.

1984 "Probleme der Soziologie literarischer Gattungen" in *Gattungsprobleme der älteren slavischen Literaturen (Berliner Fachtagung 1981)*. Ed. W.-H. Schmidt. Berlin-Wiesbaden, 291-310.

1987 "Funktionstheorie der altbulgarischen Literatur" in *Gattung und Narration in den älteren slavischen Literaturen*. Ed. K.-D. Seemann. Berlin-Wiesbaden, 185-205.

Schmidt, W.-H. and Seemann, K.-D.

1984 "Die Gattungsforschung und die älteren slavischen Literaturen" in *Gattungsprobleme der älteren slavischen Literaturen (Berliner Fachtagung 1981)*. Ed. W.-H. Schmidt. Berlin-Wiesbaden, 13-32.

1987 "Erzählen in den älteren slavischen Literaturen" in *Gattung und Narration in den älteren slavischen Literaturen*. Ed. K.-D. Seemann. Berlin-Wiesbaden, 1-25.

Sciacca, F.

1975 "The History of the Vyshgorod Cult of Boris and Gleb: A Reinterpretation of Its Origin and Development in the Eleventh Century." Unpublished Masters Essay, Columbia University.

1977 "Royal Farmers: A Folkloric Investigation into Pagan Origins of the Cult of Boris and Gleb," *Ulbandus Review* 1, 1977, 3-14.

1983 "The Kiev Cult of Boris and Gleb: the Bulgarian Connection" in *Proceedings of the Symposium on Slavic Cultures: Bulgarian Contributions to Slavic Cultures. An International Conference Dedicated to the Celebration of the Thirteen Hundredth Anniversary of the Founding of the Bulgarian State. Columbia University in the City of New York, November 14, 1980.* Sofia Press, 58-70.

1985 "The Cult of Boris and Gleb." Unpublished Ph.D. diss., Columbia University.

Seemann, K.-D.

1976 *Die altrussische Wallfahrtsliteratur. Theorie und Geschichte eines literarischen Genres.* Munich.

1984 "Thesen zum mittelalterlichen Literaturtypus und zur Gattungssystematik am Beispiel der altrussischen Literatur" in *Gattungsprobleme der älteren slavischen Literaturen (Berliner Fachtagung 1981)*. Ed. W.-H. Schmidt. Berlin-Wiesbaden, 277-90.

1987[a] "Genres and the Alterity of Old Russian Literature," *Slavic and East European Journal* 31, 2, 246-258.

1987[b] "Zum Verhältnis von Narration und Gattung im slavischen Mittelalter" in *Gattung und Narration in den älteren slavischen Literaturen*. Ed. K.-D. Seemann. Berlin-Wiesbaden, 207-221.

Septuagint

1851 *The Septuagint with Apochrypha: Greek and English.* Trans. Lancelot C. L. Brenton. London [cited from the reprint by Zonderan Publishing House, Grand Rapids, Michigan, 1970].

Serebrjanskij, N. I.

1910 "Žitie blag. knjazej Borisa i Gleba po rukopisi XV v. biblioteki Pskovo-Pečerskogo Monastyrja," *Trudy Pskovskogo Istoriko-Arxeologičeskogo komiteta. Pskovskaja starina.* Vol. 1. Pskov.

1915 *Drevne-russkie knjažeskie žitija (Obzor redakcij i teksty).* Moscow.

Seregina, N. S.

1991 "Iz istorii pevčeskix ciklov Borisu i Glebu," *TODRL* XLIII (forthcoming).

Sergij, Archimandrite

1875-1876 *Polnyj mesjaceslov vostoka.* 2 vols. Moscow.

Skazanie

1985 *Skazanie o Borise i Glebe. Vol. 1: Naučno-spravočnyj apparat izdanija. Vol. 2: Faksimil'noe vosproizvedenie žitijnyx povestej iz Sil'vestrovskogo sbornika (2ja polovina XIV v.).* Moscow.

Slovar'
　1975–　*Slovar' russkogo jazyka XI-XVII vv.* Moscow. 13+ vols.
Smirnov, S. I.
　1908　*Žitie prepodobnogo Daniila, perejaslavskogo čudotvorca.* Moscow.
Smirnova, E. S.
　1959　"Otraženie literaturnyx proizvedenij o Borise i Glebe v drevnerusskoj stankovoj živopisi," *TODRL* XV, 312-27.
Soboleva, L. S.
　1975　"Paremijnye čtenija Borisu i Glebu," *Voprosy istorii knižnoj kul'tury. Sbornik naučnyx trudov.* Vyp. 19. Novosibirsk, 104-123.
　1979[a]　"K voprosu ob èvoljucii minejnogo teksta, posvjaščennogo Borisu i Glebu" in *Sibirskaja arxeografija i istočnikovedenie.* Novosibirsk, 5-12.
　1979[b]　"Osobennosti vozniknovenija i razvitija žanra istoričeskix paremij Borisu i Glebu" in *Problemy literaturnyx žanrov. Materialy tret'ej naučnoj konferencii 6 fevralja 1979 goda.* Tomsk, 27-28.
　1981　"Istoričeskie paremii Borisu i Glebu—maloizučennyj pamjatnik Kievskoj Rusi." Unpublished Ph.D. diss., Sibirskoe otdelenie AN SSR, Institut istorii, filologii i filosofii.
Sobolevskij, A. I.
　1890　"'Pamjat'' i poxvala' sv. Vladimiru i 'Skazanie' o svv. Borise i Glebe," *Xristianskoe čtenie* 5-6, 791-804.
　1916　"Kogda napisano Nestorovo 'Čtenie' o svv. Borise i Glebe?" *IORJaS* XXI, 2, 206-8.
Solov'ev, S. M.
　1851-79　*Istorija Rossii s drevnejšix vremen*, 29 vols. rpt. 15 vols. Moscow, 1959-66.
Spasskij, F. G.
　1951　*Russkoe liturgičeskoe tvorčestvo (po sovremennym minejam).* Paris.
Sreznevskij, I. I.
　1853　"Drevnie žizneopisanija russkix knjazej X-XI vv.," *IORJaS*, II, 125-140.
　1860　*Skazanija o svjatyx Borise i Glebe. Sil'vestrovskij spisok XIV veka.* St. Petersburg, with introduction, I-XXVI.
　1863[a]　"Drevnij russkij kalendar' po mesjačnym minejam XI-XIII v.," *Xristianskie drevnosti i arxeologija*, III, 2-22.
　1863[b]　"Drevnie izobraženija svjatyx knjazej Borisa i Gleba," *Xristjanskie drevnosti i arxeologija* IX, 67-80.
　1882　*Drevnie pamjatniki russkogo pis'ma i jazyka (X-XIV vv.). Obščee povremennoe obozrenie.* St. Petersburg.
　1893-1912　*Materialy dlja slovarja drevnerusskogo jazyka.* 3 vols. St. Petersburg.
Stender-Petersen, A.
　1953　"Jaroslav und die Väringer," in *Varangica.* Arhus, 115-138.
Stepennaja kniga
　1908　*PSRL. Tom 21, č. 1: Kniga Stepennaja carskogo rodoslovija.* St. Petersburg.
Svodnyj katalog
　1984　*Svodnyj katalog slavjano-russkix rukopisnyx knig, xranjajuščixsja v SSSR (XI-XIII vv.).* Ed. S. O. Šmidt, et. al. Moscow.
Temnikovskij, E.
　1904　"K voprosu o kanonizacii svjatyx," *Vremennik Demidovskogo juridičeskogo liceja*, kn. 88, 1-75.
Thietmar, Bishop of Merseburg
　1012-1018　*Thietmari Merseburgensis Episcopi Chronicon/Thietmar von Merseburg: Chronik.* Ed. and trans. R. Holtzmann and W. Trillmich. Ausgewählte Quellen zur deutschen Geschichte des Mittelalters 9. Darmstadt, 1957.
Titov, A. A. (ed.)
　1893　"Žitie sv. Leontija, Episkopa rostovskogo." *ČOIDR*, 4, Otd. 1, 1-35.

Tixonravov, N. S.
1862 "Slova i poučenija, napravlennye protiv jazyčeskix verovanij i obrjadov," *Letopisi russkoj literatury i drevnosti*, IV, č. 3, 83-112.
1892 (ed.) *Drevnie žitija prepodobnogo Sergija Radonežskogo*. Moscow.
Tokarev, S. A.
1957 *Religioznye verovanija vostočnoslavjanskix narodov XIX-načala XX v*. Moscow.
Toporov, V. N.
1985 "Ponjatie svjatosti v Drevnej Rusi (Sv. Boris i Gleb)" in *Slavic Linguistics, Poetics, Cultural History. In Honor of Henrik Birnbaum on his Sixtieth Birthday, 13 December 1985*. Ed. M. S. Flier and D. S. Worth [*International Journal of Slavic Linguistics and Poetics*, 31-32], 451-472.
Troickij, I. M.
1889 *Skazanie vkratce o gorodax i stranax ot Antioxii do Ierusalima, a takže Sirii, Finiki i o svjatyx mestax v Palestine, konca XII veka*. In *Pravoslavnyj Palestinskij sbornik* VIII, 2, 23.
Tvorogov, O. V.
1974 "Povest' vremennyx let i Xronograf po velikomu izloženiju," *TODRL* XXVIII, 99-113.
Tuptalo, D. [Metropolitan Dimitrij Rostovskij]
1705 *Četii Minei*, 12 vols. Rpt., Moscow, 1855 and 1908 under the title *Žitija svjatyx, na russkom jazyke*. Ed. and annotated under the direction of Archimandrite Panteleimon. Kniga devjataja, 77-112.
Uspenskij, B. A.
1982 *Filologičeskie razyskanija v oblasti slavjanskix drevnostej (Relikty jazyčestva v vostočnoslavjanskom kul'te Nikolaja Mirlikijskogo)*. Moscow.
1983 *Jazykovaja situacija Kievskoj Rusi i ee značenie dlja istorii russkogo literaturnogo jazyka*. Moscow.
Uspenskij Sbornik
1971 *Uspenskij sbornik XII-XIII vv*. Ed. O. A. Knjazevskaja, V. G. Dem'janov and M. V. Ljapon. Moscow.
Vasil'ev, V.
1893 *Istorija kanonizacija russkix svjatyx*. Moscow.
Velimirovič, M.
1967 "The Influence of the Byzantine Chant on the Music of the Slavic Countries" in *Proceedings of the XIIIth International Congress of Byzantine Studies. Oxford 5-10 September 1966*. Ed. J. M. Hussey, D. Obolensky, S. Runciman. New York, 119-140.
Vernadsky, G. (trans.)
1969 *Medieval Russian Laws*. New York.
Vorob'eva, E. V. and Tic, A. A.
1974 "O datirovke Uspenskogo i Borisoglebskogo soborov v Černigove," *Sovetskaja arxeologija*, XXXVIII, 2, 98-111.
Voronin, N. N.
1957 "Anonimnoe skazanie o Borise i Glebe, ego vremja, stil' i avtor," *TODRL* XIII, 11-56.
1963 "Žitie Leontija Rostovskogo i vizantijsko-russkie otnošenija vtoroj poloviny XII v.," *Vizantijskij vremennik* XXIII, 23-46.
Voronin, N. N. and Žukovskaja, L. P.
1976 "K istorii smolenskoj literatury XII v." in *Kul'turnoe nasledie drevnej Rusi. Istoki, stanovlenie, tradicii* [Festschrift for D. S. Lixačev]. Ed. M. V. Xrapčenko. Moscow, 69-79.
Vries, J. de
1956 *Altgermanische Religionsgeschichte. Band I: Einleitung. Vorgeschichtliche Perioden. Religiöse Grundlagen des Lebens. Seelen- und Geisterglaube. Macht und Kraft. Das Heilige und die Kultformen*. Berlin.

Wellesz, E.
1962   *A History of Byzantine Music and Hymnography.* 2nd ed. London.
Wittgenstein, L.
1967   *Philosophische Untersuchungen/Philosophical Investigations* [a bilingual edition, cited in the translation of G. E. M. Anscombe]. Cambridge.
Worth, D. S.
1984   "Toward a Social History of Russian" in *Medieval Russian Culture.* Ed. H. Birnbaum and M. S. Flier. California Slavic Studies 12. Berkeley-Los Angeles, 227-246.
Xaruzina, V. N.
1906   "K voprosu o počitanii ognja u russkix krest'jan i inorodcev, s priloženiem programmy," *Ètnografičeskoe obozrenie* 18, nos. 3-4, 68-205.
Xolostenko, N. V.
1967   "Issledovanie Boriso-glebskogo sobora v Černigove," *Sovetskaja arxeologija* XXXI, 2, 188-210.
Xorošev, A. S.
1986   *Političeskaja istorija russkoj kanonizacii (XI-XVI vv.).* Moscow.
Xruščov, I. P.
1878   *O drevnerusskix istoričeskix povestjax i skazanijax. XI-XII stoletija.* Kiev.
Žukovskaja [Žukovs'ka], L. P.
1981   "Hipotezi j fakty pro davn'orus'ki pysemnist' do XII st." in *Literaturna spadščyna Kyjievskoji Rusi i ukrajins'ka literatura XVI-XVIII st..* Ed. O. V. Myšanyc. Kiev, 9-35.
1983   *Aprakos Mstislava velikogo.* Podgotovili L. P. Žukovskaja, L. A. Vladimirova, N. P. Pankratova. Moscow.
Žuravskij, B. P.
1985   "O nekotoryx zakonomernostjax knižnoj konstrukcii žitijnogo cikla o Borise i Glebe" in *Skazanie o Borise i Glebe. Vol. 1: Naučno-spravočnyj apparat izdanija.* Moscow, 104-149.

INDEX

Abel, son of Adam, murdered by his brother Cain (Gen. 4:1-16) 35, 87, 96, 106, 126, 127, 135, 136, 139
Abimelech, King of Shechem (Judges 9) 114, 119
Abraham, Patriarch (Gen. 12-26) 76, 133, 142
Abrahamse, D. 42
Abramovič, D. I. 38, 41, 43, 49, 51-53, 56, 60-62, 65, 68-70, 72, 75, 83-89, 93, 95, 97, 98, 131, 133, 136, 138
Adrian Pošexonskij, Saint (d. 1550 29
Adrianova-Peretc, V. P. 136
Afanas'ev, A. N. 37, 38, 40
Afanasij Nikitin, Tver' merchant who traveled to India (ca. 1466-1472) 26
Ahab, King of Israel (919-896 B. C.) 114, 115
Ajnalov, D. V. 15, 130, 131, 134, 137
akolouthia, see office
Aleksandr Jaroslavovič, Nevskij, Saint, Grand Prince of Vladimir (1252-1263) 131
Aleškovskij, M. X. 14, 42, 48, 49, 128, 129, 131, 133
Alexis, "the man of God," Saint (5th c.) 135
Alissandratos, J. 22, 133
Alpatov, M. V. 131
Al'ta, river 35, 53, 106, 108, 109, 132, 139
Ammann, A. M. 14, 49
ancestor worship, pagan Slavic 14, 37, 64, 83, 86, 98, 121, 127 (see also kinship)
Andrej Jur'evič, Bogoljubskij, Saint, Grand Prince of Vladimir (1157-1174) 130
Andrej of Smolensk, Saint, Prince (d. ca. 1390) 43
Anna of Kašin, Saint (d. 1368) 50
Antonij of the Caves, Saint (d. 1072/3) 24
apostrophe 96, 108, 113, 119 (see also mode)
Arkadij, Bishop of Novgorod (1156-1163) 56, 65, 67
ársael, power of certain Scandinavian kings to bring fertility, good fortune, etc. to their land 129 (see also charisma)
auctoritas 28, 77, 104
automelon, see hymnography, terms
Bamborschke, U. 18
Barbara, martyr (3rd or 4th c.) 85, 138

Bari 79
Basil, the Great, Saint (d. 79) 46
Batu (Batyj), Khan, leader of the Golden Horde (d. 1255) 53
Berlin School 9, 18, 23, 129-130
besknjaž'e, the absence of a prince 110-112
biography, 17, 24, 26, 27, 30, 40, 82, 86, 88, 90, 99, 124 (see also life)
bios, see life
Birkfellner, G. 63
Birnbaum, H. 9, 18, 140
blood revenge 36, 76, 77, 120, 127, 133, 139
Blud, Kievan general 118
bludjaščij ogon', see *ignis fatuus*
Bohemia 107, 140
Bolesław I, the Brave (Chrobry), King of Poland (992-1025) 12, 34, 106, 111, 112, 140
bonds, see lateral bonds, vertical bonds
Book of Degrees of the Imperial Genealogy, see *Stepennaja kniga*
Boris Vjačislavovič, Prince of Smolensk (d. 1078) 138
Boris (Roman) Vladimirovič, Saint, Prince (d. 1015) 7, 8, 11, 12, 20, 26, 54, 113, 118, 122-125; biographies of 79-100, 134-139; burial of 38, 39, 41-43, 129; canonization of 13-14, 38, 45-48; Christian ethical models and 120-121 (and *passim*); chronicle accounts of 102-108, 110, 111, 113, 139-142; cult of 16, 31, 39-41, 127, 130; offices for 56, 59-77, 131-133; pagan festivals and 128; posthumous miracles 39-41, 43-45, 47, 49, 51-52, 128; relations with Jaroslav 32-37; relics of 48-53, 126
Bosley, R. 134
bratoljubie, political principle whereby junior princes obey senior princes 74, 77, 134 (see also *philadelphia*)
Brjačislav Izjaslavovič, Prince of Polock (d. 1044) 34
brotherly love, see *bratoljubie, philadelphia*
Bugoslavskij, G. K. 56, 57, 67-70, 142
Bugoslavskij, S. A. 15, 79, 80, 88, 89, 130, 134, 137, 138
Bulgakov, M. P. (Metropolitan Makarij) 134
Bulgakov, S. V. 131, 138

INDEX

Bultmann, R. 18
Burislafr, Prince 33–34, 126 (see also *Eymundar Þáttr*)
Butkov, P. G. 134
Byock, J. 9
Byzantine church hierarchy 14; generic models 7, 17, 74, 77, 81, 90, 91, 99, 122–124
Byzantium 7, 17, 81, 116–117; liturgical tradition of 57, 63, 64, 72, 124; monasteries of 42
Cain, son of Adam, murderer of Abel (Gen. 4) 35, 36, 63, 71, 87, 96, 106, 117–119, 126, 127, 135, 137
calendars, saints', see *svjatcy*
canonization (*proslavlenie*) 12–14, 32, 38, 41, 44, 45, 47–50, 54, 78, 79, 95, 97, 98, 104, 123, 124, 128, 129, 139
Cathedral of the Holy Mother of God, see churches: Church of the Tithe, Kiev
Černigov 49, 52, 53, 73, 74, 130, 133
Černogubov, N. N. 131
Členov, A. M. 126
Chaloupecký, V. 134
charisma 48, 121, 141 (see also healing, miraculous)
Chase, F. 21
Cherniavsky, M. 13, 127
Christine of Tyre, Saint (4th c.) 60, 61, 69, 123, 131
chronicles: Chronicle of Hamartolus (9th century Greek monastic chronicle translated into Slavonic) 87; Kievan 101–121, 124–125, 131, 135, 139–142; *Drevnejšij svod* of 1039 103; *Načaľnyj svod* of 1093 103 (see also historiography, Lur'e, Primary Chronicle, Šaxmatov)
Church Council of 1547 45, 46
Church Council of 1549 45, 46
churches: Church of St. Basil, Vyšgorod 38–40, 42, 43, 46, 54, 95, 108, 127, 128, 137; Church of the Mother of God, Jaroslavl 50–51; Church of the Tithe (*Desjatinnaja cerkov'*, Cathedral of the Holy Mother of God), Kiev 92, 136
Cicero (M. Tullius) (d. 43) 101, 139
Čiževskij (Čyževskyj), D. 15, 26, 80, 90, 136
clan, see ancestor worship, *bratoljubie*, kinship
Cook, R. 33, 126
Constantine I, the Great, Saint, Emperor of Rome (324–337) 47, 118, 141
Constantine-Cyril of Thessalonica, Saint, apostle of the Slavs (d. 869) 27–29
Cross, S. H. 33–34, 126, 139–142
Čtenie o žitii i o pogublenii, see Lection
Cyrus and John, martyrs (d. ca. 303) 61, 62, 65
Dal', V. I. 40
David, Saint, see Gleb
David, Saint, King of Israel (ca. 1010–970 B.C.) 46, 114
David Igorevič, Prince of Volynsk (d. 1112) 138
David Svjatoslavovič, Prince of Černigov (d. 1123) 52, 53, 73, 74, 130
Delehaye, H. 91, 132, 133, 135
Demetrius, martyr (dates unknown) 62, 97, 138
Deržavin, A. 99
Desjatinnaja cerkov', Kiev see churches: Church of the Tithe
Dibelius, M. 11, 18, 126
Dionisij, Archimandrite of the Trinity-Sergius Laura 126
Dmitriev, L. A. 26, 29, 39, 40
Dmitrij Konstantinovič, Prince of Suzdal' and Nižegorod (d. 1383) 102
Dmitrij Tuptalo, Saint, Metropolitan of Rostov, hagiographer (d. 1709) 99
Dnepr, river 107, 139, 140
Drevnejšij svod of 1039, see chronicles, Kievan
družina, princes' guards, Kievan 86, 95, 104, 108, 110, 111, 137; Varangian 12, 33, 39, 40, 51, 105, 107, 109, 111, 139, 140
dvoeverie, see syncretism
dynastic model, see kinship
Ebbinghaus, A. 18
Elijah, the Prophet 40
encomiastic disposition 22 (see also eulogy)
enkolpion, pectoral reliquary cross 13–14, 130
enkomion, see eulogy
Ensslin, W. 116
Epifanij, the Wise (Premudrij), hagiographer, monk (d. before 1422) 91, 136
Eremin, I. P. 15, 127, 136, 137
etiquette, literary 17, 23, 125
eulogy 15, 22, 25, 72–76, 79, 88, 97, 98, 105, 108, 113, 119, 133
Eustace Placidus, Saint, legendary Roman general (date unknown) 92, 97
Eymundar Þáttr Hringssonar, a saga-like tale inserted in the lives of kings Olaf Tryggvason and Olaf Haraldsson in the *Flateyjarbók* 12, 33–34

Eymundr, son of King Hringr of Norway 12, 33–34
Fedor Rostislavovič, the Black (*Černyj*), Saint, Prince of Smolensk and Jaroslavl' (d. 1299) 50, 128
Fedotov, G. 13, 36, 138
Feodosij of the Caves, Saint (d. 1074) 11, 49, 60, 88, 89, 126, 129, 136
Feotikst, Bishop of Černigov 52, 73
Filippovskij, G. Ju. 42
fire worship, pagan Slavic 37–41
Flateyarbók, late 14th c. Icelandic manuscript containing the *Eymundar Þáttr* 33
Florja, B. A. 81
Forbes, N. 140
Formgeschichte critics 7, 18
Forschungsgruppe "Altere Slavische literaturen," see Berlin School)
Fotij, Metropolitan of Kiev and all Rus' (1408–1431) 139 (see also *Vladimirskij polixron* of 1421)
Fowler, A. 24
Fraehn, C. M. 37
Freydank, D. 81, 135
Frojanov, I. Ja. 110
Gardner, J. von 9, 131
Gebrauchskontext, institutional or traditional context of a medieval genre 19
General Menaion, see Menaion, General
genre: anomalies (*Unikate*) 20, 23; communicative model of 19; family resemblance theory of 18, 23, 24; genre-set 18; genre-system 14, 17, 80, 82, 103; modern vs. medieval 8, 14, 16–27, 30, 77, 80–82, 103–104, 126, 139; sovereign and vassal genres 103, 104, 125
George, martyr (d. ca. 303) 40, 62
George, Metropolitan of Kiev 14, 46, 49–51, 88, 129
Georgij, Boris' retainer 86, 95, 128, 132, 137
German, Hegumen of the Kievan Monastery of the Savior 49, 129
Gideon, judge of Israel, father of Abimelech (Judges 8:31) 114
Gleb Svjatoslavovič, Prince of Novgorod (d. 1078) 138
Gleb (David) Vladimirovič, Saint, Prince (d. 1015) 7, 8, 11, 12, 20, 26, 48, 54, 113, 118, 122–125; biographies of 79–100, 134–139; burial of 38, 39, 41–43, 127; canonization of 13–14, 38, 45–48; Christian ethical models and 120–121 (and *passim*); chronicle accounts of 102–108, 110, 111, 113, 139–142; cult of 16, 31, 39–41, 127, 130; offices for 56, 59–77, 131–133; pagan festivals and 128; posthumous miracles 39–41, 43–45, 47, 49, 51–53, 127, 128; relations with Jaroslav 32–37, 126; relics of 48–53, 115
Golubinskij, E. E. 15, 45–47, 50, 60, 128, 133, 134
Golubovskij, P. V. 58, 65, 67, 68, 133, 142
Gorskij, A. and Nevostruev, K. 44
Gregory of Nazianzus, Saint (d. 389) 37
Gregory of Tours, Saint, Bishop, chronicler (d. 594) 101, 139
Grekov, B. D. 36
Grodno 53
Gusev, P. L. 131
Hadas, M. 117
hagiography, see life
Hálfdan, "Whiteleg", King of Norway (d. 860) 129
Hamartolus, see chronicles
Hannick, Ch. 9, 63, 131
Hauck, K. 141
healing, miraculous 14, 40, 43–45, 48, 54, 61, 64, 65, 69, 97–98, 121, 123, 124, 130, 132, 133, 138, 141, 142
Heimskringla, history of the Kings of Norway by Snorri Sturluson (d. 1241) 34, 39, 129, 140
heirmos, see hymnography, terms
Helena, Saint, Empress of Rome, mother of Constantine I (d. ca. 330) 47
Hellmann, Manfred 141
historiography 81, 83, 101–121, 124–125 (see also chronicles)
Hollingsworth, P. 9
homily 71–75, 96, 97, 108, 109, 113, 116, 117, 122, 124
homologētēs, a saint who does not sacrifice his or her life 64
Hruševs'ky, M. S. 33
Hurwitz, E. 130
hymnography, terms: automelon 64, 65; heirmos 57, 58, 63; hypakoe 57; kanon 57–63, 66–71, 85, 131; kontakion 20, 25, 57, 58, 60, 61, 64, 65, 69, 132; ode, segment of a saint's kanon 59, 63, 66; oikos 57, 60, 61, 64, 69, 132; photogogikon 69, 70; prosomoion 64,

INDEX

132; sedalen (Gr. *kathisma*) 57, 60, 61, 69, 132; sticheron 25, 56, 57, 60, 62, 63, 65, 68–71, 131; *stopica* 20; theotokion 63, 69; troparion, hymn for a saint 20, 25, 57, 58, 60, 70, 71, 131; troparion, stanza 57, 63
Hypatian Chronicle 46, 72, 102, 104, 105–107, 114, 115, 118, 119, 129, 130
Ignatij of Rostov, Saint, Bishop (d. 1288) 78, 134
ignis fatuus (will-o'-the-wisp) 38
Igor' Svjatoslavovič, Prince of Novgorod-Severskij (d. 1202) 23
Ilarion, Metropolitan of Kiev (1051–1054) 48
Il'in, N. N. 12–14, 33, 34, 39, 46, 81, 103, 104, 126, 129, 134, 136
imitatio Christi 91
Ingham, N. 9, 13, 15, 17, 18, 22–24, 27, 28, 36, 81, 82, 89–91, 135–139
Ingigerd (Irene), daughter of Olaf Skotkonung of Sweden, wife of Kievan Grand Prince Jaroslav Vladimirovič 112, 140; depicted under the name of Ingigerðr in the *Eymundar Þáttr* 33, 34
Innokentij, monk, disciple of St. Pafnutij of Borovsk 58
Ioann and Loggin of Jarenga, Saints (exact dates unknown; relics of Ioann first translated in 1544) 29
Isaiah, Prophet: citations from Book of 83, 86, 116, 117, 133, 141
isocolic principle, see Picchio
Israel 114, 117
Israelites 83
Izjaslav Davidovič, son of David Svjatoslavovič of Černigov, twice Grand Prince of Kiev (d. 1161) 74
Izjaslav Jaroslavovič, Grand Prince of Kiev (d. 1078) 13, 48, 49, 51, 72, 128, 129, 130, 136, 138
Izjaslav Vladimirovič, Prince of Polock (d. 1001) 84
Jacob, son of Isaac, father of Joseph 93
Jagoditsch, R. 17, 23
Jakobson, R. O. 81
Janin, V. L. 131
Jarislafr, Prince 33–34 (see also *Eymundar Þáttr*)
Jaropolk Svjatoslavovič, Grand Prince of Kiev, murdered by his brother Vladimir I in 980 32, 34, 83, 84, 118, 126, 134
Jaroslav Vladimirovič, the Wise (Mudryj), Grand Prince of Kiev (d. 1054) 12, 13, 15, 32–39, 41–43, 45, 48, 52–54, 63, 74, 76, 77, 80, 82, 84, 86, 87, 89, 91, 95, 98, 99, 103, 105–107, 109–113, 118, 120, 123, 124, 126, 128, 129, 133–136, 139, 140
Jaroslavl' 50, 51, 128
John I, Metropolitan of Kiev (1019–1035) 12, 14, 39, 41, 43, 45, 47, 50, 54; office of 56–65, 69, 70, 96, 123, 124, 127, 131
John II, Prodromos, Metropolitan of Kiev (1076–1089) 12, 14, 79
John Chrysostom, Saint (d. 407) 37
Joseph, son of Jacob, hated by his jealous brothers (Gen. 37:4) 93
Judas Iscariot, disciple who betrayed Christ 95
Julian the Apostate (Flavius Claudius Julianus), Emperor of Rome (361–363), known for his persecution of Christians 87, 135
Kaiser, D. 36
kanon, see hymnography, terms
Kantor, M. 28, 127, 128–130, 134, 135, 138
Karger, M. K. 14, 42, 131
Kasinec, E. 9
kathisma, see hymnography, terms: sedalen
Keller, F. 61, 62, 65
Kidekša (in Suzdal') 53
Kiev, city of 106, 108, 109, 111, 112, 124, 137, 140, 141 (see also Kievan Rus')
Kievan Cave Monastery, see monasteries
Kievan Cave Patericon 24, 39, 138
Kievan Rus', principality of 12, 14, 16, 29, 32, 33, 41, 42, 48, 52, 53, 54, 65, 67, 68, 72, 77, 79, 80, 82, 87, 94, 98, 109, 113, 114, 117, 120, 122, 125, 129, 136, 137, 142
Kievan Rus'ian: bookmen 62, 63, 81, 103, 140; church protocol 47; citizens of Kievan Rus' 11, 13, 17, 31, 32, 37, 40, 42, 66, 67, 98, 118, 122; chronicles (see chronicles, Kievan); court protocol 82; cult of Boris and Gleb 8, 47, 53, 122, 126; pagan traditions 13, 36–41; historical period (882–1240) 24, 29, 30, 101; political situation 36, 103, 104, 124, 125; princes 34, 42, 54, 82, 129; saints' lives (see life); scriptoria 30; throne 12, 34, 51, 54, 84, 85, 95, 105, 106, 109, 110–113, 118; writings 17, 39, 80, 81, 103, 122, 136

Kievo-Pečerskij paterik, see Kiev Cave Patericon
kinship 36-38, 54, 73, 91, 92, 96, 98, 113, 120, 127, 129, 139
Kirill of Turov, Saint, Bishop (2nd half of the 12th c.) 37, 127
Kleimola, A. 9
Kloss, B. M. 134
Ključevskij, V. O. 21, 44, 58, 90
Komarovič, V. L. 37
Königsheil, see charisma
Konstantin, Rostov priest sent to investigate the miracles of Fedor Rostislavovič Černyj 50
Konstantin Vsevolodovič, Prince, son of Grand Prince Vsevolod Jurevič III (d. 1218) 37
Konstantin Vsevolodovič, Saint, Prince of Jaroslavl' (died during the Mongol invasion, exact date unknown) 51, 58
kontakion, see hymnography, terms
Kostroma 102
Krumbacher, K. 22, 72
Kuza, A. V. 140
Kuz'min, A. G. 136
Lamech, descendant of Cain (Gen. 4:18-24) 35, 87, 117, 118, 127, 135
lateral bonds 24-27, 30, 77, 122 (see also protogenre, vertical bonds)
Laurentian Chronicle 12, 32, 34, 37, 38, 41, 46-48, 51, 72, 79, 80, 83, 84, 88, 97, 102-114, 118, 119, 124, 125, 137, 139, 140
law: divine 117; Kievan 36; Mosaic 113, 117, 125
lawlessess (*bezakon'e*) 114-118
Lazar' of Perejaslavl', Bishop 52, 79
Leclercq, J. 64
Lection 15, 16, 38-41, 43, 47, 48, 51, 79, 82, 88-99, 104, 113, 120, 124, 130, 131, 135-139
Lenhoff, G. 21, 24, 91
Leontij of Rostov, Saint, Bishop (d. ca. 1070) 42, 58, 90
Lesjučevskij, V. I. 13, 130, 131, 133
letopis', see chronicles, historiography
life, biography of a saint 15-18, 21-30, 40, 42, 49-51, 58, 78-100, 103, 104, 122-125
Lilienfeld, F. von 135, 137
literary types (*Kunstformen*) 17
literaturnyj etiket, see etiquette, literary
Lixačev, D. S. 14, 16, 17, 23, 36, 74, 103, 104, 126, 131, 138, 140

Ljaščenko, V. G. 33
Ljubeč, battle of 35, 105, 106
Lomonosov, M. V. 20
Loparev, Xr. 26, 74, 89, 133
Lord's Prayer 21, 22
Lot, captured by four kings in Sodom and rescued by his uncle the patriarch Abraham (Gen. 14) 76, 133
Ludmila, Saint, Princess, grandmother of Wenceslas (d. 921) 39, 103
Lupus, legendary servant of St. Demetrius 138
Lur'e, Ja. S. 102, 103, 139
Maczko, S. 13, 36, 127, 133, 136, 138
Makarievskie sobory 1547-1549 gg., see Church Councils of 1547 and 1549
Makarij, Archbishop of Novgorod (1526-1542), Metropolitan of Muscovy and All Rus' (1542-1563) 30, 50, 99; see also *Velikie Minei Četii*
Mansikka, V. 131
martyr 13, 15, 22, 62, 63, 64, 69, 82, 83, 85-87, 91, 98, 99, 108, 113, 120, 121, 124, 130, 132, 133, 135, 140
martyrdom, account of martyr's death 15, 22, 73, 80, 81, 83, 85-87, 90, 93, 99, 103, 121, 124, 135, 142
martyrion, see martyrdom
Matins 52, 57, 59, 69-71, 85, 130
Maximian, co-Emperor of Rome with Diocletian (285-305) 135, 138
Menaion, General (*Obščaja mineja*) 27, 61; Ivaniči Menaia of 1547-79 56, 67-70, 142; Menaion of 1628 70; Reading, see *Velikie Minei Četii*; Service (*Služebnaja mineja*) 57, 59, 60, 62, 63, 67, 131
Menander of Laodicea (3rd c.) 133
Mercurius of Caesarea, martyr (date unknown) 87
Merkurij of Smolensk, legendary 13th century martyr 23
Methodius, Saint, apostle of the Slavs (d. 885) 29
Micaiah, Prophet 115
Michell, R. 140
Mina, Bishop of Polock 52
Mixail, Bishop of Gurgev 49, 129
Mixail Jaroslavovič of Tver', martyr, Prince (d. 1318) 37
Mixail (Mixalko) Jur'evič, Prince, son of Jurij Dolgorukij (d. 1176) 37
Mixail Klopskij, Saint (d. ca. 1456) 29
mode, narrative 18, 22, 107-109

monasteries: Kiev Cave Monastery 58, 88, 89, 97, 136, 138; of St. George, Palestine 40; Trinity-Sergius Laura 58, 91, 126
Morozova, Feodosija Prokop'evna (Feodora), noblewoman (*bojarynja*) venerated by the Old Believers as a saint 39
Moszyński, K. 38
Mstislav Svjatopolkovič, Prince of Volyn' (d. 1099) 138
mučenie, see martyrdom
mučenik, see martyr
Müller, L. 15, 43, 80, 81, 84, 87, 89, 104, 126, 128, 134, 135, 136, 140, 142
Mur'janov, M. F. 63, 67, 131
Murom 137
Muscovy 7, 30, 53, 99, 122, 123, 125, 139
names, Christian vs. dynastic 48, 62, 128–129
Narration 15, 16, 32, 38, 39, 41, 43, 48, 51, 72, 79–92, 94–100, 103, 104, 113, 120, 121, 124, 130, 131, 134–139
Narrative of Miracles 43, 46, 48, 49, 51, 52, 79, 89, 90, 130
Nasonov, A. N. 136, 139
Neofit, Metropolitan of Černigov 49, 129
Nestor, Kievan monk 15, 39, 44, 51, 88, 89, 92–94, 96–99, 104, 120, 124, 126, 135–139
Nicetas, martyr (d. 305) 62, 85, 135, 138
Nicholas of Myra, Saint, Bishop (4th c.) 79, 136
Niederle, L. 37
Nikifor, Metropolitan of Černigov 52
Nikita, Bishop of Belgorod 49, 129
Nikita of Perejaslavl', martyr (date uncertain: either 1186 or very close to the time of the first Mongol invasion) 43, 58
Nikol'skij, N. K. 46, 75, 130, 134
Nikon Chronicle 129
Nikon, Hegumen of the Kievan Cave Monastery (d. 1088) 88, 89
Nikon, Patriarch of All Russia (1652–1658) 20
Norway 33
Novgorod 33, 53, 67, 68, 105, 106, 107, 111, 112, 124, 130, 139
Novgorod I Chronicle 65, 102, 105, 106, 114, 139, 140
Novgorod IV Chronicle 105
Novgorod Sticherarion Office 65–69, 124, 131
ode, see hymnography, terms
office, proper for a saint 14, 31, 56–71, 75, 78, 90, 123, 124, 128, 131–133, 142
oikos, see hymnography, terms
Olaf Haraldsson, Saint, King of Norway (d. 1030), foster brother of Eymundr 39
Oleg Svjatoslavovič, Prince of the Drevljane, brother of Vladimir I (d. 977) 32, 126
Oleg Svjatoslavovič, Prince of Černigov and Tmutarakan' (d. 1115) 52, 72, 130, 138
Ol'ga, Saint, Princess (d. 969) 13, 49, 50
Orlov, A. S. 88
Orlovskij, I. I. 130, 131
Ostromir's Gospel Book (*Ostromirovo Evangelie*) 48
Pafnutyj of Borovsk, Saint (d. 1477/8) 58
Pamjat' i poxvala Vladimiru 49
panegyric, saee eulogy
paremia readings 36, 70, 75–77, 134
passio, see martyrdom
passion-sufferer, see martyr
Paul, Saint, apostle of the Gentiles (d. ca. 67) 62
Paxomij, Logofet, Serbian-born Athonian monk and bookman who worked in Muscovy and Novgorod (d. 1488) 91, 122, 136
Pechenegs, Turkic nomads who controlled the Pontic Steppe (10th–11th c.) 84, 94, 106–108, 140
Pekař, J. 134
Perejaslavl'-Zalesskij 43, 49, 52
perenesenie, see translation
Perì epideiktikōn 133
Perun, pagan Slavic god of thunder 40
Peter, Saint, apostle of the Gentiles (d. ca. 64) 62
Petr, Bishop of Perejaslavl' 49, 129
Petr of the Horde (Ordynskij), Saint, a Mongol of the Chingisid clan (late 13th c.) 18
Petrarch (Francesco Petrarca) (d. 1374) 20
Petrarchan sonnet 20
philadelphia, brotherly love 77, 98, 134, 135
Phocas, Greek pilgrim (late 12th c.) 40
photogogikon, see hymnography, terms
Picchio, R. 28, 126
Pisarev, S. P. 130
Pogodin, M. P. 133
Poland 12, 34, 105–107, 109, 140
Polikarp, Kievan cave monk 138
Polock 33–34, 48, 52
Polovci (Kipchaks), Turkic nomads who dominated the Pontic and Caspian Steppe

(11th-mid 13th c.) 130
Polyeleos 69, 75
Poppe, A. 9, 14, 36, 42, 45, 46, 48, 49, 89, 127, 129, 130, 131, 133, 134, 136, 138
Povest' vremennyx let, see Primary Chronicle
Poxvala i mučenie svjatyx mučenik Borisa i Gleba 73-75, 135
Pozvizd Vladimirovič, Prince, identified as one of Vladimir I's sons 84
Pravda Russkaja 36, 127
Predslava (Peredslava), Princess, daughter of Vladimir I 34, 111
Primary Chronicle 15, 16, 34, 75, 79, 81, 83, 87, 101-121, 134, 141
Pritsak, O. 34, 127
Procopius, martyr (d. 303) 61, 62
prosomoion, see hymnograpy, terms
protogenres 7, 24-26, 30, 31, 122, 123, 125
Pskov 102
Put'ša of Vyšgorod, murderer of Boris 85
Reisman, E. 13, 128
relics, veneration of 43, 48-54, 66, 76, 115, 123-124, 128, 130, 138
Revelli, G. 9, 134
Rogov, A. I. 81, 128, 134
Roman Svjatoslavovič, Prince of Tmutarakan' (d. 1079) 138
Romanus, Saint, see Boris
Romanus, the Melodist, Saint, hymnographer (6th c.) 46
Rome 118
Rostov 50, 53
Rule, Studite, Athos, Jerusalem 69
Rus', see Kievan Rus'
Rybakov, B. A. 13, 128
Rydzevskaja, E. A. 33, 126
saint, concept of 8, 11, 21, 26-30, 33, 39-41, 46-48, 53, 64, 132; eschatological vs. intercessory function of 132; pairs of 64, 132 (see also canonization, life, translation, typology of)
Savvatij of Solovki, Saint, monk (d. 1435) 78, 134
Šaxmatov, A. A. 14, 15, 75, 79, 83, 88, 103-105, 119, 121, 126, 134, 136, 137, 139, 140
Ščapov, Ja. N. 37
Schmemann, A. 132
Schmidt, K.-D. 129
Schmidt, W.-H. 9, 18, 129
Sciacca, F. 13, 42, 127, 128
"Second South Slavic" influence 30, 71, 122

sedalen, see hymnography, terms
Seemann, K.-D. 9, 18, 19, 23, 24
Septuagint 8, 114
Serebrjanskij, N. I. 49, 134
Sergij of Radonež, Saint (d. 1392) 58, 91, 136
sermo humilis 92
sermon, see eulogy, homily
Sermon on Law and Grace 48
service, for a saint, see office
Sherbowitz-Wetzor, O. 126, 139-142
Sil'vestrovskij Sbornik 51, 88
Simon, Bishop of Vladimir and Suzdal' (d. 1226) 138
Sitz im Leben 7, 8, 18, 23, 26, 29, 31, 55, 60, 77, 82, 91, 98, 99, 117
S"kazanie i strast' i poxvala, see Narration
S"kazanie čjudes, see Narrative of Miracles
Slovo poxvalno svjatoju mučeniku Borisa i Gleba 72, 73
Slovo o Merkurii Smolenskom 23
Slovo o polku Igoreve 23
Slovo o zakone i blagodati, see Sermon on Law and Grace
Slovo Xristoljubca 37
služba, see office
Smirnov, S. I. 43
Smirnova, E. S. 131
Smjadin', river 38, 46, 53, 75
Smolensk 23, 29, 46, 53, 75, 130
Snorri Sturluson, see *Heimskringla*
Soboleva, L. S. 36, 46, 61, 75-77, 134
Sobolevskij, A. I. 15, 75, 134
Sofronij, Hegumen of St. Michael's Monastery in Kiev 49, 129
Solov'ev, S. M. 126
Sophia, the Divine Wisdom 28
Sophia I Chronicle 105
Sophia II Chronicle 129
Spasskij, F. G. 63
Sreznevskij, I. I. 14
Stanislav Vladimirovič, Prince, son of Vladimir I 84
Stender-Petersen, A. 140
Stepennaja kniga carskogo rodoslovija 53, 123
Stephen, protomartyr (d. ca. 35) 62
sticheron, see hymnography, terms
stopica, see hymnography, terms
strastoterpec, see martyr
Sudislav Vladimirovič, Prince, son of Vladimir I 84
Svarožič, pagan Slavic god of fire 37

Svjatopolk Izjaslavovič, Grand Prince of Kiev (d. 1113) 52, 72, 79, 89, 128, 129
Svjatopolk Jur'evič, Prince of Turov (d. 1190) 129
Svjatopolk Mstislavovič, Prince of Polock (d. 1154) 129
Svjatopolk Vladimirovič, Grand Prince of Kiev (d. after 1022) 12, 32-37, 42, 53, 54, 62, 63, 65, 73, 76, 77, 79, 80, 83-87, 93-96, 99, 103, 105-121, 126, 128, 129, 132, 133-136, 139-141
Svjatoslav Davidovič, Prince of Černigov (d. 1143) 74
Svjatoslav Jaroslavovič, Grand Prince of Kiev (d. 1076) 49, 51, 72, 129, 130
Svjatoslav Vladimirovič, Prince, son of Vladimir I (d. 1015) 105, 108, 116, 118
Svjatoslav Vsevolodovič, Grand Prince of Kiev (d. 1194) 130
svjatcy 46, 48
syncretism 32, 38, 41, 63, 82, 86, 98, 99, 113, 120, 121, 123, 129
Tatars 76
Theophanes of Kerameos, Archbishop 74
theotokion, see hymnography, terms
Thessalonica 28, 97, 138
Thietmar, Bishop of Merseburg (d. 1019), author of the *Chronicon* 140
Tic, A. A. 131
Tipografskij Typikon 131
Titov, A. A. 90
Tixonravov, N. S. 37, 91
Tokarev, S. A. 38
Toporov, V. N. 132
topos 21, 22, 26, 27, 72, 80-82, 91, 107, 133, 135
translatio, see translation
translation 41, 46, 48-53, 66, 68, 79, 123, 129, 130
Trifon, Bishop of Rostov (d. 1468) 50
Trinity-Sergius Laura, see monasteries
Troickij, I. M. 40
troparion, see hymnography, terms
Typikon of 1641 46
typology of saints 27, 64, 83, 91
Ul'janija Osor'ina, Lazarevskaja, Saint (d. 1604) 30, 39
Urlegende 15, 80, 81, 104, 134, (see also martyrdom)
Ursaga 15, 80, 104
Uspenskij, B. A. 81
Uspenskij Sbornik 46, 51, 72, 79, 88, 126

Ustav Vladimira 37
Valdimar, Prince 33-34 (see also *Eymundar Þáttr*)
Varlaam of Xutyn', Saint (d. 1192/3) 39
Vartilafr, Prince 33-34 (see also *Eymundar Þáttr*)
Vasil'ev, V. 44, 46
Vasilij Skvorcov, keeper of the Jaroslavl' Church of the Mother of God 50-51
Vasilij Vsevolodovič, Saint, Prince of Jaroslavl' (died during the Mongol invasion, exact date unknown) 51, 58
Vassian Sanin, Archbishop of Rostov (1506-1515) 58
Veder, W. 9
Velikie Minei Četii 72, 75, 99
Velimirovič, M. 62
Vernadsky, G. 127
vertical bonds 25, 27, 30, 55, 74, 79, 82, 102, 122, 123
Vespers 57, 69, 70, 75, 76
vita, see life
Vladimir Davidovič, Prince of Černigov (d. 1151) 74
Vladimir Svjatoslavovič, Saint, Grand Prince of Kiev (980-1015) 12, 13, 34, 37, 49, 69, 70, 79, 83, 84, 92, 93, 107-111, 113, 118-120, 134-137, 139-142
Vladimir Vsevolodovič Monomax, Grand Prince of Kiev (1113-1125) 43, 52, 53, 72, 79, 129, 130
Vladimirskij polixron of 1421 139
Vorob'eva, E. V. 131
Voronin, N. N. 42, 130, 136
Vries, J. de 127
Vroon, R. 9
Vseslav Brjačeslavovič, Prince of Polock (d. 1101) 48
Vsevolod Jaroslavovič, Grand Prince of Kiev (1077, 1078-1093) 49-52, 72, 129, 138
Vyšegrad, see Vyšgorod
Vyšgorod 32, 38, 45, 46, 52-54, 62, 66, 68, 72, 74, 76, 85, 87, 89, 95, 97, 103, 105, 108, 124, 132, 133, 136-138
Wellesz, E. 57, 132
Wenceslas, Saint, Prince (d. 929) 13, 33, 81, 82, 85, 103, 128, 136, 138
Wittgenstein, L. 23, 24
work-types (*Werkformen*) 17
Worth, D. 9, 18
Xaruzina, V. N. 38
Xolostenko, N. V. 131

Xorošev, A. S.   42, 49, 129
Zacharias   95
žitie, see life
Zosima of Solovki, Saint, monk (d. 1478) 134
Žukovskaja, L. P.   46, 130

OTHER BOOKS FROM SLAVICA

Ronelle Alexander: *The Structure of Vasko Popa's Poetry*, 196 p., 1986 (ISBN: 0-89357-149-0), (UCLA Slavic Studies, Volume 14).

American Contributions to the Tenth International Congress of Slavists, Sofia, September, 1988, Linguistics, edited by Alexander M. Schenker, 439 p., 1988 (ISBN: 0-89357-190-3)

American Contributions to the Tenth International Congress of Slavists, Sofia, September, 1988, Literature, edited by Jane Gary Harris, 433 p., 1988 (ISBN: 0-89357-191-1)

American Contributions to the Ninth International Congress of Slavists (Kiev 1983) *Vol. 1: Linguistics,* ed. by Michael S. Flier, 381 p., 1983 (ISBN: 0-89357-112-1).

American Contributions to the Ninth International Congress of Slavists, (Kiev 1983) *Vol. 2: Literature, Poetics, History,* ed. by Paul Debreczeny, 400 p., 1983 (ISBN: 0-89357-113-X).

American Contributions to the Eighth International Congress of Slavists (Zagreb and Ljubljana, Sept. 3-9, 1978), *Vol 1: Linguistics and Poetics,* ed. by Henrik Birnbaum, 818 p., 1978 (ISBN: 0-89357-126-1).

American Contributions to the Eighth International Congress of Slavists (Zagreb and Ljubljana, Sept. 3-9, 1978) *Vol. 2: Literature,* ed. by Victor Terras, 799 p., 1978 (ISBN: 0-89357-047-8).

Patricia M. Arant: *Russian for Reading,* 214 p., 1981 (ISBN: 0-89357-086-9).

Howard I. Aronson: *Georgian: A Reading Grammar,* 526 p., 1982 (ISBN: 0-89357-100-8).

James E. Augerot and Florin D. Popescu: *Modern Romanian,* xiv + 330 p., 1983 (ISBN: 0-89357-124-5).

Natalya Baranskaya: Неделя как неделя *Just Another Week,* edited by L. Paperno *et al.*, 92 p., 1989 (ISBN: 0-89357-202-0).

Adele Marie Barker: *The Mother Syndrome in the Russian Folk Imagination,* 180 p., 1986 (ISBN: 0-89357-160-1).

R. P. Bartlett, A. G. Cross, and Karen Rasmussen, eds.: *Russia and the World of the Eighteenth Century,* viii + 684 p., 1988 (ISBN: 0-89357-186-5).

John D. Basil: *The Mensheviks in the Revolution of 1917,* 220 p., 1984 (ISBN: 0-89357-109-1).

Henrik Birnbaum & Thomas Eekman, eds.: *Fiction and Drama in Eastern and Southeastern Europe: Evolution and Experiment in the Postwar Period,* ix + 463 p., 1980 (ISBN: 0-89357-064-8) (UCLA V. 1).

Henrik Birnbaum and Peter T. Merrill: *Recent Advances in the Reconstruction of Common Slavic (1971-1982),* vi + 141 p., 1985 (ISBN: 0-89357-116-4).

OTHER BOOKS FROM SLAVICA

Marianna D. Birnbaum: *Humanists in a Shattered World: Croatian and Hungarian Latinity in the Sixteenth Century*, 456 p., 1986 (ISBN: 0-89357-155-5). (UCLA Slavic Studies, Volume 15).

Feliks J. Bister and Herbert Kuhner, eds.: *Carinthian Slovenian Poetry*, 216 p., 1984 (ISBN: 3-85013-029-0).

Karen L. Black, ed.: *A Biobibliographical Handbook of Bulgarian Authors*, 347 p., 1982 (ISBN: 0-89357-091-5).

Marianna Bogojavlensky: *Russian Review Grammar*, xviii + 450 p., 1982 (ISBN: 0-89357-096-6).

Rodica C. Boțoman, Donald E. Corbin, E. Garrison Walters: *Îmi Place Limba Română/A Romanian Reader*, 199 p., 1982 (ISBN: 0-89357-087-7).

Richard D. Brecht and James S. Levine, eds: *Case in Slavic*, 467 p., 1986 (ISBN: 0-89357-166-0).

Gary L. Browning: *Workbook to Russian Root List*, 85 p., 1985 (ISBN: 0-89357-114-8).

Diana L. Burgin: *Richard Burgin A Life in Verse*, 230 p., 1989 (ISBN: 0-89357-196-2).

R. L. Busch: *Humor in the Major Novels of Dostoevsky*, 168 p., 1987 (ISBN: 0-89357-176-8).

Catherine V. Chvany and Richard D. Brecht, eds.: *Morphosyntax in Slavic*, v + 316 p., 1980 (ISBN: 0-89357-070-2).

Jozef Cíger-Hronský: *Jozef Mak* (a novel), translated from Slovak, 232 p., 1985 (ISBN: 0-89357-129-6).

J. Douglas Clayton, ed.: *Issues in Russian Literature Before 1917 Selected Papers of the Third World Congress for Soviet and East European Studies*, 248 p., 1989 (ISBN: 0-89357-199-7).

Frederick Columbus: *Introductory Workbook in Historical Phonology*, 39 p., 1974 (ISBN: 0-89357-018-4).

Julian W. Connolly and Sonia I. Ketchian, eds.: *Studies in Russian Literature in Honor of Vsevolod Setchkarev*, 288 p. 1987 (ISBN: 0-89357-174-1).

Gary Cox: *Tyrant and Victim in Dostoevsky*, 119 p., 1984 (ISBN: 0-89357-125-3).

Anna Lisa Crone and Catherine V. Chvany, eds.: *New Studies in Russian Language and Literature*, 302 p., 1987 (ISBN: 0-89357-168-7).

Carolina De Maegd-Soëp: *Chekhov and Women: Women in the Life and Work of Chekhov*, 373 p., 1987 (ISBN: 0-89357-175-X).

Bruce L. Derwing and Tom M. S. Priestly: *Reading Rules for Russian: A Systematic Approach to Russian Spelling and Pronunciation, with Notes on Dialectal and Stylistic Variation*, vi + 247 p., 1980 (ISBN: 0-89357-066-4).

OTHER BOOKS FROM SLAVICA

Dorothy Disterheft: *The Syntactic Development of the Infinitive in Indo-European,* 220 p., 1980 (ISBN: 0-89357-058-3).

Thomas Eekman and Dean S. Worth, eds.: *Russian Poetics* Proceedings of the International Colloquium at UCLA, September 22-26, 1975, 544 p., 1983 (ISBN: 0-89357-101-6) (UCLA Slavic Studies, Volume 4).

Mark J. Elson: *Macedonian Verbal Morphology A Structural Analysis,* 147 p., 1989 (ISBN: 0-89357-201-2).

Michael S. Flier and Richard D. Brecht, eds.: *Issues in Russian Morphosyntax,* 208 p., 1985 (ISBN: 0-89357-139-3) (UCLA V. 10).

Michael S. Flier and Alan Timberlake, eds: *The Scope of Slavic Aspect,* 295 p., 1985 (ISBN: 0-89357-150-4). (UCLA Slavic Studies 12).

John Miles Foley, ed.: *Comparative Research on Oral Traditions: A Memorial for Milman Parry,* 597 p., 1987 (ISBN: 0-89357-173-3).

John M. Foley, ed.: *Oral Traditional Literature A Festschrift for Albert Bates Lord,* 461 p., 1981 (ISBN: 0-89357-073-7).

Diana Greene: *Insidious Intent: An Interpretation of Fedor Sologub's* The Petty Demon, 140 p., 1986 (ISBN: 0-89357-158-X).

Charles E. Gribble, ed.: *Medieval Slavic Texts, Vol. 1, Old and Middle Russian Texts,* 320 p., 1973 (ISBN: 0-89357-011-7).

Charles E. Gribble: *Reading Bulgarian Through Russian,* 182 p., 1987 (ISBN: 0-89357-106-7).

Charles E. Gribble: *Russian Root List with a Sketch of Word Formation, Second Edition,* 62 p., 1982 (ISBN: 0-89357-052-4).

Charles E. Gribble: *A Short Dictionary of 18th-Century Russian*/Словарик Русского Языка 18-го Века, 103 p., 1976 (ISBN: 0-89357-172-5).

Charles E. Gribble, ed.: *Studies Presented to Professor Roman Jakobson by His Students,* 333 p., 1968, (ISBN: 0-89357-000-1).

George J. Gutsche and Lauren G. Leighton, eds.: *New Perspectives on Nineteenth-Century Russian Prose,* 146 p., 1982 (ISBN: 0-89357-094-X).

Morris Halle, ed.: *Roman Jakobson: What He Taught Us,* 94 p., 1983 (ISBN: 0-89357-118-0).

Morris Halle, Krystyna Pomorska, Elena Semeka-Pankratov, and Boris Uspenskij, eds.: *Semiotics and the History of Culture In Honor of Jurij Lotman Studies in Russian,* 437 p., 1989 (ISBN: 0-89357-195-4), (UCLA Slavic Studies, Volume 17).

Charles J. Halperin: *The Tatar Yoke,* 231 p., 1986 (ISBN: 0-89357-161-X).

William S. Hamilton: *Introduction to Russian Phonology and Word Structure,* 187 p., 1980 (ISBN: 0-89357-063-X).

Pierre R. Hart: *G. R. Derzhavin: A Poet's Progress,* iv + 164 p., 1978 (ISBN: 0-89357-054-0).

OTHER BOOKS FROM SLAVICA

Michael Heim: *Contemporary Czech*, 271 p., 1982 (ISBN: 0-89357-098-2) (UCLA Slavic Studies, Volume 3).

Michael Heim, Zlata Meyerstein, and Dean Worth: *Readings in Czech*, 147 p., 1985 (ISBN: 0-89357-154-7). (UCLA V. 13).

Warren H. Held, Jr., William R. Schmalstieg, and Janet E. Gertz: *Beginning Hittite*, ix + 218 p., 1988 (ISBN: 0-89357-184-9).

M. Hubenova & others: *A Course in Modern Bulgarian, Part 1*, viii + 303 p., 1983 (ISBN: 0-89357-104-0); *Part 2*, ix + 303 p., 1983 (ISBN: 0-89357-105-9).

Martin E. Huld: *Basic Albanian Etymologies*, x + 213 p., 1984 (ISBN: 0-89357-135-0).

Charles Isenberg: *Substantial Proofs of Being: Osip Mandelstam's Literary Prose*, 179 p., 1987 (ISBN: 0-89357-169-5).

Roman Jakobson, with the assistance of Kathy Santilli: *Brain and Language Cerebral Hemispheres and Linguistic Structure in Mutual Light*, 48 p., 1980 (ISBN: 0-89357-068-0). (New York University Slavic Papers, Interdisciplinary Series, Volume IV)

Donald K. Jarvis and Elena D. Lifshitz: *Viewpoints: A Listening and Conversation Course in Russian, Third Edition*, iv + 66 p., 1985 (ISBN: 0-89357-152-0); *Instructor's Manual*, v + 37 p., (ISBN: 0-89357-153-9).

Leslie A. Johnson: *The Experience of Time in Crime and Punishment*, 146 p., 1985 (ISBN: 0-89357-142-3).

Stanislav J. Kirschbaum, ed.: *East European History: Selected Papers of the Third World Congress for Soviet and East European Studies*, 183 p., 1989 (ISBN: 0-89357-193-8).

Emily R. Klenin: *Animacy in Russian: A New Interpretation*, 139 p., 1983 (ISBN: 0-89357-115-6). (UCLA Slavic Studies, Volume 6)

Andrej Kodjak, Krystyna Pomorska, and Kiril Taranovsky, eds.: *Alexander Puškin Symposium II*, 131 p., 1980 (ISBN: 0-89357-067-2) (New York University Slavic Papers, Volume III).

Andrej Kodjak, Krystyna Pomorska, Stephen Rudy, eds.: *Myth in Literature*, 207 p., 1985 (ISBN: 0-89357-137-7) (New York University Slavic Papers, Volume V).

Andrej Kodjak: *Pushkin's I. P. Belkin*, 112 p., 1979 (ISBN: 0-89357-057-5).

Andrej Kodjak, Michael J. Connolly, Krystyna Pomorska, eds.: *Structural Analysis of Narrative Texts (Conference Papers)*, 203 p., 1980 (ISBN: 0-89357-071-0) (New York University Slavic Papers, Volume II).

Demetrius J. Koubourlis, ed.: *Topics in Slavic Phonology*, vii + 270 p., 1974 (ISBN: 0-89357-017-6).

Ronald D. LeBlanc: *The Russianization of Gil Blas: A Study in Literary Appropriation*, 292 p. 1986 (ISBN: 0-89357-159-8).

OTHER BOOKS FROM SLAVICA

Richard L. Leed, Alexander D. Nakhimovsky, and Alice S. Nakhimovsky: *Beginning Russian, Vol. 1,* xiv + 426 p., 1981 (ISBN: 0-89357-077-X); *Vol. 2,* viii + 339 p., 1982 (ISBN: 0-89357-078-8); *Teacher's Manual*, 45 p., 1981 (ISBN: 0-89357-079-6).

Richard L. Leed and Slava Paperno: *5000 Russian Words With All Their Inflected Forms: A Russian-English Dictionary*, xiv + 322 p., 1987 (ISBN: 0-89357-170-9).

Edgar H. Lehrman: *A Handbook to Eighty-Six of Chekhov's Stories in Russian*, 327 p., 1985 (ISBN: 0-89357-151-2).

Lauren Leighton, ed.: *Studies in Honor of Xenia Gąsiorowska*, 191 p., 1983 (ISBN: 0-89357-102-4).

R. L. Lencek: *The Structure and History of the Slovene Language*, 365 p., 1982 (ISBN: 0-89357-099-0).

Jules F. Levin and Peter D. Haikalis, with Anatole A. Forostenko: *Reading Modern Russian*, vi + 321 p., 1979 (ISBN: 0-89357- 059-1).

Maurice I. Levin: *Russian Declension and Conjugation:* A Structural Description with Exercises, x + 159 p., 1978 (ISBN: 0-89357-048-6).

Alexander Lipson: *A Russian Course. Part 1,* ix + 338 p., 1981 (ISBN: 0-89357-080-X); *Part 2,* 343 p., 1981 (ISBN: 0-89357-081-8); *Part 3,* iv + 105 p., 1981 (ISBN: 0-89357-082-6); *Teacher's Manual* by Stephen J. Molinsky (who also assisted in the writing of Parts 1 and 2), 222 p., 1981 (ISBN: 0-89357-083-4).

Yvonne R. Lockwood: *Text and Context Folksong in a Bosnian Muslim Village,* 220 p., 1983 (ISBN: 0-89357-120-2).

Sophia Lubensky & Donald K. Jarvis, eds.: *Teaching, Learning, Acquiring Russian*, viii + 415 p., 1984 (ISBN: 0-89357-134-2).

Horace G. Lunt: *Fundamentals of Russian*, xiv + 402 p., reprint, 1982 (ISBN: 0-89357-097-4).

Paul Macura: *Russian-English Botanical Dictionary*, 678 p., 1982 (ISBN: 0-89357-092-3).

Thomas G. Magner, ed.: *Slavic Linguistics and Language Teaching*, x + 309 p., 1976 (ISBN: 0-89357-037-0).

Amy Mandelker and Roberta Reeder, eds.: *The Supernatural in Slavic and Baltic Literature: Essays in Honor of Victor Terras,* Introduction by J. Thomas Shaw, xxi + 402 p., 1989 (ISBN: 0-89357-192-X).

Vladimir Markov and Dean S. Worth, eds.: *From Los Angeles to Kiev Papers on the Occasion of the Ninth International Congress of Slavists*, 250 p., 1983 (ISBN: 0-89357-119-9) (UCLA Slavic Studies, Volume 7).

Mateja Matejić and Dragan Milivojević: *An Anthology of Medieval Serbian Literature in English*, 205 p., 1978 (ISBN: 0-89357-055-9).

OTHER BOOKS FROM SLAVICA

Peter J. Mayo: *The Morphology of Aspect in Seventeenth-Century Russian (Based on Texts of the Smutnoe Vremja)*, xi + 234 p., 1985 (ISBN: 0-89357-145-8).

Arnold McMillin, ed.: *Aspects of Modern Russian and Czech Literature Selected Papers of the Third World Congress for Soviet and East European Studies*, 239 p., 1989 (ISBN: 0-89357-194-6).

Gordon M. Messing: *A Glossary of Greek Romany As Spoken in Agia Varvara (Athens)*, 175 p., 1988 (ISBN: 0-89357-187-3).

Vasa D. Mihailovich and Mateja Matejic: *A Comprehensive Bibliography of Yugoslav Literature in English, 1593-1980*, xii + 586 p., 1984 (ISBN: 0-89357-136-9).

Vasa D. Mihailovich: *First Supplement to A Comprehensive Bibliography of Yugoslav Literature in English 1981-1985*, 338 p., 1989 (ISBN: 0-89357-188-1).

Edward Mozejko, ed.: *Vasiliy Pavlovich Aksenov: A Writer in Quest of Himself*, 272 p., 1986 (ISBN: 0-89357-141-5).

Edward Możejko: *Yordan Yovkov*, 117 p., 1984 (ISBN: 0-89357-117-2).

Alexander D. Nakhimovsky and Richard L. Leed: *Advanced Russian, Second Edition, Revised*, vii + 262 p., 1987 (ISBN: 0-89357-178-4).

The Comprehensive Russian Grammar of A. A. Barsov/ Обстоятельная грамматика А. А. Барсова, Critical Edition by Lawrence W. Newman, lxxxvi + 382 p., 1980 (ISBN: 0-89357-072-9).

Felix J. Oinas: *Essays on Russian Folklore and Mythology*, 183 p., 1985, (ISBN: 0-89357-148-2).

Hongor Oulanoff: *The Prose Fiction of Veniamin Kaverin*, v + 203 p., 1976 (ISBN: 0-89357-032-X).

Temira Pachmuss: *Russian Literature in the Baltic between the World Wars*, 448 p., 1988 (ISBN: 0-89357-181-4).

Lora Paperno: *Getting Around Town in Russian: Situational Dialogs*, English translation and photographs by Richard D. Sylvester, 123 p., 1987 (ISBN: 0-89357-171-7).

Slava Paperno, Alexander D. Nakhimovsky, Alice S. Nakhimovsky, and Richard L. Leed: *Intermediate Russian: The Twelve Chairs*, 326 p., 1985, (ISBN: 0-89357-144-X).

Ruth L. Pearce: *Russian For Expository Prose, Vol. 1 Introductory Course*, 413 p., 1983 (ISBN: 0-89357-121-0); *Vol. 2 Advanced Course*, 255 p., 1983 (ISBN: 0-89357-122-9).

Jan L. Perkowski: *The Darkling A Treatise on Slavic Vampirism*, 169 p., 1989 (ISBN: 0-89357-200-4).

Gerald Pirog: *Aleksandr Blok's* Итальянские Стихи *Confrontation and Disillusionment,* 219 p., 1983 (ISBN: 0-89357-095-8).

OTHER BOOKS FROM SLAVICA

Stanley J. Rabinowitz: *Sologub's Literary Children: Keys to a Symbolist's Prose,* 176 p., 1980 (ISBN: 0-89357-069-9).

Gilbert C. Rappaport: *Grammatical Function and Syntactic Structure: The Adverbial Participle of Russian,* 218 p., 1984 (ISBN: 0-89357-133-4) (UCLA Slavic Studies, Volume 9).

David F. Robinson: *Lithuanian Reverse Dictionary,* ix + 209 p., 1976 (ISBN: 0-89357-034-6).

Don K. Rowney & G. Edward Orchard, eds.: *Russian and Slavic History,* viii + 303 p., 1977 (ISBN: 0-89357-036-2).

Catherine Rudin: *Aspects of Bulgarian Syntax: Complementizers and WH Constructions,* iv + 232 p., 1986, (ISBN: 0-89357-156-3).

Gerald J. Sabo, S.J., ed.: *Valaská Škola, by Hugolin Gavlovič, with a linguistic sketch by L'. Ďurovič, 730 p., 1988* (ISBN: 0-89357-179-2).

Ernest A. Scatton: *Bulgarian Phonology,* xii + 224 p., 1975 (reprint: 1983) (ISBN: 0-89357-103-2).

Ernest A. Scatton: *A Reference Grammar of Modern Bulgarian,* 448 p., 1984 (ISBN: 0-89357-123-7).

Barry P. Scherr and Dean S. Worth, eds.: *Russian Verse Theory Proceedings of the 1987 Conference at UCLA,* 514 p., 1989 (ISBN: 0-89357-198-9).

William R. Schmalstieg: *Introduction to Old Church Slavic, second edition,* 314 p., 1983 (ISBN: 0-89357-107-5).

William R. Schmalstieg: *A Lithuanian Historical Syntax,* xi + 412 p., 1988 (ISBN: 0-89357-185-7).

R. D. Schupbach: *Lexical Specialization in Russian,* 102 p., 1984 (ISBN: 0-89357-128-8) (UCLA Slavic Studies, Volume 8).

Peter Seyffert: *Soviet Literary Structuralism: Background Debate Issues,* 378 p., 1985 (ISBN: 0-89357-140-7).

Kot K. Shangriladze and Erica W. Townsend, eds.: *Papers for the V. Congress of Southeast European Studies (Belgrade, September 1984),* 382 p., 1984 (ISBN: 0-89357-138-5).

Michael Shapiro: *Aspects of Russian Morphology, A Semiotic Investigation,* 62 p. (7 x 10" format), 1969 (ISBN: 0-89357-004-4).

J. Thomas Shaw: *Pushkin A Concordance to the Poetry,* 2 volumes, 1310 pages total, 1985 (ISBN: 0-89357-130-X for the set).

Efraim Sicher: *Style and Structure in the Prose of Isaak Babel',* 169 p., 1986 (ISBN: 0-89357-163-6).

Mark S. Simpson: *The Russian Gothic Novel and its British Antecedents,* 112 p., 1986 (ISBN: 0-89357-162-8).

David A. Sloane: *Aleksandr Blok and the Dynamics of the Lyric Cycle,* 384 p., 1988 (ISBN: 0-89357-182-2).

OTHER BOOKS FROM SLAVICA

Greta N. Slobin, ed.: *Aleksej Remizov: Approaches to a Protean Writer*, 286 p., 1987 (ISBN: 0-89357-167-9).

Theofanis G. Stavrou and Peter R. Weisensel: *Russian Travelers to the Christian East from the Twelfth to the Twentieth Century*, L + 925 p., 1985, (ISBN: 0-89357-157-1).

Gerald Stone and Dean S. Worth, eds.: *The Formation of the Slavonic Literary Languages, Proceedings of a Conference Held in Memory of Robert Auty and Anne Pennington at Oxford 6-11 July 1981*, 269 p., 1985 (ISBN: 0-89357-143-1) (UCLA Slavic Studies, Volume 11).

Roland Sussex and J. C. Eade, eds.: *Culture and Nationalism in Nineteenth-Century Eastern Europe*, 158 p., 1985 (ISBN: 0-89357-146-6).

Oscar E. Swan: *First Year Polish, second edition, revised and expanded*, 354 p., 1983 (ISBN: 0-89357-108-3).

Oscar E. Swan: *Intermediate Polish*, 370 p., 1986 (ISBN: 0-89357-165-2).

Jane A. Taubman: *A Life Through Verse Marina Tsvetaeva's Lyric Diary*, 296 p., 1989 (ISBN: 0-89357-197-0).

Charles E. Townsend: *Continuing With Russian*, xxi + 426 p., 1981 (ISBN: 0-89357-085-0).

Charles E. Townsend and Veronica N. Dolenko: *Instructor's Manual to Accompany Continuing With Russian*, 39 p., 1987 (ISBN: 0-89357-177-6).

Charles E. Townsend: *Czech Through Russian*, viii + 263 p., 1981 (ISBN: 0-89357-089-3).

Charles E. Townsend: *The Memoirs of Princess Natal'ja Borisovna Dolgorukaja*, viii + 146 p., 1977 (ISBN: 0-89357-044-3).

Charles E. Townsend: *Russian Word Formation, corrected reprint*, viii + 272 p., 1975 (ISBN: 0-89357-023-0).

Janet G. Tucker: *Innokentij Annenskij and the Acmeist Doctrine*, 154 p., 1987 (ISBN: 0-89357-164-4).

Boryana Velcheva: *Proto-Slavic and Old Bulgarian Sound Changes*, Translation of the original by Ernest A. Scatton, 187 p., 1988 (ISBN: 0-89357-189-X).

Walter N. Vickery, ed.: *Aleksandr Blok Centennial Conference*, 403 p., 1984, (ISBN: 0-89357-111-3).

Essays in Honor of A. A. Zimin, ed. D. C. Waugh, xiv + 416 p., 1985 (ISBN: 0-89357-147-4).

Daniel C. Waugh: *The Great Turkes Defiance On the History of the Apocryphal Correspondence of the Ottoman Sultan in its Muscovite and Russian Variants*, ix + 354 p., 1978 (ISBN: 0-89357-056-7).

Susan Wobst: *Russian Readings and Grammatical Terminology*, 88 p., 1978 (ISBN: 0-89357-049-4).

DATE DUE

HIGHSMITH # 45220